FIRST-TIME

D1128123

JOHNS HOPKINS STUDIES IN ATLANTIC HISTORY AND CULTURE

RICHARD PRICE

GENERAL EDITOR

ALSO BY RICHARD PRICE

Maroon Societies: Rebel Slave Communities in the Americas
Saramaka Social Structure
An Anthropological Approach to the Afro-American Past (with Sidney W. Mintz)
The Guiana Maroons: A Historical and Bibliographical Introduction
Afro-American Arts of the Suriname Rain Forest (with Sally Price)
To Slay the Hydra: Dutch Colonial Perspectives on the Saramaka Wars
Narrative of a Five Years Expedition against the Revolted Negroes of Surinam
by John Gabriel Stedman (edited with Sally Price)
Two Evenings in Saramaka: Afro-American Tale-Telling from the Suriname Rain Forest
(with Sally Price)

FIRST-TIME

The Historical Vision of an Afro-American People

RICHARD PRICE

THE JOHNS HOPKINS UNIVERSITY PRESS

BALTIMORE AND LONDON

© 1983 by Richard Price
All rights reserved
Printed in the United States of America

Originally published in hardcover and paperback, 1983
Second printing, paperback, 1989

The Johns Hopkins University Press, 701 West 40th Street
Baltimore, Maryland 21211
The Johns Hopkins Press Ltd., London

Library of Congress Cataloging in Publication Data
Price, Richard, 1941-
First-time.
(Johns Hopkins studies in Atlantic history and
culture)
Bibliography: p. 183
1. Saramacca tribe—History. I. Title. II. Series.
F2431.N3P73 1983   988'.3   83-29
ISBN 0-8018-2984-4
ISBN: 0-8018-2985-2 (pbk.)

TITLE PAGE ILLUSTRATION:
Saramaka *apínti* drum collected 1928–29. Courtesy of the Museum of African Art,
Smithsonian Institution, Melville J. Herskovits Collection. Photo by Antonia Graeber.

FOR ALL THOSE SARAMAKAS
WHO DIDN'T LIVE TO SEE THE PEACE,
AND FOR ALL THOSE WHO DID.

Those people who didn't live to see the Peace, they must not be jealous. Their hearts must not be angry. There is no help for it. When the time is right, we shall get still more freedom. Let them not look at what they have missed. Let us and them be on one side together, those First-Time people! It is to them we are speaking.

—Tebíni, 1976, quoting words first spoken in 1762

CONTENTS

ILLUSTRATIONS

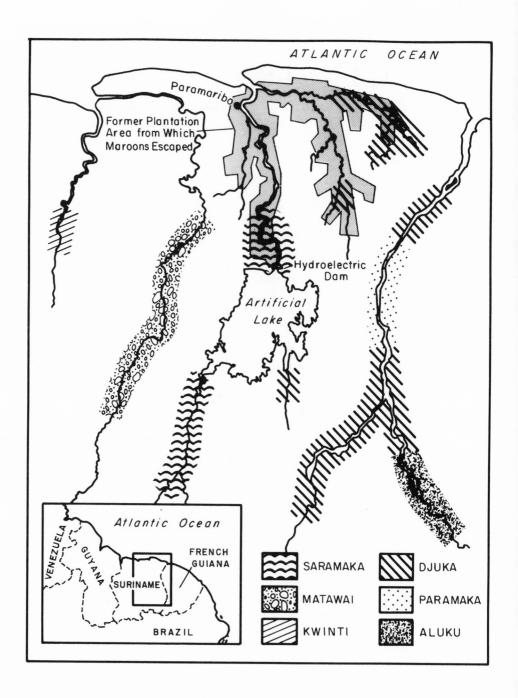

The Saramaka and other Suriname Maroons

The Saramaka are now one of six Maroon (or "Bush Negro") tribes in Suriname that together constitute more than 10 percent of the national population. During the 1960s, approximately half of traditional Saramaka territory was flooded in order to produce cheap electricity for Alcoa's new smelter near the capital. Six thousand people were forced to leave their homelands, some settling in special "transmigration villages" to the north of the lake, others establishing villages near its southern border. (The English word *maroon* derives from the Spanish *cimarrón,* a term originally used in Hispaniola to refer to domestic cattle that had taken to the hills; by the early 1500s, it had come to be used in plantation colonies throughout the Americas to designate slaves who successfully escaped from captivity.)

FIRST-TIME

THE SARAMAKA—about twenty thousand people—live in the heavily forested interior of the Republic of Suriname in northeastern South America. Their ancestors were among those Africans who were sold into slavery in the late seventeenth and early eighteenth centuries to work Suriname's sugar, timber, and coffee plantations. They soon escaped into the dense rain forest—individually, in small groups, sometimes in great collective rebellions—where for over one hundred years they fought a war of liberation. In 1762, a full century before the general emancipation of slaves in Suriname, they won their freedom.

THOSE TIMES
SHALL COME AGAIN

*There was a day in time when the last
eyes to see Christ were closed forever.*

—Jorge Luis Borges

In a sacred grove beside the village of Dángogó, shaded by equatorial trees, stands a weathered shrine to the Old-Time People (*Awónêngè*), those ancestors who "heard the guns of war." Whenever there is a collective crisis in the region—should the rains refuse to come on time or an epidemic sweep the river—it is to this shrine that Saramakas repair. As libations of sugar-cane beer moisten the earth beneath newly raised flags, the Old-Time People are one by one invoked—their names spoken (or played on the *apínti* drum), their deeds recounted, their foibles recalled, and the drums/dances/songs that they once loved performed to give them special pleasure.[1]

Literally thousands of individual Saramakas must have heard the guns of war between the 1680s and the coming of the Peace in 1762. Yet the names invoked at Awónêngè number merely in the scores. All history is thus: a radical selection from the immensely rich swirl of past human activity. The uniqueness of this book lies in its taking seriously the selection that is made by those people who gather together at this shrine. It is about those distant people and those long-ago events that Saramakas today choose to think about, talk about, and act upon; but it is also about the ways that Saramakas transform the general past (everything that happened) into the significant past, their history. This book is an attempt to communicate something of the Saramakas' own special vision of their formative years.

Saramakas are acutely conscious of living in history, of reaping each day the fruits of their ancestors' deeds, and of themselves possessing the potential, through their own acts, to change the shape of tomorrow's world.[2] All evil, they believe, originates in human action, which makes Saramaka historicity a two-way street. Not only does each misfortune, illness, or death stem from a specific past misdeed, but every offense, whether against people or gods, bears someday its bitter fruit. If a man is killed, his spirit will dedicate itself to wreak vengeance eternally upon the kinsmen of the killer (and likewise with the spirits of offended snake gods and other deities). Nor need the initial crime be murder; it can almost as easily be petty theft or an offense against someone's honor. In Saramaka, events are the very stuff of history (not, as Valéry [1962: 476] would have it, "only the froth on things").[3] The ignoble acts of the dead intrude daily on the lives of the living, who must learn to accept them and to handle the evils they engendered. Any illness or misfortune calls for divination, which quickly reveals the specific past act that caused it. And in the lengthy process of making things right once more, the ancestors speak, the gods dance, and the past comes alive, palpable and visible.

Yet the past that so insistently intervenes in everyday life is (in practice, though not in Saramaka theory) temporally restricted. The specific events that Saramakas believe affect their daily lives can be shown to have occurred in the relatively recent past, during no more than the last hundred years. Whether we examine the avenging spirits that relentlessly trouble the living, or the friendly dead who help them in their daily tasks, the great majority turn out to have died recently, most within the memory of people still alive.[4] A little reflection will show that such a system requires for its functioning the periodic "retirement" of the more ancient symbols of group identity (whether avenging spirits or friendly ancestors) as the process of social segmentation moves forward in time. And I have reason to believe that in Saramaka this has always been the case. Two hundred years ago, it would have been those people who had lived (and died) in wartime who were playing the active interventionary role in daily life. But by 1840, for example—following the major northward movement of villages and the striking growth of new social groups that occurred in the first post-peacetime generations—these wartime figures would no longer have been able to serve as effective local symbols; the new emergent groups would have needed new, exclusive markers for their identity. Saramaka memories retain fascinating traces of what happened at that temporal watershed. One man recounted that

> Fankía heard the guns of war. When they brought her down from the Upper River [in the great migration of the 1770s] she was still a "large-apron-girl" [teenager]. Well, she lived there [in the new village near the present Dángogó] until she was very very old. They used to lift her up and lay her out in the sun, for warmth. She would begin to shake her body like this [demonstrates dance movement with torso]. And when they would ask her why, she'd say that she could hear them playing [drums] for her in the land of the dead. Well, she lived until she died, and they raised up her coffin [in divination]. She told them that the Old-Time People had a message for the living about how they should henceforth speak with them. They should build a shrine according to the specific instructions she would give. And whenever they wanted to talk with the Old-Time People, they should pour libations at its base. And until today, the first name invoked at the shrine of Awónêngè must always be Fankía, who heard the guns of war.

This event, which independent evidence permits me to date to the mid-1840s when Fankía would have been 85–90 years old, seems to have helped formally to divide the Old-Time People (henceforth to be worshiped at this special shrine) from the more recent dead, who played a more active role in the daily lives of the living (and who would be worshiped at shrines in the villages themselves).[5] In the years since the 1840s, several generations of ancestors who at one time played important roles in the lives of the living must have been quietly "retired"—for the most part simply forgotten. Today only two groups of ancestors, separated by more than a century of lived experience, remain in sharp focus: those relatively recent dead who continue to intervene in daily life today, and the Old-Time People, whose very special place in Saramaka life was institutionalized, with Fankía's help, a century and a half ago.

FIRST-TIME

The past as a precise idea has
meaning and value only for the
man who is aware that he has a passion
for the future.

—Paul Valéry

For Saramakas today, First-Time (*fési-tén*)—the era of the Old-Time People—differs most sharply from the recent past in its overwhelming inherent power.[6] Stretching roughly to 1800, First-Time is not more "mythologized" or less accurately recalled than the more recent past; but knowledge of First-Time is singularly circumscribed, restricted, and guarded. It is the fountainhead of collective identity; it contains the true root of what it means to be Saramaka.[7] Once Améiká, a man in his seventies, remarked in my presence:

First-Time kills people. That's why it should never be taught to youths. . . . That's why, when you pour a libation at the ancestor shrine, you must be careful about speaking in proverbs [because you may not be aware of all their hidden implications]. There are certain [people's] names that, if you call them, you're dead right on the spot! There are names that can't be uttered twice in the course of a whole year! It is with such things that we were raised.

Likewise, Captain Góme—an affable and knowledgeable "Christian," then only months away from his eightieth birthday—once interrupted a whispered recounting of "the two things that Alábi killed at Sentéa Creek [in 1770]" to say:

I don't want "children" to hear this. The water and the shore! [a veiled reference to the "two things" he had just explained to me]. I will not tell them! My mother's brother [a key relative in this strongly matrilineal society] used to say, "talk with them but don't *tell* them. Because if you tell them, those things will rise up and come listen!"

The imminent danger of First-Time resides, in part, in its specialized uses in social action. The recent past (roughly the last hundred years) that intrudes on everyday life tends to affect only individuals, domestic groups, and, occasionally, whole village units. First-Time, though called upon less frequently, relates to larger and older collectivities, most often the "clans" (*lô*) that trace their ancestry matrilineally back to an original group of rebel slaves.[8] First-Time most often comes alive in the restricted but highly charged arena of interclan politics. It was the migratory movements of the First-Time people that established land rights for posterity; it is the details of how they held political office that provide the model on which modern succession is based; and it is the particular alliances and rivalries among the wartime clans that shape the quality of their descendants' interaction today. Any dispute between clans—whether over land, political office, or ritual possessions—immediately brings knowledge of First-Time to the fore. In these settings, when corporate property and prestige are at stake, such knowledge becomes highly perspectival; the point of knowing about a First-Time event is to be able to use it in support of one's clan. To cite a simple but exemplary case: the members of the Matjáu clan describe with meticulous detail the way that Gúngúúkúsu, the Wátambíi clan ancestor, greeted their own man Ayakô on the occasion of their first postrebellion reunion in the forest. Since Saramaka etiquette requires the "guest," not the "host," to extend the first greeting, this historical fragment effectively preserves Matjáu precedence in the forest (viz-à-viz Wátambíis), as well as the entitlements to land thus entailed.

First-Time provides the "charter," as well, for the most powerful ritual possessions of each clan, many of which date back to that formative period. It is to these powers, and the First-Time ancestors associated with them, that knowledgeable Saramakas appeal in times of real crisis. Learning the details of their history provides an unmatched degree of personal security, for one need thereafter never be alone: the Old-Time People and their enormous powers will be standing by one's side. As one elder confided to me, after recounting the minutiae surrounding the death of Afadjétosúme, an early Matjáu clan captain, near Berg en Dal (a former plantation on the lower Suriname River):

If you are ever in real trouble near there, it is his name you must call. And the trouble won't be more than you can handle. You say, "Afadjétosúme, well, the thing that was too much for you to handle here, it's trying to do the same to me." And he'll take care of it.

Such specialized knowledge of the past, then, means power in a very direct sense; it permits some measure of control over the vagaries of the unpredictable present.

Knowledge of First-Time is preserved in a number of special forms, largely unfamiliar to a non-Saramaka, among which narrative (straightforward storytelling) ranks rather low.[9] The major forms that such knowledge takes are illustrated throughout this book, but a preliminary listing may be useful at this point:

1. Genealogical nuggets—"Yáya, she bore Abíni," or "Adjágbò called Ayakô *tío* [mother's brother]."
2. Personal epithets or clichés—"Fankía heard the guns of war," or "Ayakô cut the reeds at Túlíobúka."
3. Commemorative place names—"Makambí Creek" (where the Lángu clan warrior Makambí was laid

to rest, following a battle, by the Nasí clan leader Kwádjaní) or "Dáume" (the village that harbored Kúngoóka, a latecoming maroon born in Dahomey, West Africa, who brought them their greatest spiritual possession).

4. Lists—verbal maps, as it were—of which lands are owned by which clans. To quote a typical fragment spoken by the tribal chief to a subordinate: "From just above Dáume rapids all the way to Baáku Creek, just below Tjíbihédi, at that stone, that's where the Abaísa clan's lands end. And right there, from the mouth of Gádu Creek all the way to the tip of Ómi Sandbank, below Malobí, that is Matjáu clan territory." Behind such apparently dry lists, however, hides some of the most detailed knowledge of the movements, deeds, and personalities of the First-Time people, for it is these details that explain and justify, when necessary, the bare maps themselves.

5. Strings of names, serving a similarly rich mnemonic function, but relating to the holders of particular staffs of office—for example, "The first to hold this staff was Mbutí. When he died, there was [and a list of eight others follows]."

6. Proverbs and speech fragments, often in esoteric language, that refer elliptically and perspectivally to First-Time events and relationships. (Many examples are found in the subsequent chapters.)

7. Drum (and until recently horn) slogans—First-Time people's praise names as well as proverbs referring to specific incidents—now played on the *apínti* drum at specified ritual and political occasions.

8. Songs (and drums) of several kinds: those actually dating from First-Time that are still sung at shrines such as Awónêngè to bring pleasure to the Old-Time people; those sung in the esoteric Papá language during funerals, to commemorate specific First-Time events; and those sung at the shrines of particular *óbia*s and gods who were powerful in First-Time, as part of the maintenance and continued glorification of their cult.

9. The ever-changing and largely spontaneous prayers spoken to the First-Time ancestors in times of genuine need. The act of preserving specific memories of their personalities and deeds to speak of at their shrine is considered one part of living people's holding up their end of the tenuous bargain that links them to these First-Time ancestors. Without correct (and flattering) worship, there will be no assistance and succor.[10]

THE TRAINING OF THE SARAMAKA HISTORIAN

*Because they [the Saramaka] are a free
people, they take very seriously the
traditions of their forefathers.*

—C. Kersten, missionary to the Saramakas, 1770

The pursuit of First-Time knowledge is a strictly solitary endeavor, and in any clan the number of older men considered really to "know things" can be counted on a single hand. (Women and youths, with few exceptions, are prohibited *a priori* from entering deeply into the world of First-Time knowledge.) Within any clan, each expert's knowledge is idiosyncratic, learned from a unique network of older kinsmen and reflecting that individual's particular strengths as a historian. Over the course of his adult lifetime, each interested man must construct his own images and analyses of "what really happened" two and three centuries ago, based on bits and pieces of relevant songs and rites, disputes, and celebrations that he makes it his business to attend to, as well as on the supplementary narratives he is able to wheedle out of his often-reluctant older kinsmen. The Saramaka historian-in-training hoes a very long row; those that take it on as a vocation, like the very finest of our own historians, seem positively driven by an inner need to make sense of the past, quite apart from the prestige that may incidentally accrue from their special mastery.[11]

First-Time knowledge is a valuable commodity, and those who possess pieces of it share them only sparingly with others. Question-asking about First-Time was traditionally prohibited. As Peléki—a middle-aged Matjáu clan man then being groomed as a possible successor to Tribal Chief Abóikóni—explained:

Asking about things in detail simply did not occur. The old folks would tell you things. You just sat there without a sound, listening. And that was all.

Several of the most knowledgeable Saramaka historians explicitly credit their accumulation of special knowledge to their own natural curiosity and "shameless" insistence in pressing their elders. A 1978 discussion with Captain Góme, the elderly historian from the Awaná clan, provides a fine illustration of the triumph of such persistence over the convention of not-asking.

I had just mentioned a First-Time incident I had recently uncovered. (The previous year, in the Algemeen Rijksarchief in The Hague, I had come upon two brief allusions to a 1779 request by the Awaná captain, Alábi, that had moved me deeply: Alábi was reported to be asking the whites to relinquish into his own care a sister, Tutúba, who had been captured decades before and forced into slavery, where she now languished.)[12] Upon my mention of "Tutúba," the old man's eyes sparkled with tears of joy, and he sang out:

Tutúba, Tutúba u mi o, mmá   Tutúba, my Tutúba, [little] momma
Míí o, u o míti a goónlíba?   Child, oh. Will we ever meet again on this earth?

And Góme excitedly told me:

This is what Alábi's mother used to sing as she pined for her stolen daughter. Alábi learned his sister's name from his mother. Tutúba, Alábi's sister. The child the whites caught and carried off! But not everyone [i.e., hardly anyone] knows about this. I learned it from my mother's brother, Willem Sampie. My mother's brother once told me, "The story of Tutúba. You must not forget it as long as you still breathe. The sister of Alábi [their own Awaná ancestor who later became tribal chief]. They captured her in battle, took her to the city, and put her into slavery. Well, her name was Tutúba." Now the reason we don't use this name, don't give it to children, is that the people of today might misuse it. Alábi's name is public—he was tribal chief. But Tutúba's name must be kept hidden, so people won't misuse it. Tutúba [reminiscing]: They say she wasn't "red" [light-skinned]; she was absolutely black! She died here, on the Upper River [after she was returned to Alábi]. She died before her brother.

Góme then pressed home his point:

Very few people know Alábi's sister's name! [In fact, I found no one else who did.] They'll only know Tjazímbe [his mother's mother] and Akoomí [his mother]. . . . The only reason I know it is because I was such a shameless [dèê-wóyo] youngster. I'd say, "But Mother's Brother, could it be that Alábi didn't have even one other sister?" He'd say [disapprovingly], "Child, there are certain things . . ." [indicating he was not about to answer]. But I'd ask him over and over. And finally one day he told me.

The research procedures of the apprentice Saramaka historian (like those of his Western counterpart) include a good deal of plain sitting (often after having traveled a considerable distance for the privilege). "First-Time things," Peléki once mused to me, "don't have only one head. . . . Your ears must truly grow tired of the thing before you will really know it." Likewise, Asipéi, a Wátambíi clan elder in his late sixties, stressed the need for patience when he used to go to be instructed by his mother's brother: "I'd be there right at cock's crow to 'converse.' But this 'conversing' meant that he simply told me whatever he felt like. You can't get up from your stool quickly if you really want to hear things!" Certainly, the necessity to sit passively for long periods is one reason why the pursuit of First-Time knowledge is not for everyone. I once overheard Captain Góme, spurred on by our own discussions of First-Time, chiding a relative who was then in his forties: "Your hour is already late. You don't have the patience to sit down and listen to the words of old men. . . . Then one day a 'child' will ask you things. And you will have absolutely nothing to tell him!"

Such research requires tact, strategy, and patience, the skills of a master elicitor. As Peléki once put it, "Every older man has a very particular way you must approach him [about First-Time knowledge]. . . . [One must] know exactly where to walk [what to say] so they will speak. . . . exactly where not to walk lest they won't say a word" (see 169 below).[13] Here is Peléki effectively using flattery on Tebíni—an elder raised by his father's clan, the Matjáus, and perhaps the greatest living Saramaka historian—to try to persuade him to divulge a First-Time fragment regarding the Nasí clan.

> [Peléki to me:] The old man here [Tebíni, who was sitting alone with us], he *knows* things about Muyánwóyo Creek . . . *really* knows them. Because he has told things to the Nasí elders [Muyánwóyo is in Nasí territory] that absolutely amazed them. . . . Well, today's people, they tend to be like that [like those Nasís]; they no longer know things. But the Truth is always something special! When you hear it, you're dumbstruck. Because the places and place names that he [Tebíni] explained to them— why a certain place has a certain name—they were absolutely amazed. They'd been calling that place by its name all these years but they no longer knew why. So they *believed* him. [Tebíni chuckles modestly, but with genuine pleasure.]

Cock's crow, with an older man speaking softly to a younger kinsman: this is the classic Saramaka setting for the formal transmission of First-Time knowledge. (Cock's crow is the hour or two that precedes dawn, when most villagers are still asleep in their hammocks.) Although the bulk of any man's First-Time knowledge is in fact pieced together from more informal settings— from overheard proverbs and epithets, from songs and discussions of land tenure—discreetly prearranged cock's crow discussions are, conceptually, the epitome of First-Time learning. It is at such times that a captain is supposed to instruct a potential successor, a grandfather his grandson, or a mother's brother his sister's son. Indeed, the standard phrase with which a Saramaka denies knowledge of First-Time is "I never sat down with oldfolks at cock's crow."

The knowledge transmitted at cock's crow is deliberately incomplete, masked by a style that is at once elliptical and obscure.[14] It is a paradoxical but accepted fact that any Saramaka narrative (including those told at cock's crow with the ostensible intent of communicating knowledge) will leave out most of what the teller knows about the incident in question. A person's knowledge is supposed to grow only in very small increments, and in any aspect of life people are deliberately told only a little bit more than the speaker thinks they already know.[15] On pages 129–34 I provide an extended illustration of the masking of information typical of a cock's crow narrative by comparing an example taken from a tape-recorded session with other, more fully elaborated kinds of materials. (And there are other examples regarding narrative content throughout the book.) Here, I wish only to signal the most salient feature of the style of cock's crow discourse—its recurrent, pervasive historiographical "digressions."

Well over half of cock's crow speech consists of what a Western historian would consider "footnote material"—detailed discussion of sources and prior authorities. In this book, I have generally deleted such materials from the historical fragments presented, since they tend to be rather repetitive and, for someone not familiar with the sources in question, intrusive. I instead present at this point some representative examples, taken off tape recordings, of such historiographical discursions.

Here is Captain Kála (then in his seventies, holder of the original Peace Treaty Matjáu clan staff) instructing Abátelí, his classificatory grandson (then in his forties), at cock's crow; the subject is land tenure along the Pikílío, but Kála interrupts his list of places and owners to stress,

> I am *telling* you things here. Asápampía [Kála's late "mother's brother"], Amanábèntá [another late "mother's brother"]—I knew them when I was already full-grown, when I was already interested in [First-Time] things. . . . Now Kositán [his late "older brother"], it seems like only yesterday that he died. . . . Kositán would tell things exactly as they happened, because he really took his mother's brothers to heart. Now, Tebíni of Kámpu, when he tells you something, there may now be times when old age confuses it, but as for *true* Matjáu clan things, there is no one alive like Tebíni to tell them. Old man Afukáti [now deceased], Man, he *knew* things. Bitjénfóu [his late "mother's brother," and the holder of Kála's captain's staff during the early twentieth century], that whole group of people. Now when you take their words, you're not taking lie-talk. Asápampía knew things until he could read books without ever having been to school! Now, to get back to the lands along this river. . . . [and he continues with land tenure]

A few moments later, Kála again interrupts his listing to discuss exactly *where* he had heard things from Asápampía. After a several-minute-long speech about how he had gone to coastal French

Guiana, paid for a ship with his own money, and so on—all so that he could "hear" Asápampía (who was working there at the time) firsthand—Kála notes:

> Well, he used to *tell* me things. Now you [Abátelí] have come to hear things from me. And I am telling you things of "the inner Pikílío" [the real McCoy]. . . . Now, other people will try to tell you things too, but you shouldn't pay attention. Because if some day you tell people the things that I am telling you here, the person is not alive who will laugh at you. No way.

Or, let us listen in on the elderly tribal chief "interrupting" a cock's crow discussion of land tenure with a younger kinsman:

> Akwánkwáni, when I lived with him he would *tell* me. The old man called Faándja, I slept two nights with him, and I *heard*. A man from Malobí called Goónkíima, I slept with him for a week and I heard. Gosí and I lived together [in the same place] for over twenty years, and I heard things from his own mouth. . . . [He returns for a few moments to the land tenure talk but digresses to say:] It's my old age that you hear talking here. The age that let me see seven mother's brothers as well as the other elders that I knew. Well, it's for them [on their authority] that I am speaking here.

Clearly, the elders that a man knew, and the fame of these teachers, have much to do with establishing the worth of his own historical knowledge. Even when a person is denigrating his own knowledge in comparison to another's, he uses this idiom. I once overheard the tribal chief say, "Tebíni . . . he saw the very oldest generation. He knew them all! Unlike me, who lived with my father's people [the Fandááki], whose knowledge really doesn't go back very far." Constant allusions to authority, a repeated shoring up of ones bona fides, pervade every discussion of First-Time. My calling them "interruptions," "digressions," or "footnote material" is not intended to diminish their import; in this nonliterate society, they are a central datum for the Saramaka listener, a crucial part of his critical apparatus. They are the single leitmotif running through all cock's crow instruction.

In any Saramaka narration, the citation of specific sources complements these more general appeals to authority. "My 'great grandfather,' Kositán, heard this from his own father, Adobóiti, who was a [member of the clan called] Abaísa"; or "[the late] Captain Maáku used to tell us boys this." Such specific citations often include copious details about the travel arrangements to set up the meeting, who was sitting where, what they were wearing, and so on—all lending a sense of veracity and immediacy to the account.[16] And Saramaka historians "criticize" such sources in much the same way as their Western counterparts: [Tebíni, skeptically:] "Where did he say he heard that story?" [I supply the information.] "That's a no-good place! [an unreliable source] Of course it isn't true!" Similarly, I have witnessed accusations of "false footnoting"—of the citation of spurious sources—by one man criticizing (behind his back) the words of another. As in our own system, a person's scholarly integrity in this regard can be his most valuable possession, and any such accusation is taken most seriously.[17]

THOSE TIMES SHALL COME AGAIN

Why, the dumbest black bastard in the
cotton patch knows that the only way to
please a white man is to tell him a lie!
—Ralph Ellison, *Invisible Man*

Saramaka collective identity is predicated on a single opposition: freedom versus slavery. The central role of First-Time in Saramaka life is ideological; preservation of its knowledge is their way of saying "Never again." As I overheard one man reminding another, "If we forget the deeds of our ancestors, how can we hope to avoid being returned to whitefolks' slavery?" Or, in the memorable words of Peléki, speaking at the time to me (see *170–76* below), "This is the one thing Maroons really believe. It's stronger than anything else. . . . This is the greatest fear of all Maroons: that those times [slavery and the struggle for freedom] shall come again."

"Those times," as Saramakas are well aware, refers to the harshest realities. Maroons recaptured by the colonists were routinely "punished" by hamstringing, amputation of limbs, and a variety of deaths by torture. To cite but one example, a recaptured maroon, "whose punishment shall serve as an example to others," was sentenced

> to be quartered alive, and the pieces thrown in the River. He was laid on the ground, his head on a long beam. The first blow he was given, on the abdomen, burst his bladder open, yet he uttered not the least sound; the second blow with the axe he tried to deflect with his hand, but it gashed the hand and upper belly, again without his uttering a sound. The slave men and women laughed at this, saying to one another, "That is a man!" Finally, the third blow, on the chest, killed him. His head was cut off and the body cut in four pieces and dumped in the river. (Herlein 1718:117)

For Saramakas today, talk about First-Time is very far from being mere rhetoric, preserved for reasons of nostalgic pride. Rather, First-Time ideology lives in the minds of twentieth-century Saramaka men because it is relevant to their own life experience—it helps them make sense, on a daily basis, of the wider world in which they live. For more than a century now, every Saramaka man has spent many years of his life in coastal Suriname earning money by logging, construction work, and many other forms of low-paid wage labor (see Price 1975). There, he meets *bakáas*—"outsiders," white and black—who treat him in ways that he fits comfortably into a First-Time ideological framework. Asipéi, a dignified man in his sixties, described an incident that may appropriately stand here for dozens of similar ones I heard recounted. When he was a boy, visiting the city with his mother's brother, an urban Afro-Surinamer derisively called him a "monkey," to which his uncle replied angrily but with pride: "Where you live, you pay to drink water, you pay to have a place to shit; but in the forest where I live, I drink the finest water in the world whenever I like, I defecate at my leisure." For all those respected Saramaka historians or ritual specialists, for all those renowned woodcarvers or dancers who are forced by economic necessity (and lack of Western schooling) to clean out toilet bowls in the French missile-launching base at Kourou, First-Time ideology cannot but remain a powerful relevant force. And for *all* Saramakas, the recent construction of the great hydroelectric project (that flooded fully half of the lands their ancestors had fought and died for, and that caused the forced resettlement of thousands of their people) represented an expectable continuation of the kind of behavior that their First-Time ancestors routinely suffered at the hands of the *bakáas.* Continuities of oppression, from original enslavement and torture to modern political paternalism and economic exploitation, have been more than sufficient to keep First-Time ideology a living force.

The fear of group betrayal, forged in slavery and the decades of war, remains a cornerstone of the Saramaka moral system. Proverbs and folktales are filled with morals about not trusting other people, and self-defensive posturing and manipulation permeate interpersonal relations (see also Price 1975:31–37). "Testing" people, whether kinsmen, friends, or a spouse, is a pervasive and acceptable aspect of interpersonal relations; one man "plants" a valued object to see if his new wife will be tempted to steal it, another confides some manufactured gossip about himself to a friend with the express purpose of seeing whether it gets leaked out. This sort of thing is common among close kinsmen as well. With outsiders, as would be expected, deception and prevarication become very much a matter of course. An anthropologist who has lived with the Alúku, a neighboring Maroon group, describes a "layer of spurious culture," which they have "created to shield [their] custom from the outside world," and notes that in their dealings with outsiders they "have made a high art of institutionalized prevarication" (T. Price 1970:65–66). It is for these reasons that until recently many village names recorded on official maps of Saramaka were either obscene expressions or the names of nearby cemeteries. And Saramaka men spend hours swapping stories of personal experiences they have had on the coast regarding what Afro-Americans in the United States used to call "puttin' on ol' massa." The quintessential formulation of this ethic is contained in a folktale that I will have reason to refer back to several times in the course of this book.[18]

There was a great hunter called Bási Kodjó. He had hunting dogs that were killing off all the Bush Cows in the forest. [The Bush Cow is a mythical animal, resembling—but fiercer than—a tapir.] Finally, the Bush Cows held a council meeting. They said, "What can we do to kill this man? Soon there will be none of us left." One of them, a female, spoke. "I'll go to him. I have a plan to lure him back here so we can kill him." And she changed herself into a beautiful woman, in order to trick Bási Kodjó.

She arrived in his village with a basket on her head, saying that the man who could knock it to the ground would become her husband. She was really beautiful! No one could do it. Finally Bási Kodjó tried, and the basket fell. So this beautiful woman [really the Bush Cow in disguise] became his wife. Every night, when they were in their hammock, making love, she would ask Bási Kodjó what his secret was, how it was that he was able to kill so many Bush Cows without their ever hurting him. Each night she asked, and each night he told her a little more. She was so beautiful!

Often, during the night, the woman would go out behind the house to stare at the row of Bush Cow skulls that her husband had nailed against the rear wall as trophies. She would weep and weep, silently, for her dead relatives. When she had finished crying, she would return to the house, and Bási Kodjó would ask, "Where have you been?" "I went to urinate," she would say. But every few minutes she would go back out and just stare at those skulls and weep.

Every night, she asked Bási Kodjó over and over, "Those animal skulls at the back of your house. How in the world did you kill those animals? They're fiercer than any animal alive!"

One night, Bási Kodjó finally told her, "Woman, those animals live in savannahs. I go all the way to the middle of the savannah and fire my gun. When they come charging, I toss my gun aside and climb an awara [palm] tree. The animals circle round and furiously chew at the trunk to fell it. Meanwhile, my mother is back in the village, stirring the boiling pap that she feeds to my hunting dogs at the proper moment, to excite them. When I see that the palm tree is about to fall, I turn myself into a chameleon, sitting on the trunk, and I call out '*fííí*,' and this makes the trunk grow even thicker than it was at first. I do this until I know that the dogs have had time to gobble up all the boiling pap, and really feel it. Then I let the tree fall. By then, the Bush Cows have realized that I am the chameleon, so I turn into a spot of sand. When they try to eat that up, I use my final disguise and turn myself into a. . . . " Just then, Bási Kodjó's mother shrieked from her house, "Bási Kodjó. Bási Kodjó. Hurry. Snake. Snake!" [It was really the god in her head that was calling out.] Bási Kodjó jumped out of his hammock and ran to kill the snake. When he got to his mother's house she pulled him close and whispered, "There's no snake. But I must warn you. That beautiful woman is not really a woman! Don't tell her the last thing you know how to turn yourself into. Instead, tell her that you become a *nóuna*." Bási Kodjó returned to his wife. She said, "That thing you were about to tell me, the very last thing you turn yourself into, when the Bush Cows come charging at you, what is it?" He said, "I become a *nóuna* [a nonsense word, a word with no meaning]." At last, she was satisfied. They slept.

In the middle of the night, the woman arose very quietly and went to her basket and took out a razor. She prepared to cut Bási Kodjó's throat. Bási Kodjó's gun said, "I will shoot her *kpóó*!!" His cutlass said, "I will cut her *vélevélevélevéle*!" His magical belt [*óbiatatái*] said, "I will tie her *kíli-kílikílikíli*." All the posts of the house groaned loudly *hiiiii*. Bási Kodjó awoke with a start, saying, "What's going on?" She answered, "I have no idea. I was asleep." Not a single thing in the house slept during the rest of the night.

At dawn, the beautiful wife asked Bási Kodjó to go off to the forest with her to collect awara palm seeds. He told his mother to prepare the pap for the dogs. And they set off. The woman led him deeper and deeper into the forest until they finally reached the savannah. Bási Kodjó climbed the awara tree and began picking fruit. Suddenly, the woman turned back into her natural form, a Bush Cow, and called out to her relatives. In a moment, the savannah was black with Bush Cows, all coming to eat Bási Kodjó. Quickly, he turned himself into a chameleon. She told them he was now the chameleon. So they began felling the tree. When it finally fell, they couldn't find the chameleon. She said, "Eat that spot of sand. *It* is Bási Kodjó." After a while, they could not find the sand. Bási Kodjó had turned himself into a tiny awara palm thorn, and hidden himself by sticking himself into a leaf. She said, "Destroy the *nóuna*. He's turned himself into a *nóuna*." The Bush Cows milled around in confusion. None of them knew what a *nóuna* was!

Meanwhile, Bási Kodjó's hunting dogs, who by then had finished eating their boiling pap and had been untied, arrived on the scene and they ripped every last Bush Cow to shreds. Except for one. Bási Kodjó saw that this last Bush Cow was pregnant, and he called off the dogs. This Bush Cow was hiding in a cave near a stream. She called out, "Bási Kodjó, have mercy. You're about to kill your own offspring!" He grabbed her by one side, ripping off the whole leg, and then shoved her back into the cave.

Now you know the importance of *nóuna*.

The core meaning of this tale, and the heart of Saramaka morality, is that knowledge is power, and that one must never reveal all of what one knows. And this holds doubly for First-Time, and with outsiders.

FIELDWORK

*In the arts, the unimplicated observer has
been reduced to a minor convention; in the
sciences to an unreachable limiting case.
But in much of sociology, anthropology, and
political science he lives on, masquerading
as a real person performing a possible act.*

—Clifford Geertz

For some two years in the mid-1960s, Sally Price and I lived in Saramaka, carrying out ethnographic fieldwork on an unusually wide range of issues, from "social structure" and "religion" to "language" and "art" (see, for a partial list of the resulting publications, Price and Price 1980:227). Only one subject was explicitly forbidden, from our earliest encounters with the oracle of Gaán Táta right up to the week of our final departure—First-Time.[19] I diligently avoided systematic exploration of the distant past (though it greatly interested me and though its emanations were everywhere around me) as part of holding up my end of the fieldwork bargain that we had struck with our hosts.

During the subsequent years, as a fledgling professor at Yale and Johns Hopkins, I learned more about the early history of Afro-Americans, in particular maroons, elsewhere in the hemisphere (see, for some of the results, Mintz and Price 1976 and Price 1979b). And I decided to try to persuade Saramakas to explore First-Time in depth with me. When I broached the possibility, on brief trips in 1974 and 1975, I was sufficiently encouraged to proceed. In one sense, the elder Saramakas I knew best had always expected me to work on First-Time; how else could I become a man of knowledge? Nevertheless, they expected me to do it only when I was ready—when *they* thought I was ready—and the time now seemed right.

During much of our first two years in Saramaka, we had posed an enormous threat to our hosts, far more than we realized at the time. Many truly believed that we had come to kill them on the spot; others believed that we had come to learn their secrets so that we could bring great armies to destroy them; and all of our hosts knew that our presence, in spite of the frequent rituals to which they subjected us, might sufficiently anger the gods and ancestors so that they would wreak wholesale destruction upon them. As Captain Kála used to pray at the ancestor shrine, during those early days of our stay,

Whitefolks have never come to Dángogó. The ancestors always said whites must never come as far as Dángogó. No outsider [black or white] has ever slept in Dángogó. The Old-Time People simply cannot "see" whitefolks. The war we fought, it's not finished yet. . . . What in the world are we to do with these people? I have never buried a white person. If they die, how will I know how to bury them?

Yet eventually our initially reluctant hosts were seeing us, at least much of the time, as individual human beings with our own idiosyncratic personalities, and not just as "whitefolks." And there was a widespread—if sometimes grudging—respect for the way that we took pains to conduct ourselves in everyday life. As the tribal chief said in his parting speech to us in 1968, Sally had not committed adultery and had strictly held to the menstrual taboos; I had hunted and fished like a real man, sharing with our neighbors. We hadn't walked where we had been told not to (the shrine for the First-Time ancestors, the upriver site of the First-Time villages) and I hadn't talked about what I wasn't supposed to (First-Time).[20] Given the historical circumstances, we felt that we had been treated with considerable grace and generous hospitality. We also felt that we had made several lifelong friends, a feeling that time has since borne out.

By our return to Suriname in the mid-1970s, the world of Upper River Saramaka, where we had lived for two years, had changed. Government officials or tourists dropped in and out of the once-isolated villages almost on a monthly basis, film crews occasionally came and went, Saramaka men often wore long pants in the villages, and people were listening to radios and spending considerable time on the coast in the capital. I too had changed: I was now a professor and chairman of a department rather than a student; I was known to be an "authority" for outsiders on Saramaka life (Saramakas had been given copies of the books and papers I had written); and I was considered to be in a position to help them in various ways with outside officials. Our earlier stay—the social relations it involved, the fears it raised—had by now become in some sense part of Dángogó's past; a new chapter was beginning. While we had once been objects of fear and concern, we were now, at least for many Saramakas, honored guests. Here is Captain Kála—perhaps my fiercest adversary during the often-difficult first two years, and a strict upholder of the First-Time ways—greeting me with a proverb on our return in 1978.[21]

Asó pipí mi sa djóubi. Asó pipí mi sa djóubi.[22] When you first came to Saramaka, people would say, "Abátelí [Kála's grandson, our initial direct 'host' in Dángogó] has brought a person to me, Dangasí [another of Kála's names], and all of Saramaka will be destroyed." How come [they said that]? Saramaka territory has a tjína [taboo] against whitefolks. Well, they've brought him to the village they call Dángogó Háfupási, a true slavery-time village. Outsiders do not come here! [People said] Abátelí and I took him, brought him, put him here to kill every single living Saramaka.[23] Then, on a day [otherwise] like any other, you [RP] come back, bearing all sorts of "gifts" [for everyone]. Asó pipí mi sa djóubi. [He then explains the proverb:] Rice granary says that. When it's dry season and you begin to make a garden, you risk death at every turn. When you clear the underbrush, your machete can kill you, a snake can bite you, a tarantula can bite you; every sort of thing can kill you when you're clearing the underbrush! [Then] when you go to fell a tree, well, every single tree can kill you; the axe in your very hand can kill you. You do all those things [take all those risks] right through the time when you burn the garden [the final stage before planting]. And then the rice grows. You harvest it until you're all finished; you load it up in your granary. Until the granary is chock full! Then it [the granary] says its praise name for you. Asó pipí mi sa djóubi. Because the way you loaded up the granary until it was absolutely full, you can't possibly eat it all by yourself. When you cook it and eat it, until you can't eat more, you toss the leftovers to the fish. Let's say people come to visit you from another village. Well, you cook them some of it, even though they didn't do the work. You throw some to the chickens for them to eat. There are rats in the granary, tree squirrels too. They all eat it. It's available for everyone. Asó pipí mi sa djóubi. The American came out from his country and arrived in Saramaka. [People said] Abátelí and I put him here to destroy the world. But today [in contrast]: asó pipí mi sa djóubi. [They're all reaping the benefits.] First-Time language! I, Dángasí, say so!

My own activities in Saramaka shifted significantly between the initial fieldwork of the 1960s and the 1976 and 1978 research seasons (when I obtained most of the specific oral material for this book). While before I had spent considerable time in hunting, attending oracle sessions, and participating in other tasks appropriate for a man of my age, I now worked singlemindedly on First-Time, seeking out selected elders for private conversation. With the knowledge and approval of Tribal Chief Abóikóni, Captain Kála, and the other Matjáu clan elders who had become, in a sense, our spiritual guardians, I began work with men who had known me (at least by reputation) from the previous decade (Because of knowledge I had since gleaned from written sources, I was now in a position to offer Saramaka historians a most precious gift, new information about their own early past) (Although I gave such information sparingly—as is always appropriate in discussions of First-Time—I nevertheless had, and have, considerable qualms about any "interference" in their system of knowledge [see below].) After an additional research

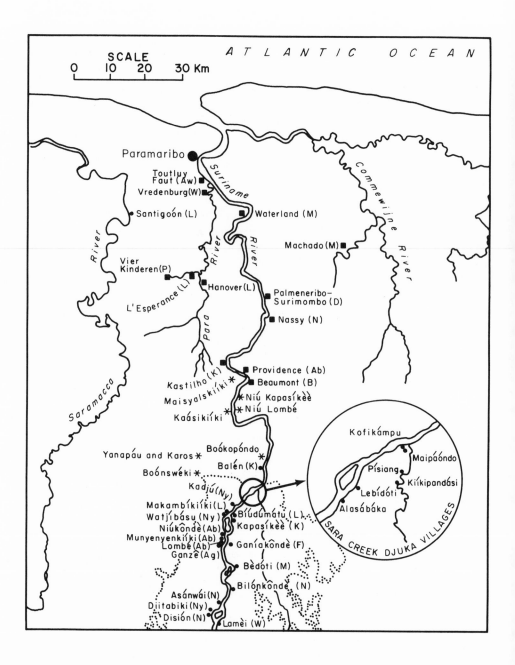

Major Saramaka Villages

Dots (●) indicate villages as they existed in 1963, on the eve of the closing of the hydroelectric dam. Asterisks (*) indicate new villages of people forcibly relocated during the mid-1960s because of the lake. Dominant clans are shown in parentheses, using the following abbreviations: Ab=Abaísa; Ag=Agbó; Aw=Awaná; B=Biítu; D=Dómbi; F=Fandááki; K=Kasitú; Kw=Kwamá; L=Lángu; M=Matjáu; N=Nasí; Ny=Nyafái; P=Papútu; Pa=Paatí-nêngè; W=Wátambíi. Also depicted (with a ■) are the major plantations, when known, from which the First-Time ancestors of these clans escaped. (This map summarizes information supplied by many dozens of Saramakas over a twelve-year period. It represents the first systematic attempt to depict the location of Saramaka villages cartographically.)

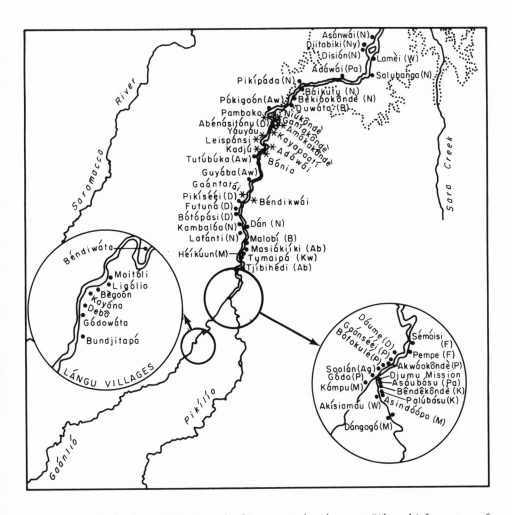

year in the Netherlands in 1977–78, much of it spent in the Algemeen Rijksarchief, my store of First-Time information had increased enormously, enough so that even without offering much in the way of specifics, I now possessed a considerable reputation as a historian among knowledge-able Saramakas. An exchange of information became, for some old men, the principal motive for "sitting down" with me and not only did I know original whitefolks' views on First-Time events, but I was fast building up a storehouse of Saramaka knowledge about the period that in its breadth exceeded the knowledge of any single Saramaka. Fortunately, the growth of my own knowledge coincided with an independent realization by some elders that knowledge of First-Time (at least the nonritual parts of it) had better be written down soon or else be lost forever.[24] Indeed, at a 1978 gathering (*kuútu*) in the tribal chief's reception hall, I was asked on behalf of the Matjáu clan to write such a book for them; flattered with a characteristic rhetorical declaration that I was now a Matjáu, I was formally asked to be their official chronicler.

It was this kind of official approval, which contrasted so strikingly with the explicit prohibitions of the 1960s on my discussing First-Time at all, that permitted me to proceed. Nonetheless, it did not really make any easier the act of eliciting First-Time knowledge from wary elders, as people very much kept their own counsel about how much, and exactly what, they wished to share with me. All of my discussions with Saramakas about First-Time must be firmly situated in their basic ideological context: "First-Time kills," "Never tell another more than half of what you know," and "Those times [the days of war, the days of whitefolks' slavery] shall come again." Some of the strongest fears about divulging information were perspectival: the tribal chief was at first reluctant to have me traveling the river to speak with other clans about First-Time, as it might "confuse" Matjáu priorities; and members of other clans were often afraid I would carry back what they might tell me to Matjáus, or to other clans.[25] The methods of work imposed by practical considerations ruled out most traditional modes of historical transmission; I could not, like a Saramaka, simply wait a lifetime and piece together what I had seen and heard. I had to seek people out, explain myself, and actively persuade them to share information, with little to offer except my own historical knowledge, compensation for their time (in money or, if they preferred, in "gifts"), and the excitement of joint discoveries—for some the most important inducement of all. I had to keep telling myself, as the Saramaka hunting proverb says, that "if you don't stir up a hole, you won't find out what's inside"; but I could never afford to forget its cautionary counterpart: "If you shake a dry tree, you'd better watch out for your head."[26]

With the men I worked with most often, I developed various routines that helped ease for both of us the basic inappropriateness of the enterprise.[27] I soon realized, for example, that the great historian Tebíni was not fully comfortable speaking about First-Time while looking directly at me; so I worked with him in the presence of one or another younger kinsman whom Tebíni could formally address as he spoke. Sometimes—particularly when we became involved in an exchange of pressing interest to him—Tebíni would indicate that my concerns with propriety were exaggerated and that he (like Góme, see above) shared my traditionally "inappropriate" impatience with the convention of not asking questions. When I once insisted on learning about a detail, but at the same time apologized for my audacity, he waved off the apology:

> I'm like that too, you know. That's how I would sit down with my father's older brother [Captain] Bitjé[nfóu], until sleep would overtake him. Then he'd rise and finally go to his hammock. He'd be sitting there on his *fútu bángi* [an old-fashioned one-piece stool][28] telling us things. . . . He'd say, " 'Son,' are you dozing off?" And I'd say, "No way, 'Father.' " I would really listen in those days! I wanted to know things in detail [like you].

Having a third party present in my discussions with Tebíni turned out to be helpful in other ways as well. Rhetorically, it provided the necessary answerer who could lend the speaker full attention (since I was often scribbling and working hard to digest what I was hearing); but more important, it provided a crucial source of new questions.[29] With time, Tebíni, like several other elders, was willing to discuss almost any First-Time issue, but neither he nor the others often brought up a "new" issue on their own. An important part of my job, then, became the discovery of fragments or traces, puzzles or songs (some overheard in proverbs or witnessed at rites, some found in the archives) that would spark a reaction. Some of my best sessions with Tebíni were attended also by Peléki—then in his fifties, visually impaired after a serious bout with syphilis that ruined his once-strong chances for succession to the office of tribal chief, and nourishing a true passion for First-Time history. An intensely serious man, Peléki followed Tebíni's disclosures with rapt interest, always ready with the appropriate words of flattery to cajole a particular fragment out of him (see above), and able to ask about new matters related to the subject at hand about whose very existence I was often ignorant. One evening, for example, Tebíni was describing the original migration of the Nasí clan, noting that they were the first people to come south by canoe rather than on foot; I would have left it there, but Peléki interrupted to ask, "Is that the thing they say about making the first canoe?" And Tebíni answered affirmatively, "That's when they made the Silk-Cotton Tree canoe!" and proceeded to discuss this famous incident (see 86 below). In a game in which knowing the right questions was halfway to winning, middle-aged Saramakas often pitched in by helping to nudge new items out of their closemouthed elders.

By 1978, Tebíni was old enough to be physically and psychologically up one day and down the next, but he had truly come to enjoy our nighttime exchanges. On a good day, he would greet me in the evening in some unexpectedly playful way (just as he would, in a good mood, when visiting an old age-mate); he might clear his throat, enter and sit down, and say out of the blue, "*Máti*

[Friend, his term of address for me], I'm here. I'm Bímboasilá-u-Musútu [Bímboasilá-from-Musútu]. I'm here! That's what a [certain] *apúku* [forest spirit] always says [when he 'arrives' to possess a person]!" And when Tebíni got excited about a story he was telling me, seeing me writing (and never fully clear about how tape recorders worked), he'd say, "Friend. Take it down *exactly*. Because some day you will 'tell it' [in a book]."[30]

Something of the tone of these collegial discussions may be gleaned from the numbered fragments that constitute the heart of this book, though they have been edited for repetition and historiographical discursions. I have, however, deliberately left one excellent extended example intact—Tebíni, Peléki, and I engaged in a discussion about an apparently obscure fact—in order to illustrate something of the tone of our joint research efforts (see *169* below). This aura of collegiality—mutual respect always tempered by an appropriate measure of reticence—marked my historical conversations with a number of other men besides Tebíni and Peléki. Among these I would single out Captain Góme of the Awaná clan, Basiá [Assistant Headman] Bakáa of the Dómbis, Asipéi of the Watambíis, Mètisên of Lángu, and a number of Matjáus—Tribal Chief Agbagó (also known as Abóikóni), Captains Kála and Faánsisónu of Dángogó, Basiá Tandó, and the quixotic Otjútju (whose unique readiness to talk about forbidden things opened up many new avenues for me and was matched only by his willingness to ply me with highly politicized, consciously distorted versions of First-Time events). With each of these men I developed complex relations, many spanning a twelve-year period. Indeed, with these people it would be more accurate to envision a series of intermittent/interrupted conversations that continued over the years than more standard anthropological "interviews." Through time, as my own knowledge grew, I set aside certain former interests in favor of others that began to emerge as more important. The chronological development of my discussions with any of these men is a record of deepening understanding and mutual comprehension. With each of them, I eventually enjoyed relations that permitted a serious exchange of ideas about First-Time.

Necessary statement to lend authenticity to his work

There were, however, other research encounters marked more by mistrust and fear than collegiality, and I would be remiss not to give them their full due here as well. In certain villages where I had been known only by reputation, I was greeted with interest and cooperation; I had not, for example, really known Captain Góme or Basiá Bakáa well before 1978, but both quickly became valued colleagues (as well as being gracious hosts).[31] In other such villages, however, where I had come to spend a few days, I met polite hospitality combined with a firm deter-mination not to cooperate. Traveling with a Saramaka friend (sometimes accompanied by Sally)—that is, without the non-Saramaka entourage considered normal for outsiders—I pre-sented each new village with an anomaly: a white man who not only spoke their language well but was familiar, in certain respects more so than they, with details of their own people and places and battles that had been hidden from whitefolks for centuries. Listening later with Matjáu friends to some of the tapes from these downriver sessions, I came to realize just how frightened some of these groups of elders were of me and of my knowledge. And I was also reminded, again, just how strong First-Time ideology remains, and the extent to which it lends deep meaning and dignity to these men's lives. What I learned in such situations was always less than I hoped; fear is hardly conducive to truth-telling. Nevertheless, I occasionally sowed seeds that later bore fruit, as when a man subsequently came to me alone to talk seriously, or when I picked up fragments of stories I was later able to fill out in detail with other people.

fn. These men are nominally Christian as such have "enormous respect" for book learning

When I appeared in such a village, having first sent word ahead, I was always direct in stating my intentions, once the appropriate small talk and exchange of gifts had been completed. Here is an example translated from a tape made with the Nasís of Kambalóa, traditional rivals of the Matjáus; present in the house of elderly Captain Aláfo were our host, his yet older kinsman Aseedu, two middle-aged men, our Matjáu friend Abátelí who accompanied us on this trip, Sally, and I. After a few minutes of small talk I formally addressed one of the middle-aged men, who served as my answerer.

The way I'm living on the Pikílío. [So?] I am in the hands of the Matjáu people. [Exactly.] With them I live. [Truly.] I sit down with the old folks: [Truly.] the tribal chief, [So?] the captains, [So?] other old men. [So it is.] And they tell me things: [Well so?] how Matjáus lived in First-Time. [Precisely.] Sometimes they tell me things about the Nasí people too. [So?] But when I weigh and examine what they say about that, [Truly.] I take only half as true. [So?] Because any clan, when they tell things, [So?] seeks to make itself higher, right? [Yes, they'll try to make themselves higher.] Isn't that the way with human beings? [Yes, exactly.] Well, that's why I've run down here to you. [Truly.] Because some of the things I've heard, [So?] I wonder if that's the way they really happened. [Exactly.] Also, when I went to the Queen's Country (Netherlands), [So?] I found so many things about Nasí people. [Exactly.] On paper. [So?] From First-Time. [Well so?] And they don't match up with what I heard upriver. [They don't match up!] I think that only you can know [So?] what really happened. [That's true.] So, I will give to you, [So?] and you will give to me. [All right.] And we'll see if it all fits together. [If it all fits together.]

After such a speech I would be asked to proceed, and it was usually only after the next several minutes that my hosts really began to realize, with mixed amazement and fear, what was at hand.

I usually opened with a relatively neutral fact that I thought would particularly interest them, something I had found in the archives but which they might not have preserved in detail. In the Nasí case, for example, I discussed their first two post-Treaty captains' staffs. The aged Aseedu answered (formally addressing one of the younger men) in a rhetoric typical of such encounters:

Well, you know? We can't say it's not true. You know why? His "ancestor" [the pen and notebook] is in his hand. But ours are no longer here. We know nothing, really. Whitefolks know everything. Look at us here, We just don't know the truth any more. If he has things to tell us, let him speak. But it's not that we have anything we can tell him. Let him speak. Our own elders simply never taught us. [And he continued in this vein for several minutes.]

In such situations, after sharing with my hosts a series of facts, I might ask a question. For example, with an Abaísa group, at this same stage of an initial interview I asked about where their ancestors had "walked" in their migration from slavery. There was embarrassed laughter; then an old man said, "This thing. We won't find it!" And another chimed in, "Let *him* just keep telling *us*." When I pleaded that they must contribute as well, I was met by further protestations of ignorance: "If only you had come here in the days when people knew things. Our oldfolks are all dead and gone; we who are left on this earth know nothing at all."

Often, during this stage of a meeting, some middle-aged man who sensed my frustration would attempt to help out by addressing his elders. Here is an Abaísa example:

You know what the man wants? After he's told you something, if your elders have told you that, you say, "Yes, that's what we've heard," or "No, it's *this* way we've heard it." But you mustn't just listen and say you've never heard it. That's not what he wants.

In this case, as in others, an older man interrupted fiercely to insist:

He'll tell us, and we'll say if it's true. . . . My own elders used to say, "Not everyone knows these things" [that is, non-Abaísas do not]. My mother's brothers used to say that! Let *him* tell us only.[32]

Several times during such sessions, an older man would arrive, sit down, and, sensing what was at stake, interrupt the proceedings. Once, in Masiákííki, an elder exclaimed, using a series of vaguely connected images:

Don't blow the horn, eh! Don't make waves like a motorboat! This canoe will not be carved [fashioned from its trunk] quickly. Don't point the canoe straight downstream. Better to walk like an old man, with a staff [that is, slowly].

But even the most frustratingly guarded encounters sometimes eventuated in important sharing of knowledge. In one of my initial Abaísa group discussions, which truly seemed to be going nowhere, I finally told a detailed story about Abaísa ancestors that I had heard from other Saramakas, asking them at its conclusion whether it matched their own traditions.

[Old man:] So you've heard.

[I:] So I've heard.

[O:] So you've heard. [*long silence*] Basiá [assistant headman], have you heard this?

[Basiá Lántifáya:] No, I haven't heard this. . . . [*Mumbling:*] But the one about slavery times. That I've heard.

[Younger man:] I will ask the man here. Did the woman [their apical ancestress, Ma Kaála, whom I had just been telling them about] come out of Africa *with* her husband?

[I:] I don't know; it's not in the "book." But I have heard that his name was Father-in-law Andolé.

[B, *in amazement:*] Exactly!

[I:] But I still don't understand what the "slavery" story is.

[B:] That *is* it. [*silence*]

[I:] But I want to know what happened. [*silence*]

[B:] You want to know it.

[I:] Yes. I want to know it. [*silence*]

[B, *to others:*] He wants to know it.

[Others:] He wants to know it. [*long silence*]

[B, *finally, clearing his throat:*] Well, what we've heard. . . .

And he then proceeded to give me my fullest version ever of the Abaísa escape from slavery (see 39 below).

These "difficult" encounters always left me emotionally drained, as they undoubtedly did my reluctant hosts. My elderly Dómbi friend, Améiká, aptly remarked after the officials of his village had forbidden him to discuss First-Time with me in 1978, "*Íngi dòôngò ma án lási ên amáka*" ("The Indian may be drunk but he still knows where his hammock is"). Améiká was saying that the officials may be foolish from one perspective—after all, it is 1978, not 1778—but you have to give them credit for keeping their priorities straight, for not forgetting what really matters. As I hope to have made clear already, cooperation was *always* a matter of degree in my historical discussions with Saramakas, and the ideology of First-Time was never far from the surface. Toward those men who chose to have nothing to do with what must have seemed a dangerous and bizarre project, I join Améiká in extending my respect. As I think back on my more difficult encounters or listen again to the tapes that are so frustrating if viewed solely from the perspective of gathering facts, I am struck by the overwhelming dignity of these quiet elderly men. If I learned less from them than I would have liked about First-Time, I learned from them something far more important. And I hope that my own conduct successfully reflected the grace and tact with which I was always treated, even by my sternest intellectual adversaries.

BOOKMAKING ✓

> . . . *one of the greatest fallacies that*
> *surrounds the study of the past; the notion*
> *that there is such a thing as a detached*
> *researcher, that it is possible to discover*
> *and analyze and interpret without getting*
> *caught up and swept away.*
>
> —David Bradley, *The Chaneysville Incident*

It has been said of the late French ethnographer Alfred Métraux that after traveling to the Amazon to become the student of his Indians, he used to return to Paris wanting nothing more than to become the Indian of his students.[33] The complex process of "translation" between cultures that characterizes all ethnographic teaching and writing becomes doubly problematical in a book like this one. The act of its creation embodies the selfsame paradox as a Saramaka elder telling a younger kinsman a fragment from First-Time. For traditional men, it is the supreme good to "know" (and a true pleasure to "learn"), but it is an equally grave danger to "tell." As Otjútju once mused:

> There are certain *papá* songs of which it is said, "If you sing this you will die," yet people still [must] sing them! . . . When an elder [referring to First-Time] says to a person, "Tomorrow [meaning 'some-time soon'] I will teach you," a week won't go by before the youth is dead. Or, perhaps the elder will say "When my pregnant wife delivers her baby, then I will teach you." And then the woman dies! And it [the knowledge] is finished.

Damned if they do (tell, sing), because of terrible perceived dangers, and damned if they don't, because the knowledge would be forever lost, Saramakas steer an unsteady middle course, reluctantly sharing partial disclosures with selected kinsmen. I faced a similar dilemma.

⟨Saramaka men are acutely aware of the ongoing and irreversible loss of knowledge; it is a vivid part of their own experience and the subject of frequent discussion among them⟩ Asipéi nicely captured the sense of personal loss in this comment about a particular piece of ritual knowledge (which could as easily have concerned a fragment of First-Time historical knowledge):

> There is one thing my elders did with us [our generation] that I cannot forgive. The really good knowledge that they had they did not teach us. They simply carried it away [when they died]. But our own eyes were clear enough [we were old enough] to learn things. Take my mother's brother Máko-yá. He and my own mother had the very same mother and father. Could he and I have been any closer? Well, he was the master of the *óbia* [medicine] for rib [side] pain. But he carried it away! He didn't share it with us. . . . When he was very sick [dying], the day his side was really hurting him, he sent for me. He said, "Call Asipéi for me." So I went and I sat down. He said, "Man, the way my side is really giving me pain, I want to teach you the *óbia*, so that you can prepare it for me." So I said, "I'm ready." He said, "Pull up your stool." And I sat down right next to him. Then he began to shake all over [in great pain]. He said, "Man, leave me for now. I can't catch my breath long enough to talk to you." I said, "Uncle, the pain just gets worse and worse. . . . If you don't tell me now, there may not be a chance. Tell me now so I can prepare the *óbia* for you, so you can get some relief." He said, "Man, leave me now. I simply can't talk." [The exchange continues with more of the same.] Those people! They had stout hearts! So, I went away. Later I returned. He was worse! The next day even worse! And the *óbia* stayed with him [forever]. Our mothers' brothers didn't give us their knowledge. They carried it away with them. They denied it to us.

The decision to write this book was inextricably bound up with this historiographical process. The issues it raised for me ranged from the potential impact on the Saramaka system of knowledge of my codifying in writing these particular fragments, to the potential consequences of identifying by name the men who had shared their knowledge with me. None of these issues are simple, all have a strong moral component, and only time will tell if my carefully considered decisions have been wise. Insofar as possible, however, they were made with the advice and consideration of the people whose words are represented in this book.

Consider the issue of identifying speakers by name. Twelve years ago, when I wrote my first book about Saramaka, there was simply no question; people made clear that they did not want their names to be written down in any "whitefolks' book," and—though I personally found the solution dehumanizing—I duly avoided using any names at all (when necessary, calling individuals as well as clans "A," "B," "X," and so on). By the time of my 1978 discussions with contributors to this book, the issue had shifted: people were torn between awareness, on the one hand, of traditional sanctions against telling things to whitefolks and talking about First-Time to *anyone* not in their clan, and, on the other hand, pride in their own knowledge and that of their clan, and the wish to be remembered by their juniors as men of wisdom. While Saramakas did not, and could not, fully understand the ultimate products of much of the kinds of general eth-nographic information I explored with them during the 1960s (for example, articles on kinship theory or demography), they had a keen idea of how a book about First-Time might look. In regard to history, it was always much easier to be explicit about my goals—for example, comparing Saramaka versions to those found in contemporary archives; and as colleagues (however unequal, in many and complex ways) we could join the search together. The solution I adopt here grows out of my discussions with Saramakas, but is clearly my own responsibility: in this book I identify speakers by their real names, with the sole exception of cases (regarding particular historical fragments) in which the speaker specifically asked to remain anonymous.

Or, consider the potential impact of this book on the Saramaka system of knowledge. By presenting certain Saramaka versions of events and not others, and by introducing contemporary written evidence, I run the risk of establishing a "canonical" or "authorized" version of Saramaka history. In 1978, on my second night in Saramaka that year, I wrote down the following bleak thoughts in my field notebook:

> I am struck forcefully and painfully, and really for the first time ever in the field, by the ways in which my authority (the authority of my findings [archival, oral]) influences or crystallizes or freezes "the truth" for those Saramakas who hear it. It would, for example, be impossible for someone to work on Kwasímukámba [an important story for which I had found considerable archival corroboration, see *170–76* below] with Matjáus ever again and not get the story as *I* tell it now. The moral choice on my part is a difficult one; on the one hand, the wish/obligation to share and exchange knowledge with the people who share it with me; on the other hand, the danger of interfering in a *system* of knowledge, in the very way it functions. The main justification for my telling Saramakas even as much [outside, written] information as I do is the rapidity with which the system is dying [as the old men pass away]. But this is hardly a fully persuasive argument.

Insofar as the contents of this book, and not just its physical form, will reach Saramaka, this issue remains alive. My decision to publish is made with a strong sense of the speed with which First-Time knowledge is disappearing, with the reassurance that the main participants in my learning have approved publication, and with the expectation (based on past experience) that the book's contents will only very gradually and very partially penetrate to the level of those elders who most directly participate in the system of knowledge.

Other, related moral issues abound. There is the basic question of whether the publication of information that gains its symbolic power in part by being secret does not vitiate the very meaning of that information. Does publication of these stories, these very special symbols, fundamentally diminish their value and meaning? While a Saramaka elder always tells First-Time selectively, and carefully chooses his recipients, the publication of a book by its very nature deprives its author of control (except perhaps via the language in which it appears) over its audience. It is inevitable that these stories will ultimately cross traditional clan boundaries in Saramaka; and all of them are being given, immediately and at once, to white and black outsiders, the traditional collective enemy.

These issues are as germane to small details as to major events. Consider the name of the great Matjáu hero, Lánu, of whom it is said, "His name must never be spoken." Should it appear in this book? Captain Góme, in a speech already quoted, showed his concern about the potential misuse by his descendants of his ancestor Tutúba's name, and his general wish, therefore, to keep it hidden (though he approved its publication in this book). Tebíni (and other elders) not only told me Lánu's name, they agreed to its publication. Góme and Tebíni (as well as others) are in a sense especially entrusted with such knowledge and with its distribution. Should I proceed on this authority? Or should I accept the view—which I could surely elicit from any number of Saramakas if I tried—that Tebíni (and the others) have violated a trust and, in this sense, are "traitors"? Or again, the Dómbi captains of the village of Sééi ordered Améiká not to speak to me about First-Time in 1978 (see above), but other Dómbi officials—a captain and a *basiá* in a nearby village—were pleased to contribute. By publishing their words, am I violating some trust with that first group? The question of "informed consent" in social science research—much debated recently by professional societies as well as congressional committees—becomes particularly thorny in anthropology: is it individuals or is it groups who constitute the appropriate unit for consent in terms of property that is in part corporate? How much knowledge of the outside world is necessary before consent becomes truly informed?

None of these questions have simple answers. Some of them regress on more general questions of social science or anthropological ethics, and all refer back, ultimately, to philosophical and political positions. The responsibility for making the materials in this book public, after I have considered all these issues, must be mine alone. In addition, however, there are special responsibilities that devolve upon the readers of such a work, who by the very act of reading become partial custodians of its knowledge and potential power. A word about these may not be out of place here.

I would wish to remind Saramakas who read or hear portions of this book to be sure not to treat it as a bible, but rather as an incomplete and early attempt to bring together the fragments of First-Time knowledge that I have been able to learn. It is intended, ultimately, as a celebration of the Saramaka historiographical tradition, as an example of how successful Saramakas have been collectively in preserving a vision of First-Time truths. And it is meant to encourage a whole new generation of Saramaka historians to continue the search and to broaden and deepen our understanding.

Likewise, I would want to urge outsiders (whether they are Surinamers, Dutch, Americans, or whatever) who in the course of their work or leisure come into contact with Saramakas to respect the special "unspeakable" status of this knowledge. For this group of readers, the book will have served its purpose if it brings greater respect for the historical accomplishments of Saramakas and for their traditions of scholarship. The knowledge itself, unlike that in a book on, say, social structure or art, is not intended to be discussed lightly with Saramakas. For anyone who has read this far, it should be clear that discussion of this knowledge requires a special code and etiquette as well as a real facility with the language. When Tebíni, for example, concluded that Lánu's name could be published, it was certainly on the assumption that it would not be spoken in Saramaka any more frequently than it is today. Very generously, he assumed that readers would share my own verbal discretion.

And finally, for the very great majority of readers who will never have the opportunity to meet Saramakas except through books, this study is intended as a tribute to their dignity in the face of oppression, and to their continuous rejection of outsiders' attempts to define them as objects. It depicts, in their own words, a people fashioning against all odds a new world of their own making. They were ordinary men and women who were called upon to perform extraordinary deeds. And because of their accomplishments, all of us may consider ourselves the richer.

This book ends, necessarily abruptly, in 1762, with the making of the Peace. A second volume of a rather different character continues the story to 1800 (Price n.d.). As I worked on early Saramaka history in the Dutch archives during a year at the Netherlands Institute for Advanced Study in 1977–78, it became clear that 1762 represented a major division not only in Saramaka thought but also in the kinds of written materials available to the historian. Before 1762, contemporary materials are limited to reports of military expeditions against the Saramakas, raids conducted by them, punishments of recaptured maroons, and so on. After the Peace, however, two remarkably rich new sources appear: the diaries of the Moravian missionaries who began living with Saramakas in 1765 and continued their presence through the end of the century, and the reports of the government officials who, for most of the rest of the century, were permanently stationed among them. The second book, which focuses on the latter half of the eighteenth century, draws on these unusual written sources, in combination with the same kinds of oral materials used more heavily here, to reconstruct a picture of Saramaka society and culture. The great increase in documentation after the Peace lends a far richer texture to that account. While the events themselves become, in a sense, less dramatic than those depicted in the present book, the description of social and cultural institutions becomes far more complete, and a whole way of life becomes visible.

In reading the present work, it is important never to forget the extreme earliness of the period under consideration. For some latecoming Saramaka clans (for example, the Fandááki), history begins only after the Peace, and they do not appear in these pages at all. Likewise, the complex history of missionization dates only from 1765 and is therefore not part of the present work, though it is—in the consciousness of certain Saramaka groups—the beginning of their significant history. In considering the early events that inform this book, we are always dealing with the outer limits, the far edges, of Saramaka historical knowledge. It is a period at once crucial to the formation of their collective identity and, in terms of any oral tradition, very long ago.

In the present book, my unit of analysis is the event. Taking fragments (often a mere phrase) from many different men, comparing them, discussing them with others, challenging them against rival accounts, and eventually holding them up against contemporary written evidence, I try to begin to develop a picture of what the most knowledgeable Saramakas collectively know, and why they know and preserve it. Constant comparison—challenging and discussing accounts of events with Saramakas—rather than passive text-gathering was my *modus operandi.* I quickly found out that information was stored or embedded in particular forms (songs, land tenure lists, and so on) and was often not available to the speaker in other forms. "Different people," as Cohen matter-of-factly states of East African oral historians, "carry in their heads different modes and systems of arranging and simplifying the complex and massive information that the past remits to the living" (1977:15). If, for example, I asked Tebíni the name of a certain captain's successor, he might honestly deny knowledge, yet the information would turn out to be embedded in a song or a narrative fragment that he knew well, and would be told me weeks later apropos of something else. It was simply not recoverable for him in the form in which I had asked.

Even the men most respected for their control of First-Time knowledge vary enormously in the depth and breadth of their repertoires. Cohen's comments on the traditional system of historical knowledge in Busoga (Uganda) apply as well to Saramaka and are worth quoting at length:

> The preservation and transmission of such information was not consistent but rather varied according to the relationship of individual or group to particular facets of the past, to the positions of observers and listeners in the past. The preservation of information varied too with the substance and meaning of things past. . . . The allocation of a political office and land to a particular person or lineage, and the possibly related dispossession of another, were not likely to be forgotten by any of the principal participants in the affair, nor by their descendants. Their place in society and their rights to the office and land were preserved, and are preserved today, not in deeds, papers, or documentary titles of appointment, but in the corroborated memories of men and women around them . . . . Tradition in Busoga is much less the arcane survivals of an oral past than the lively and ever-functioning intelligence upon which society and man rest. The transmission of historical information is not along orderly chains of transmission but across and through the complex networks of relationship, association, and contact that constitute social life. (1977:8–9)

For such reasons, what any Saramaka individual knows about the distant past is distinctly idiosyncratic. Many elders, including some important captains, knew very little at all about pre-1762 history. And the very most knowledgeable men tend to know little beyond the web of interests that touches on their own, and sometimes their father's, clan.[34] All this leads to a paradox: much of the knowledge contained in this book would amaze (and be new to) any single living Saramaka; yet, at the same time, I am quite certain that it represents only the very tip of the iceberg that Saramakas *collectively* preserve about First-Time.

Today this iceberg is melting with startling speed. As Saramaka social and economic life is transformed, especially in relations with the world beyond tribal boundaries, so too is the meaning and value of First-Time knowledge. As Captain Góme says, "The hour is already late." The interest of middle-aged and younger men turns to different rewards, in some ways more easily achieved; at the same time, spurious information floods the system of knowledge. It is certain that the Saramaka world in which I had the privilege to work will never be the same (and not only because of the consequences of my own considered intervention which, in this broader context, must seem rather inconsequential); tourists, missionaries, government officials, and visiting scholars are all actively if unknowingly contributing to major revisions of First-Time knowledge. To cite but one example, the tribal chief now truly believes (because he was once shown, by an outsider he respected, *National Geographic* photos to "prove it") that the name of his Matjáu clan derives from "Masai," the handsome East African people he saw in the photos. And this is not an unusual case. The vocation of the Saramaka historian such as Tebíni or Góme, who spends years of his life trying to piece together a vision of "what really happened," is fast giving way to simple answers picked up from prestigious outsiders. In the process, the ideological core of First-Time is being vitiated. In the new world that younger men are making for themselves, knowledge of how to run a lathe or a tractor becomes more relevant than details of land tenure or esoteric songs. What was once a gradual loss of knowledge by means of a gentle reshaping of past experience to fit new social ends—an integral and normal part of an ongoing system—has now become a runaway process that may well point ultimately toward wholesale disappearance.

Complaining about the way that "whitefolks' modernization" brings about loss of traditional knowledge all over the world—Saramakas are perhaps most vividly conscious of this in regard to Suriname Amerindians—Tebíni once told me about an experience he had while in Lagos (on his first visit to Africa as part of a 1977 Suriname delegation to FESTAC—the Second World Black and African Festival of Arts and Culture). Tebíni had long been proud of preserving the memory of two of the "original African" styles of greeting brought by his ancestors (which are no longer used or analyzable in Saramaccan): "Bótè," to which one answers "Sikenai bótè," and "Lélembu," to which one answers "Lélembu Kizambíi." "With these words," he likes to say, "we came here."

> I tried them out on an old African [in Nigeria]. But he just stood there. I said them again. He just stared. I said to him [scolding, in Saramaccan]. "You've learned English so you no longer know our own language!"

Tebíni and other men of knowledge are also bitterly aware of what modernization threatens to do to their own oral traditions. Some years ago, shortly before his death, the tribal chief's older "brother" Kositán addressed a large political gathering. Among his words, as remembered today, was a poignant image of the disappearance of First-Time knowledge.

> The canoe of knowledge [*sábibóto*] of the Matjáu clan. . . . As it was about to "go" forever, I caught a glimpse of it just as it passed that tree there [he indicated a tree downstream from the landing place]. Not a single other person still here [alive] even saw its wake. Only me.

I often think of how much later it was when I caught my own glimpse of that canoe, which was even farther downstream, and ever increasing its rush toward the open sea.

NOTES

1. In this book, I use a modified version of the Saramaccan orthography first proposed by Voorhoeve (1959). Vowels have "Italian" values except that è = ɛ (the vowel in English "met") and ò = ɔ (the vowel in English "all"); vowel extension in speech is indicated by vowel repetition in writing; a nasalized vowel is indicated by V*m* before labial consonants and by V*n* before nonlabial consonants; single prenasalized consonants are indicated by *mb, nd, ndj, ng,* and *ny.* Both *kp* (*kw*) and *gb* (*gw*) are single consonants. An acute accent (´) indicates high tone; low tones are unmarked.

Translations from Saramaccan, Sranan, Dutch, French, and German—unless otherwise indicated—are my own responsibility.

2. This Saramaka sense of living in nonreversible time, and its consequences, are discussed at greater length in Price 1975.

3. Saramakas do preserve immensely rich memories of many other (non-event-centered) aspects of their past, from the way their ancestors spoke or cooked to the way they got married or built canoes, but these are largely embedded in other institutions and are not deliberately preserved. Unlike the materials in this book, which Saramakas consciously preserve, they must be gleaned from what Bloch felicitously called "witnesses in spite of themselves" (1953:61). (Two very fine examples of histories based on this special kind of evidence, from different parts of the world, are Cohen 1977 and Dening 1980.) The companion volume to the present book draws heavily on such materials to reconstruct the daily life of Saramakas during the eighteenth century (Price n.d.).

4. From an anthropological perspective, this restriction is easily grasped; as social groups divide, forming new villages or kin groups, they require new markers for their own identity—an avenging spirit whose wrath falls solely on their members, an ancestor who is exclusively their own. The segmentation of the spirit world thus becomes part and parcel of the segmentation of social groups. And the process makes equally good sense from the perspective of Saramaka logic; particular ancestors or gods "naturally" want to be linked most intimately to their closest kinsmen or neighbors. (For a detailed discussion of the role of avenging spirits in the process of lineage segmentation, see Price 1973.)

5. Fankía herself represents a remarkable link with the distant past. Though thousands of people must have heard the guns of war, by the early nineteenth century their numbers would have sharply dwindled. The fact that Fankía's name is always followed by this epithet suggests that at one time—c. 1840—she became (like Borges's "witness" in this section's epigraph) the sole survivor. And it is this temporally transient but very special status that made her the perfect medium to communicate the new wishes of the Old-Time People. (My dating of the death of Fankía, a woman of the Wátambíi clan, is made possible by matching additional details remembered by Saramakas about this shrine-building with contemporary written accounts that are discussed in de Beet and Thoden van Velzen 1977:108–11.)

The focus on the shrine of Awónêngè in these opening pages in part reflects a regional bias, stemming from my own primary residence in the field. Related shrines were apparently being erected during the 1840s by various Saramaka subgroups, but Awónêngè has always been the most important such shrine and remains the central place of worship for those ancestors who actually heard the guns of war. (This focus, of course, is a neo-Frazerian literary device as well; anthropologists, too, have their ancestors.)

6. In Saramaccan, *tén* means "time," *fési* means "face," and *a fési* (literally "at face") means "in the past," but with a strong sense of relative priority. In this book, *fési-tén* might have been rendered as "Face-Time" or "Past-Time," but the implication of relative priority makes "First-Time" a more appropriate gloss.

7. Tribal Chief Abóikóni (Agbagó), now well into his nineties and one of the most skilled of all Saramaka men-of-words, likes playfully to contrast First-Time and more recent events (mimicking in his basso profundo the missionaries he has heard) as "*Ouru-* [Old-]" versus "Niu-Testament." In fact, *fési-tén* is to some extent a relative term; anything not "modern" can in certain speech contexts be labeled *fési-tén*, even though it may date back, say, only to 1900. The core referent of the term, however, is clearly the days of war, the formative years of the Saramaka way of life.

8. The members of a clan, from several hundred to several thousand people, never convene, yet they constitute a "corporation." The ownership of every piece of tribal territory is vested in one or another clan, and any member of a clan has rights to be granted farming land within its traditional territory, no matter where he or she currently resides. Hunting and fishing rights are also vested in clans. Moreover, the religious-political offices of *gaamá* (tribal chief), *kabiténi* (captain, or headman), and *basiá* (assistant headman) are conceptualized as clan possessions. Clan members share a strong sense of belonging, a fierce pride in their clan's name and history—its heroes, battle victories, and religious secrets. And clan membership is symbolized less formally as well: for example, a man traveling on the river should receive warm hospitality in a strange village from any member of his clan, and a stranger should be permitted to eat freely from the fruit trees of any village controlled by his or her clan.

I list here, for convenient reference, the original (pre-Peace Treaty) land-owning clans, with the "client" or "guest" clans that now reside on their lands: the *Matjáu* (who hosted the *Wátambíi, Kasitú, Paatí-nêngè* [the people who live in the village of Asáubásu], *Papútu,* and *Nyafái*); the *Abaísa* (who hosted the *Fandááki* on lands that were originally theirs); the *Lángu* (made up of Kadósu and Kaapátu plus the people who later split off to become the *Kwamá*); the *Nasí* (who hosted their companion clan, the *Biítu*); the *Dómbi* (including those who later split off to found the village of Dáume); and the *Awaná* (made up of Tíifóu- and Tobiási-nêngè, and often considered by outsiders to include as well the Íngi-písi people and those *Agbó* who are not connected to the village of Soolán). The geographical distribution of these clans is schematized on pages 16–17.

9. In recent years, Africanist historians have attempted to develop general classifications of the oral forms in which the past is preserved. For my purposes, I find their distinctions—for example, between "cliché" and "episode"—unnecessarily limiting, even in their most sophisticated formulations (e.g., Miller 1980).

10. All these forms, designed at least in part to preserve *events* from the distant past, contrast with "witnesses in spite of themselves," which tend to be richer in preserving memories of institutional arrangements. To cite a single example: Memory of an obsolete hunting snare, described in an eighteenth-century dictionary of Saramaccan (Schumann 1778: s.v. *sekra*), is preserved today only in an obscure proverb: "The jaguar's in the *seéka* trap." As a seventy-year-old explained it to me:

It [a *seéka*] must have been set something like a *bákisi* [fishtrap]. Let's say you had been an important

person but then you get chronically ill; you're all washed up. People will say, "The jaguar's in the *seéka* trap." Anyone who wants to can come and shoot you with an arrow. Even little kids! You once were so powerful, but now you're helpless: "The jaguar's in the *seéka* trap."
More generally, I have found that songs, proverbs, and children's games are particularly rich "witnesses in spite of themselves" to the eighteenth-century way of life (see Price n.d.).

11.   It may be useful to contrast the solitary nature of the Saramaka historian's vocation with the collective efforts of elders in certain other societies to preserve secret and dangerous knowledge. In Pueblo society, for example, it is small groups that strive to maintain a monopoly on such knowledge: "Religious knowledge is necessary for political power within the community. If this knowledge can be restricted to a very small group, that group can control the community" (Brandt 1980: 131). In Saramaka, however, where the idea of a "body" of First-Time knowledge or the idea of a "group" of initiates is largely absent, individuals tend to operate independently in the acquisition, dissemination, and use of such knowledge, even when it is offered up or called upon in the service of a social group. Because of the noncollective nature of the learning and use of First-Time knowledge, disagreements and confrontations are largely avoided; it is accepted that different Saramaka historians will have different versions, and it is up to the listener to piece together for himself the version of an event that he, for the time being, accepts.

12.   The report of the official request notes that Tutúba, then just a girl, had been shot during a battle that had taken place some 30–40 years previously, and that she was now "a grizzled and of-no-practical-service Negress . . . [with] three children: a son named Jan, a slave carpenter; a slave daughter named Jacoba; and a mulatto daughter named Betje who herself has two mulatto sons" (SvS 208, 28 December 1779; see also SvS 370, 17 December 1779).

13.   Here, and throughout the book, italicized numerals refer to the numbered fragments that begin on page 45 below, and numerals followed by a "C" refer to the adjoining commentary.

14.   My knowledge of cock's crow discourse comes from my own experiences, from descriptions given by Saramaka men, and—most important—from tape recordings made for their own use, sometimes surreptitiously, by Saramaka men being instructed by an elder. I am very grateful for their permission and encouragement to use these primary documents, which provide a crucial control over information expressly intended for my ears.

15.   The reasons for this general circumspection are undoubtedly complex, in part a product of a heritage of oppression, in part a widespread Afro-American cultural legacy from Africa (see Price 1975:33–36 and Price and Price 1980:168–69, *passim*).

16.   This particular kind of "footnoting"—citing the exact place and circumstances in which one heard a story—is widespread in everyday Saramaka life and is not just a feature of First-Time rhetoric. A man recounting a local scandal introduces the story with a detailed account of who told him and exactly what he was doing when he heard it; a woman interrupting a folktale with a condensed piece of another tale begins by stating that she was an actual eyewitness to the episode; and so on. (See Price and Price 1980:220.)

17.   My insistent use of the model of Western scholarship in describing Saramaka historical thought is neither romanticism nor a literary device. Those men who pursue this vocation adhere to critical canons that are no less stringent than those of their Western colleagues. Dealing with oral rather than written materials, they have developed a different critical apparatus, but it is fully comparable in rigor and in general intent; both are tools toward the constructing and understanding of "what really happened," and that understanding is then used for various ends. The exploration of the rules or conventions that different societies use "to regulate the inherent debatability of the past" is still in its infancy (Appadurai 1981), as is the more general study of historiography among nonliterate peoples (see, for a particularly penetrating exception, Rosaldo 1980). The present study is intended, in part, as a contribution to this field.

18.   The tale, as presented here, is condensed from much longer oral versions. As I am interested here in content, not style, this procedure seems defensible. Folktales (*kóntu*) are told at wakes, and are clearly distinguished conceptually by Saramakas from what is considered to have "really happened."

19.   While this prohibition was always expressed to me straightforwardly—after all, "whitefolks have no need to know about First-Time"—its most common symbol between Saramakas was *nóuna*. Once one man had summarized the tale for me, and we had heard a fuller version at a wake (told precisely like any of scores of Saramaka tales), we often recognized supposedly veiled allusions to it in speech. Visitors to the tribal chief's older sister, our closest neighbor, might press their hands in hers and say, "Be good to these people but never forget *nóuna*." Her retort that "it is always with me" would prompt an exclamation of pleasure: "First-Time isn't dead yet!" And the tribal chief, chatting with Asipéi—a man with whom I often worked in 1967—once said to him, "Teach him [me] everything—but never *nóuna*."

20.   Ten years later, our behavior was still being cited rhetorically as an ideal model whenever outsiders

committed an antisocial act. There was, for example, widespread indignation at what was seen as rude and inappropriate behavior by a team of Afro-American filmmakers/explorers who made several visits (until they were declared *personae non gratae*) during the 1970s; several fledgling anthropologists were also expelled during the period; and an urban Surinamer who had made a clandestine arrangement to photograph the forbidden shrine of Awónêngè caused a major scandal, ending only when his wealthy father agreed to pay one of the largest compensatory fines in Saramaka legal history. During the complex discussions that took place in the wake of this last incident, as in the other cases, our own behavior was frequently cited as a contrast. Here, for example, is Captain Asêni, at age 60 the most junior of the three Dángogó captains but the one with most direct jurisdiction over the shrine to the Old-Time People. (I translate from tapes of the legal proceedings, made by Saramakas.)

> [with emphasis] I am speaking of the way Lisáti [my Saramaka name, from Richard] came here and lived for three or four years, always being careful to hold exactly to the "laws" [rules]. . . . He is a professor! He understands the thing called "respect." He does not violate laws! . . . Unlike this other fellow. If he [the latter] takes a single thing he saw [on his morning] in Dángogó and writes it down, we will see that he dies. . . . If he shows a single photo, he should die. If he draws what he saw, he must die. . . . He actually went into Awónêngè and took photos until he was finished! . . . Well [in contrast], Lisáti used to put on his breechcloth until it was [adjusted] just right, he would walk right by the edge of Awónêngè [going to visit Kandámma]. And he'd deliberately turn his back. He'd get right up to the big mango tree there. But he never went inside [the sacred grove]. Never, never.

21.   I was fortunate to have been wearing my tape recorder over my shoulder and I switched it on as Kála greeted me. (Later I received his permission to use this tape here.) Note that the visits that Sally and I made to Saramaka were always viewed by Saramakas as the work visits of a man accompanied by his wife. Although many Saramakas knew that Sally was conducting research for her own book, their firm ideas about sex roles meant that we were normally seen as a man and his dependent—"Lisáti" and "Lisáti-muyêè" ("Richard" and "Wife-of-Richard"). For a discussion of Saramaka sex roles, see S. Price 1983.

22.   This was the only occasion I heard this particular *nòngô*—a typical proverbial nugget—which is not analyzable in Saramaccan. Like many *nòngô*, it is preserved as a single linguistic unit—undoubtedly spoken slightly differently by different Saramakas—a "witness in spite of itself" to the African mother tongue of one of the original Maroons.

23.   From the time of our arrival in Saramaka, Kála had been preoccupied with the special responsibility our presence imposed. In 1967, I wrote down this fragment of an angry speech he made to a group of men:

> We all know that white-skin people don't like black-skin people. Only two kinds of people had slaves—Americans and Dutch. They came to Africa with big ships. But they never fought to get slaves; cheat, all they did was cheat them. You don't think blacks would enslave blacks! The whites just came the way Lisáti has come to us, sat down and ate with them, gave them drink, danced a lot, and then carried them off to the ships. Not one captain on the whole [Suriname] river would have Lisáti. I'm the only one; Bótópási, Tutúbúka, Abénásitónu, Djumú [Christian villages]—those are the places he could go. They would take him, *bakáa* with *bakáa* ["outsider with outsider"]! But any other Saramaka village? Never! All the other captains say to me, "Kála, what's happening that you've taken in a *bakáa* in Dángogó?" Well, Tribal Chief Agbagó [Abóikóni] sent him here; he thought, "If he's got to be somewhere, let's keep him with my own kinsmen. [Kála is the tribal chief's brother.] Then we will know just what he's doing."

My relationship with Kála was always multifaceted. In spite of his occasional rhetorical outbursts, we shared many intimate moments. For long stretches of weeks, we ate all of our meals alone together—with our wives carrying the food in to us—and spent countless hours in conversation.

24.   A few Saramakas were trying, on their own, to set down oral traditions. At least two Matjáus were keeping rival notebooks with scraps of First-Time stories, which they dictated and which were painfully inscribed by their school-going children; a nonliterate Awaná man offered testimony to an anthropologist in Paramaribo expressly to be written down so it would not be lost; and a Christian Saramaka included some information relating to First-Time in a locally published mini-ethnography (Jozefzoon 1959). All such attempts, however, recorded only radically "sterilized" versions of events; references to the spiritual world and other dangerous matters were systematically deleted. Nevertheless, these sources, like the similarly "sterilized" versions of First-Time events recorded in the early twentieth century by the outsiders Morssink (n.d.) and Junker (1922/23, 1923/24, and other articles), proved helpful in my research because they signaled events that deserved further exploration.

25.   Since most First-Time knowledge belongs to one or another clan (is in a real sense owned by them), it is not surprising that the most often-expressed fear of telling me things was that other members of the clan would somehow find out and the teller be held responsible. Among Saramakas of different clans, First-Time information is exchanged only with the greatest circumspection. Within a clan, elders enjoy trading stories

about encounters in which they devised clever ways of masking First-Time information from members of another clan.

26.   The first proverb, alluding to the special technique of stirring up a hole with a stick to drive out potential prey, is normally expressed in standard Saramaccan as *"E i án bulí baáku, i án o sa andí dê a déndu."* (The Herskovitses used it, in a "Srananized" form designed for whitefolks, as the epigraph for their book on Saramaka—see Herskovits and Herskovits 1934:67.) The second proverb is normally spoken only in esoteric "First-Time" language as *"Wása úsu wása,"* which translates into normal Saramaccan as *"Téé i ta séki dèê páu, i músu mêni i hédi."*

27.   "Inappropriate" because of the pace at which I needed to amass knowledge, the different critical apparatus I used, and the fact that I was not only an outsider from the perspective of each clan, but also from the perspective of the Saramaka nation as a whole.

28.   Price and Price 1980, fig. 120, depicts Captain Bitjénfóu's own *fútu bángi*, still kept by his descendants and originally carved ca. 1880 by his predecessor, Captain Bongoótu.

29.   All Saramaka speech is characterized by stylized contrapuntal patterns. Normal speech is punctuated by one of the listeners, who must offer supportive comments such as "That's right," "Yes, indeed," or "Not at all." Even when men living on the coast send tape-recorded messages back to their villages, pauses are left after each phrase, and the "conversation" assumes its proper two-party form once it is played. In formal settings, stylized responses become more frequent, and responsibility for providing them is assumed by someone who is not a principal participant; discussions with the tribal chief, for example, are always conducted with the rhetorical aid of a third party who explicitly represents all other witnesses to the event. (See Price and Price 1980:167–68.)

30.   Though by the 1970s tape recorders, like outboard motors, were common among younger men, people of Tebíni's generation showed little interest. Indeed, my use of a tape recorder did not enhance my image as a serious scholar in a world that had since slavery times associated whitefolks' knowledge with writing. As Tebíni's peer, Améiká of the Dómbi clan, once joked, "Tape recorders are just dumb-man's paper! That's what I call tapes: 'dumb-man's paper.' " Likewise, Saramakas possess an enormous regard for the power of the written word—which they are unable to read. The tribal chief harbors with great secrecy certain papers that he was given on a trip to the Netherlands; they turn out to be summaries of several public documents prepared by an archivist at the Algemeen Rijksarchief. And several other elders possess similar sets of "secret" papers, given to them or a kinsman by some outsider, and which members of other clans are forbidden to see.

31.   That both these men were nominally Christian may well be related to their swift willingness to enter into First-Time discussion with me, once they understood my scholarly purpose. The respect of Christian Saramakas for "book learning" is enormous.

32.   It would be wrong to read this insistence on my telling them simply as a strategy designed for outsiders; it is a standard part of the everyday Saramaka historiographical process. Here, for example, is Captain Kála teaching Abátelí at cock's crow, setting up a point he wants to make:

Just the other week, when we did the thing at the shrine of Gaán Táta [a ceremony recently held at Dángogó], Tebíni and [Tribal Chief] Agbagó and I tied our hammocks in a single house. I went there expressly to sleep with them [and learn things]. And that [the point he is about to make to Abátelí] is the first thing I asked them. . . . "Well," Tebíni said to me . . . "Man, you have asked well. But tell me what *you* have heard. [After all], you knew Asápampía, so tell me what *you've* heard. If it's not correct, I will tell you where the truth is." And then I really told them! [Kála then tells Abátelí the story.]

Characteristically, Kála came away "dry," in terms of learning anything new from Tebíni.

33.   The original remark was made by Tardits in a brief obituary (1964:19) and was later cited by Mintz in his introduction to a new edition of one of Métraux's works (Mintz 1972:2): "On pourrait presque dire que Métraux, après avoir été l'étudiant de ses Indiens, ne voulait être que l'Indien de ses étudiants."

34.   In the later stages of my fieldwork, I was repeatedly surprised at finding that Tebíni or the tribal chief or Góme, for example, were completely unfamiliar with particular events or the names of particular people I had come to know a good deal about.

OF SPEAKERS/TO READERS

*I deny utterly that primitive man is
endowed with historical sense or
perspective: the picture he is able to
give of events is like the picture of
the European war as it is mirrored in
the mind of an illiterate peasant
reduced solely to his direct observations.*

　　　　　—Robert H. Lowie

*In the primitive societies studied
by social anthropologists there are
no historical records.*

　　　　　—A. R. Radcliffe-Brown

THE VOICES IN THIS BOOK

Abátelí

Agbagó

Aláfo

Améiká

Asipéi

Abátelí born ca. 1934, Dángogó Matjáu, with a Dómbi father. Our initial host in Dángogó, and my frequent teacher-companion in hunting, canoeing, and gardening. Even by the late 1970s, Abátelí was too young to have learned much about First-Time. A fine singer, with a "name" known up and down the river, Abátelí often accompanied me on my visits to downriver villages.

Agbagó born ca. 1886, Dángogó Matjáu, with a Fandááki father. Also known as Abóikóni, he has been tribal chief since 1951. A great orator and repository of proverbial knowledge. The paragon of Saramaka grace, dignity, and wisdom. He has been our firm friend since 1966.

Aláfo born ca. 1898(?), Kambalóa (Nasí). As captain, he was our host in Kambalóa in 1978 and a leading voice in the group discussion there.

Améiká born ca. 1905, Pikísééi Dómbi, with a Nasí father. As Abátelí's father, he has often been our host in Pikísééi, where he is an important elder.

Andoma, Paulus born ca. 1885, died 1975. Matawái *basiá* from the village of Vertrouw. My translation of his words is from the Dutch transcripts kindly provided by Miriam Sterman.

Anikéi (Awági) born ca. 1926, Sémóisi Fandááki with a Papútu father. He has lived for years in Paramaribo, where he does woodcarving for sale and, as specialist in *apínti* drumming, leads the Saramaka drum/dance/song delegations that since the mid-1970s have traveled under government auspices to West Africa, the United States, and the Caribbean.

Aseedu born ca. 1895(?), Kambalóa (Nasí?). I met this old man but once, during a group discussion of First-Time at Kambalóa in 1978.

Faánsisónu

Kála

Asipéi born ca. 1912, a Wátambíi with a Fandááki father, who has always lived in his grandfather's village of Dángogó. A matter-of-fact, respected, extremely solid citizen, Asipéi was my single most important teacher of things Saramaka during the 1960s. I discussed First-Time with him only on rare occasions, always during the late 1970s.

Bakáa born ca. 1915, Bótópási Dómbi, with a Nasí(?) father. He is *basiá* (assistant headman) of Bótópási, and was recommended by Captain Bayo as *the* local man with whom to discuss First-Time. Our warm and very instructive conversations in 1978 were also attended by Captain Bayo, who seized the opportunity to hear new fragments, both from Bakáa and from my archival work.

Bayo born ca. 1925, Bótópási Dómbi. Captain of the "Christian" village of Bótópási. Extremely affable, Bayo quickly told me he knew little of First-Time but would introduce me to Bakáa.

"Captain of Haarlem" born ca. 1920. My translation of his words is from the Dutch transcripts kindly provided by Chris de Beet and Miriam Sterman.

"Disiforo" ["Diriforu?"] a Kadósu [Lángu] captain who was informant to government official L. Junker ca. 1917 (see Junker 1922/23).

Djógilési born ca. 1890, Sántigoón Kaapátu [Lángu]. Said in 1978 to be "the oldest living Kaapátu," he was interviewed about First-Time by Otjútju—not at my behest. Otjútju was kind enough to lend me the tape of this discussion to transcribe.

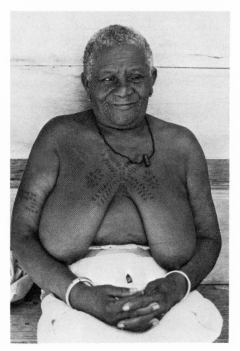

Kandámma

Lántifáya

Elias Kodjo Asikada born 1829, important Wátambíi captain. Brutally murdered by a madman when in his 80s, he continues to haunt his killers' descendants in Asindóópo as the much-feared *kúnu* (avenging spirit) known as Dódomáu. In 1888, he gave the testimony included in *15* to a city official.

Emanuel, Leo born 1923, Matawái from the village of Boslánti. My translation of his words is from the Dutch transcripts kindly provided by Chris de Beet and Miriam Sterman.

Faánsisónu born ca. 1912, Dángogó Matjáu, with a Lángu father. Headcaptain for the whole Upper River, a great speaker, fine humorist, and immensely popular man. I only rarely discussed First-Time with him. He holds the captain's staff originally given to Afadjétosúme (see *197–201* below).

Góme born 1898, Tutúbúka Awaná, with a father from the "Íngi-písi" segment of Awanás. Dignified captain of Tutúbúka, and our gracious host in 1978. A true lover of First-Time discourse, and a fine teacher.

"Grandompie" born ca. 1835, Gódo Papútu captain who was the most frequent informant and closest Saramaka "friend" of government official Junker in the period 1917-early 1920s (see Junker 1922/23).

Kála born ca. 1899, Dángogó Matjáu, with a Matjáu father. Also called Dangasí. Directly responsible for our conduct and well-being during our first years in Dángogó, Captain Kála—who holds the original Peace Treaty Matjáu staff—and I have always had a complex, somewhat adversarial relationship. It is only in recent years that we have occasionally discussed First-Time.

Otjútju

Peléki

Kandámma born ca. 1897, Dángogó Matjáu, with a Matjáu father. The acknowledged master of the folktales (*kóntu*) that are told at wakes, she told me the version of *nóuna* used on pp. 13–14 one day, while lying, ill, in her hammock. She and Tebíni are considered to be the greatest *adunké* singers on the Upper River, and it is she who sings these songs at the rites at Awónêngè for the First-Time people.

Lántifáya born ca. 1910, Masiákííki Abaísa. Our gracious host in Masiákííki in 1978 and leader of the group discussion of First-Time Abaísa history there.

Mètisên born ca. 1912, Béndiwáta Kaapátu [Lángu], brought up in his father's village, Bundjitapá [Kadósu-Lángu]. A leper and Christian who has lived for years at Djumú Mission, Mètisên has always been a polite and interested partner in discussing First-Time with me.

Otjútju born ca. 1936, Dángogó Matjáu, with a Fandááki father. Also called Belfon. Very much caught between the worlds of the coast and Saramaka, Otjútju has, since its inception in the 1960s, managed the airstrip at Djumú Mission and kept a small store there. He gave me some of my most important leads about First-Time, though his information sometimes turned out upon examination to be spurious.

Peléki born ca. 1923, Dángogó Matjáu, with a Dángogó father. Master *apínti* drummer, and in 1966 widely thought to be next in line for the office of tribal chief, Peléki suffered severe bouts of illness in the late 1960s, leaving him nearly blind. With the help of his children, he tends a store at Djumú Mission. The son of a Dángogó captain, Peléki has always played the role of student more than teacher in our discussions of First-Time, for which he has always shown an inexhaustible enthusiasm.

Tandó

Tebíni

Tandó born ca. 1928, Dángogó Matjáu, with a Dángogó father. *Basiá* for many years, a fine drummer and *papá* player, Tandó is a solid citizen, a *bon vivant*, and a man whose interests in First-Time are serious.

Tebíni born ca. 1898, Fandááki with a Matjáu father from Kámpu, where Tebíni has always lived. As a historian of First-Time, he has no peer on the Upper River, and probably nowhere in Saramaka. Dignified, quiet, something of a loner, Tebíni is a lover of historical knowledge for its own sake, an impassioned seeker after "what really happened." Before his memory began to deteriorate in 1979–80, he was the last serious link to the generation of men who led Saramaka in the early years of this century. He was, without doubt, my greatest teacher of First-Time.

Tembái born ca. 1913, Maipá Kwamá, with a Matjáu father. I met him but twice, at Maipá, during 1978. He was the leading spokesman against the Maipá elders' revealing First-Time information to me, but he told me a fine version of Wíi's story, part of which I use in this book (see *194*).

ON READING SARAMAKA HISTORY

The remainder of this book is divided into two parts, running simultaneously across two channels that divide each page horizontally. The upper channel, set in Garamond Book type, carries the "texts." The lower channel, set in Garamond Light type, carries my "commentaries."

The texts present discrete fragments of Saramaka knowledge, organized in such a way as to describe the development through time of various social groups. Each fragment is set off by an identifying number, and its source indicated. Regarding these texts, my translating and editing procedures have been aimed at preserving a Saramaka perspective. I often delete repetitive rhetorical features such as "well," "now," or "but"; I delete the conventional second-person contrapuntal interjections; and I am sometimes guilty of concretizing an elliptical or vague referent in a text to make it intelligible to someone who has less background knowledge than the person for whom the fragment was originally spoken. Except when intelligibility is threatened, however, my translations tend toward the literal. I strive to avoid romanticism and sentimentality when it is not intended by Saramakas, yet to render their poetic metaphors with something of their inherent power. Like the other Saramaka translations in which I have had a hand (see, for example, Price and Price 1980:82–83, 184–87, *passim*), those in this book tend to be rather direct.

There is considerable variation in the depth of my knowledge about the events reported in the texts. Some, such as the exploits of Kwasímukámba, I have explored quite fully, with many men, on many different occasions. A few I have heard only as a single fragment, unconfirmed by other speakers. Whenever possible, I try in my commentaries to indicate something of the status of my knowledge about each. In cases when my knowledge of an event, based on oral fragments, is particularly rich, the problem of presentation becomes especially complex. As a matter of principle, I eschew composite versions, even when they would be more richly textured and dramatically satisfying than the words of a single man spoken at a particular moment. For example, I present Otjútju's version of Lánu's initial escape without interlarding it with fragments I have heard from Tebíni or others because it better preserves a single vision or perspective on the event. When I wish to present full, contrastive versions, I do so separately, seriatim, using a single title to group together fragments that relate to a single event.

A series of texts that strictly replicated Saramaka modes of presentation would be largely impenetrable for the average reader, even with explanatory notes. In the opening section, I tried to give some idea of the general features of Saramaka ways of talking about First-Time, and I continue to give examples intermittently throughout the book (but my interest in organizing this book as I have is to remain faithful to the Saramaka conceptual organization of the past on a more general level). It is I who order the diverse texts, deriving the chronology from internal indicators matched with documented dates (see Cohen 1977:166–86 for a detailed discussion of such techniques). I do so, however, within a framework of ideas about time and history that is a fundamental aspect of Saramaka thought.

In this same vein, I should stress that the clan-based organization of these texts rests on a partial anachronism—justifiable, however, as part of my conscious efforts to maintain a Saramaka perspective. The modern members of a clan, looking backward, tend to assume a perfect fit between modern clans and the significant units of First-Time social interaction; but in fact there has been some redefinition of clan boundaries, shifts in group identities, and additions of new personnel. Indeed, hardly any of the current clans had taken on their full shape before the Peace, and their current designations in some cases (for example, "Awaná") did not yet exist. Although I defer the detailed analysis of processes of group formation to another book (Price n.d.), in the present work I consistently draw upon my latest understanding of the actual composition of particular eighteenth-century groups. And, as appropriate, I mention these realities in my commentaries in discussing the nature of Saramaka selectivity about their distant past.

My commentaries in the bottom channel of each page are intended to serve several functions. First, I use them to explain those unfamiliar Saramaka assumptions or concepts that seem minimally necessary to make sense of the particular text. This is always a very partial endeavor; to understand any text fully would presume an ethnographic knowledge—including metaphysical concepts, political ideas, and so on—far beyond the means of this book to provide. Here, I try simply to indicate the most directly useful information at the moment it becomes relevant. Second, I try to spell out something of the special meaning of each fragment to those Saramakas who preserve it, discussing why it is told in the form(s) it is by these particular people. And third, I introduce information from contemporary written sources—chronology, geography, and other facts—to help work toward a picture of "what really happened" against which we can measure and grasp the complex processes of selection used by Saramakas in regard to their distant past.

The available written sources from the first half of the eighteenth century pose problems not unlike my oral materials, in their fragmentation, incompleteness, and obscurity. Rather than providing a solid made-by-colonists whole-cloth backdrop against which we can consider Saramaka selectivity, they permit only intermittent, if vivid, glimpses of the way the colonists regarded Saramakas, and the measures they took to foil them. The reasons are several and worth spelling out. A large portion of the materials in the Algemeen Rijksarchief dating from this period are in woeful condition, and many volumes have been permanently sealed. Other once-available archives of central importance to Saramaka history (for example, those pertaining to the eighteenth-century Portuguese Jewish community) have disappeared forever. And the major historical works published during the eighteenth century that are based on documentary sources raise as many doubts as they settle, as they are either explicit polemics (for example, Nassy's 1788 defense of the Suriname Jewish community) or quite generally uncritical of their sources (for example, Hartsinck's standard 1770 history of the colony, based on official correspondence received in the Netherlands). The fact that even the available archives are truly voluminous, very largely unindexed, and often in archaic Dutch written in difficult handwriting further complicates the task. I often find myself in the frustrating position of having a half-dozen scraps of written evidence about an event (a raid by Saramakas, a military expedition against them) without being able to consult the main report about it, which is contained in a sealed archival volume, or is simply "missing."

Under these circumstances, matching Saramaka memories of a particular battle or raid with archival accounts can be a daunting task. I have found archival records of more than fifty major military expeditions against Saramakas between 1710 and 1762; and this does not include the countless small commandos that were sent out after Saramaka raids or mass escapes from plantations. Likewise, I have historical records of more than one hundred plantation uprisings and Saramaka raids on plantations during this period. (Nevertheless, my archival research is quite incomplete, because of insufficient time, difficulties with handwriting, sealed volumes, and so on.) The detailed maps that routinely accompanied the reports of military expeditions against Saramakas have been removed from the archives and, apparently, lost forever. Moreover, much of the available information about village moves and composition and about internal Saramaka events in general, as reported in the archives, turns out upon inspection to be deliberately falsified. Close study of the information held by the government about Saramaka activities during the mid-eighteenth century reveals that much of it was "planted" by Saramaka secret agents. It was common for Saramakas to send spies to be deliberately captured by the whites, in order to reveal information under "interrogation" (and often just before being executed). In this way, for example, the whites learned (falsely) in 1751 that the Saramakas had moved their villages by four days' march since the military expedition of the previous year and, in a separate interrogation, that the three white men who had been sent out as emissaries (whom the Saramakas had in fact killed) were still alive and being held prisoner. The eighteenth-century historian Hartsinck, who drew solely on such documents—the correspondence of the governors, interrogations at the Court of Policy, and so on—tended to accept these accounts at face value.* Hence all subsequent histories based on his work (and this includes almost all published historical work on Suriname, including the historical portions of Stedman 1796, and much of Wolbers 1861) must be read with more than usual caution.

In my commentaries I tend not to dwell on such historiographical problems regarding the written records, rather presenting my best-considered conclusions based on the evidence as I have been able to weigh it. Nevertheless, the reader should be aware that behind the identification of, say, the 1738–39 raid led by members of the Nasí clan on the plantation of the Jew Peyreyra lies far more than a correspondence between one or two bits of information (a plantation name, a geographical location); in all such cases, I have carefully considered a complicated bundle of evidence, often including apparently contrary facts (for example, from a late eighteenth-century writer), which I am ultimately able to dismiss by critical consideration of the sources.

My separate but simultaneous presentation of texts and commentaries represents a carefully conceived experiment. In principle, a person could read only the upper (Saramaka text) portion of each page, from the beginning of the next section right through to the end of the book, without once referring to the commentaries. I hope, however, that most readers will be sufficiently patient to try out the following procedure, for which the presentation was designed. First, read a text (or bundle of texts) indicated by a single title, for example, "Lánu's Escape." Then turn back and read the commentary indicated by that same title. And finally, reread the text with the commentary in mind before going on to the next text and continuing the process.

Why this complex procedure? One goal is to preserve the integrity of the Saramaka texts— which means avoiding constant interruptive footnotes or comments. Moreover, each commentary takes on meaning only after certain features of the particular text have become familiar; and likewise, any text becomes fully intelligible only with the help of its commentary. With a goal of helping the reader enjoy, appreciate, and more fully understand the Saramaka vision of their distant past, I have chosen this presentation as the most promising of several possible solutions. The texts are sufficiently brief so that the recommended double reading should not prove burdensome. And the second time around, I hope they will be seen through new eyes, focused on a vision that more closely approximates what the Saramaka elder who is speaking the fragment or singing the song would have expected from his listener.

---

* Nor was Hartsinck overly concerned with his details regarding Saramakas. He describes how "Claas"—an important Saramaka chief—had three villages in 1730 (1770:761–62), while Lavaux, who had himself visited the area, had depicted five on his famous and widely available map; he simply deleted (possibly to strengthen his own arguments, see 158C–161C below) the important fifteenth article from the supposedly complete printing of the 1762 treaty in his book (1770:809; compare R. Price 1983:document 11); and so on.

The Events

THE HEROIC YEARS
1685–1748

THE HEROIC YEARS

1685–1748

MATJÁU BEGINNINGS, 1685–1735

Because the bulk of my time in Saramaka has been spent living with Matjáus, my information on their early years is richer than for other groups and probably represents a fuller proportion of the knowledge they collectively possess about their own beginnings. Nevertheless, the past fifty years have undoubtedly witnessed a major loss of sharpness and detail concerning their First-Time ancestors: with the early twentieth-century demise of the cults devoted to the great Matjáu fighting and healing *óbias*, the single major context for the transmission of stories about these people disappeared. Yet key aspects of their memory are kept alive because these people and events of two and three centuries ago remain firmly woven into the fabric of ongoing Matjáu life, in terms of everything from local land tenure and interclan political relations to proverbial speech. And occasional rituals specifically devoted to the earliest ancestors maintain particular aspects of their identities through drum rhythms, songs, and dances. Nevertheless, an intense aura of danger and power continues to surround these figures and their exploits, and mention of them tends to be both highly elliptical and brief.

Matjáus conceive of their collective identity as having originated in a tiny band of escaped slaves who lived for some time just outside the bounds of the cultivated plantation area, on the creek now called by them Matjáu Creek (see map, p. 57). The name of their first great leader, Lánu, is considered so powerful that it is rarely spoken; indeed, it is most unusual for a non-Matjáu, no matter how knowledgeable historically, ever to have heard it, and most Matjáus would not know who he was. In references to Lánu—whether in ritual or historical discussion—another name is almost always substituted, normally the teknonym of Lánu's younger brother Ayakô, "Dabítatá" (Dabí's father), who was the leading Saramaka chief during the final years of the war against the whites, in the middle of the eighteenth century. Here is Peléki, telling me how his "mother's brother," the late Captain Gidé, used to "interrupt" accounts of early Matjáu history:

> He would say, "Man, Matjáus did not used to speak Ayakô's name. And one *never* says Lánu's name on the Pikílío. Those two people. Their names cannot be spoken. They were First-Time people, so 'ripe' [*lépi* = ritually powerful] that their names can't be called. If you speak their names, war will come or who knows what will happen." So, we call him [Ayakô] "Dabítatá." If someone [Lánu] did something, they'll say it was "Dabítatá." Because they're so afraid of Lánu's name that it can't be spoken.

Because of such name substitution and masking, Matjáu historians themselves in many cases no longer know which of these men is supposed to have performed a particular act. Indeed, in discussions of these early years, the names of still-more-junior relatives are often substituted because a person considers it too dangerous even to say "Dabítatá," still further confusing identities for posterity.

Eighteenth-century Saramakas understood that death held very different meanings for them and for their enemies. Lánu is said to have instructed his brother not to tell the whites when he died (5), and eighteenth-century documents make clear that the deaths of wartime leaders were in fact routinely masked from outsiders. In addition, Saramakas believed that their African-born leaders did not exactly "die"—they disappeared, in their familiar form, but continued to play a central role in the lives of the living. Today Saramakas claim that their most powerful early ancestors were not buried at all. Otjútju, for example, described how "one day Lánu entered the forest, and they never saw him again. They didn't find him to bury." Likewise, Captain Góme, speaking of the Awaná clan's equivalent figure (see 96) said, "No one knows where Vumá 'went.' They didn't find him to bury. Perhaps he went back to Africa. We simply don't know. He just disappeared." (Since Vumá, like certain other African-born Saramakas, could fly [see 96, 166], the possibility of his returning to Africa was considered quite matter-of-factly.)

The rhetorical device of name substitution, then, stems both from desires to confuse the enemy and from complex aspects of the belief system. The dangers surrounding the speaking of First-Time people's names (and the related avoidance of referring directly to First-Time events) become a major source of "noise" in the transmission and learning of knowledge about the Matjáu (and other Saramaka) past.

A local Matjáu ancestor shrine

THE EVENTS

Lánu's Escape

1. His wife—I don't know if she was a girlfriend or a real wife—worked in the white man's house. Once, she gave her husband a drink of water. ([whispering:] But they tell me that it was really sugar cane juice, because that was the "water" the white man normally drank.) Well, they saw that and said, "The woman gave Lánu sugar cane juice!" and they whipped her. They beat the woman until she was dead. Then they carried her to him and said, "Look at your wife here." Then they whipped Lánu until he lost consciousness, and they left him lying on the ground. Then, the spirit of his wife came into his head, and he arose suddenly and ran into the forest. The white man, seeing this, said, "Lánu's gone!" But his men said, "He won't live; he's as good as dead already."

When Lánu went into the forest, he ran this way and that, calling out to his wife, trying to find her. This woman was from Dahomey; they called her Osíma of Dahomey. Well, he kept calling out and calling out until he got deep into the forest. Finally, the forest spirit [*apúku*] named Wámba called out in reply. And Wámba came into Lánu's head, and brought him directly to where some Indians lived. These Indians welcomed him, took care of him, and gave him food. And he lived with them there. (Otjútju 13 August 1976) ✤

Lánu's Escape (1)

This fragment was told me by Otjútju, whose personal history is intimately and intricately bound up with the protagonists of the event. Saramakas believe that every person has a *nêséki* (normally an ancestor, but I know cases involving forest spirits or even deceased hunting dogs) who, like the mother and father, contributes at the moment of conception to that person's fundamental character (see Price 1975:51–52). Otjútju's *nêséki*, Bôò (his mother's mother's mother's mother, who died shortly before his birth), had as her own *nêséki* Lukéinsi (the daughter of Adjágbò), who served as the late-eighteenth-century medium for the forest spirit Wámba. Bôò's life was strongly influenced by her relationship—through her *nêséki*—to Wámba; and her association with the forest spirit has been relevant at several key junctures when she has been credited with intervention in the life of Otjútju. His own knowledge of Lánu's exploits has been built up very gradually, over the full course of his lifetime, by hearing fragments of information spoken or sung by a variety of people during those rituals for his own well-being that were addressed to his *nêséki* (and to her own *nêséki*'s forest spirit). During such rites, there would have been frequent incidental and elliptical references to Wámba's role as a special protector and advisor of the fledgling Matjáu group.

This Matjáu fragment, incidentally, preserves the memory of a plantation "law" that seems to have held, in the eyes of both masters and slaves, an extraordinarily heavy symbolic significance—the prohibition on slaves' tasting the sweet product of their labors. As Stedman wrote of Suriname slaves during the eighteenth century,

> The other danger is that should a Negro Slave dare to taste that Sugar which he produces by the Sweat of his Brow, he would run the hazard of paying the expense by some hundred lashes, if not by the breaking out of all his teeth. . . . [later in the book:] As to the Breaking out of their *Teeth* for Tasting the Sugar Cane Cultivated by themselves, or Slitting up their nose & Cutting off theyr Ears from private Peek, these are Look'd upon as Laughable Trifles, not Worth so much as to be Mention'd. (1988:257, 532)

The severity of Osíma's and Lánu's punishments, as preserved by Matjáus, conforms to scores of examples recorded by European observers of plantation slavery in Suriname. ✤

"Flagellation of a Female Samboe Slave." Engraving by William Blake after a drawing by John Gabriel Stedman, who witnessed the depicted punishment in 1774 and wrote: "[She was] lacerated in such a shocking Condition by the Whips of two Negro Drivers, that she was from her neck to her Ancles literally died over with blood—It was after receiving 200 lashes . . . [and almost immediately afterwards she was given another two hundred, yet] her only Crime had consisted in her firmly refusing to submit to the loathsome Embraces of her despisable Executioner [her white overseer]" (1988:264, 266).

THE EVENTS

Ayakô's Flight

2. [Lánu's younger brother] Ayakô had a sister [called Sééi] on the same plantation. One day she was at work, with her infant son tied to her back. The child began crying, but the white man didn't want her to sit down to nurse it. But it kept on crying. She kept working. The child kept crying. Then the white man called her. "Bring the child here and I'll hold it for you." So she took the child off her back, handed it to him, and returned to work. He grasped the child upside down by the legs and lowered its head into a bucket of water until he saw that it was dead. Then he called the woman and said [gruffly], "Come take the child and tie it on your back." So she did so. She returned to work until evening, when they released the slaves from work. The child was dead, stiff as a board.

Well, Dabítatá [Ayakô] saw this and said, "What sadness! My family is finished. My sister has only one child left, and when she goes to work tomorrow, if the child cries, the white man will do the same thing again. I'll be witness to the final destruction of my family. [At

---

Ayakô's Flight (2–6)

While Lánu is something of a shadowy figure in current Matjáu historiography (partly because for so long he has been considered too powerful to talk about), his younger brother Ayakô remains known as a rather full person (though knowledge of his exploits and character is also carefully protected and masked).

The first paragraph of 2 has been grafted by the teller onto the more usual Matjáu account; I have never heard it from another Saramaka. Other Matjáus, when queried, denied it had anything to do with Ayakô, noting that it was a popular slavery story among coastal Afro-Surinamers, and not a specifically Saramaka story at all. This, then, is a nice example of creative embellishment of an important historical event by making use of folkloric materials. (Stedman describes a similar incident as fact, citing the name of the child-murderer [1988:267–68].)

Fragment 2, like many others I have heard, stresses the importance of family in the Matjáu conception of their original forebears—Ayakô is depicted as escaping with his sister and her child, having been explicitly motivated by wanting to preserve the nascent matrilineage. And it commemorates the supportive role played during those early days in the forest by the Matjáu "great óbia" known as Mása Lámba. Lámba was part of a complex of Matjáu war óbias (including the great agó óbia Akwádja, closely associated with the forest spirit Wámba) that were transferred by the Matjáus to the Kasitú clan, their collective "children," at the end of the eighteenth century, in an act that helped cement the special relationship of the two groups (see 143C–146C). Though largely inactive today, Mása Lámba is remembered and praised in part because of the importance of this political relationship. Its distinctive drum rhythms, however, are also played and danced by Matjáus today at (rarely held) rites for their original collective ancestors at the Dángogó shrine of Awónêngè, to commemorate the óbia's role in confusing the enemy and making themselves unfindable. During the wars, it is said, the whites would hear the Mása Lámba drums and follow, but always in the wrong direction. I was told also that within the memory of living people, whenever rites were held in honor of Mása Lámba at its shrine outside the Kasitú village of Palúbásu, a deer would appear out of the forest as a sign that Mása Lámba was content.

Fragment 3, like several of my other Matjáu accounts, reports that Ayakô served as plantation overseer, or driver. The praise name attributed to him in 2 lends support to this tradition: okúndo bi okúndo is the verbal form of the drum slogan played on the apínti (talking) drum to summon

this point in his narrative, Kála began pouring a libation of rum; and he then prayed to the ancestors for several minutes to ask indulgence for speaking to me of these events before taking up where he had left off.] Now when I was in Africa, I wasn't a nobody. I will make a special effort, and see if since I left there what [power] I had has been spoiled." Then he prepared himself [ritually] until he was completely set. And he escaped. He ran off with his sister and her baby daughter. ([Whispering, to me:] It was not considered humanly possible to escape from those slave quarters, but he did it!)

When he got to the edge of the forest, he called out his praise name: "I'm the one! *Okúndo bi okúndo.* The largest of all animals. I may not have iron [tools] but I can still raise my family!" Then he entered the forest and continued till evening. All he carried was the [great *óbia*] Lámba gourd. Whenever they were hungry, they simply ate from that gourd. That was our food in those days. Lámba fed us. (Kála 5 July 1978)

3. Ayakô was made overseer of Plantation Waterland. He was in charge of all the slaves. It was at the time they were marching the slaves each day to dig the canal at Para. The work

---

to council meetings the important village officials known as *gaán* ("big") *basiá*, a title that derives etymologically from Sranan (coastal Suriname) *basya*, the term for "black overseer," or "slave driver," on plantations (see Voorhoeve and Lichtveld 1975:169). The heaviness of canal-building labor is cited as the specific motive for escape in the traditions of several Saramaka clans, though various actual coastal canals are mentioned, even within the traditions of any such group. (This fact, plus the frequency with which documentary sources attest to major canal-building projects during the colony's first half-century, reduces the possibility of using such construction dates for purposes of establishing the chronology of escapes.) These widespread stories stand as collective witness to the perception by slaves that this particular form of supervised gang labor—moving tons of waterlogged clay with shovels—was the most backbreaking of the tasks they were called upon to accomplish (see also Rodney 1981:2–4). It is worth noting that the great majority of escape accounts give a specific provocation, most often the imposition of a particularly onerous physical task or the wanton cruelty of the master (or his staff), usually practiced upon a *kinsman* of the person who then escapes. The formulaic Saramaccan phrase used in capping the telling of such an incident translates laconically as; "They couldn't bear the punishment any more, so they escaped."

Several already familiar themes appear in *4–6*: the fraternal relationship of Ayakô and Lánu, the extraordinary ritual powers of Lánu (who was supported by the forest spirit Wámba), Lánu's absolute hatred of whites, with whom his enmity was sworn to be eternal, and the supportive role of the Indians who harbored them. Matjáus are well aware that Indians and Africans were plantation slaves together. Indeed, I have been told that "the Indians escaped first and then, since they knew the forest, they came back and liberated the Africans." With certain individual exceptions (see *164–65*), the relationship between early runaways and those Indians who lived relatively near the coastal area is depicted by Matjáus as solidary. The final fragment also includes first mention of the mysterious African Kwémayón, who played an important role as spiritual advisor to the Matjáus during their first decades in the forest. The image of the great leader/ warrior (himself possessed of vast powers) traveling with his personal ritual specialist (in this case Ayakô and Kwémayón) appears again in the historical accounts of other groups: the Lángu leader Kaási had his Indian *óbiama*, Piyái (see *50–51*), and the famous late-eighteenth-century rebel leader of the Alúkus, Boni Okilifu, had his own special *óbiama*, Djaki Atoomboti (Pakosie 1972:5). ✣

was too heavy. It was there that they couldn't take it any more. So they made a plan and escaped. (Tebíni 11 July 1978)

4. Ayakô ran away to seek his older brother, Lánu. He found him and saw that he had been well taken care of by the Indians, that he had done well there. He, too, found many things to eat there. (Otjútju 13 August 1976)

5. Lánu had a serious talk with Ayakô, saying, "I shall never return to where there are whites, but if you wish to go take [liberate] people, you may. But never will I and the whites meet again." He also warned Ayakô, "When I die, do not ever tell the whites that I have died." (Otjútju 3 August 1976)

6. Lánu prepared Ayakô to go back to the plantation, for he was a great óbiama. From this trip, Ayakô brought back a man called Kwémayón, another great óbiama who remained thereafter always at his side. (Otjútju August 1975) ✤

Plantation Waterland, 1708, only a few years after its driver, Ayakô, escaped. The drawing, by Dirk Valkenburg, is labeled, "This view of Waterland is seen by standing before the kitchen. 1 the mill and boiling house from the front. 2 the gallery on the river side. 3 the gallery on the land side. 4 the distillery. 5 a slave house" *(Rijksmuseum Amsterdam, Rijksprentenkabinet)*.

Fish Story

7. Dakúmbe fón Damáwan	Dakúmbe drugged Damáwan Creek
Awéi bó tobôsi	Awéi bó tobôsi
Adjawé bó tobôsi	Adjawé bó tobôsi*

There's a creek . . . near Plantation Waterland called Damáwan. When they were living there, a man took a wife. She became pregnant. So he went hunting and came to this creek. His name was Dakúmbe. He saw so many fish there! So he went and told his wife. Well, she was pregnant [so it was forbidden for him to drug streams]. But she said he had to go drug the creek. He refused. "I simply can't go drug the creek and bring you fish. I came and married you. I made you pregnant. Now you want me to drug a creek. I simply can't." She said, "Go drug it." He said, "No." But she kept after him until he finally went. He drugged the creek! The woman had made him do it. Well, fish were killed in that creek until it was something to see. And he took some fish back to his wife. And she died while pregnant [for a Saramaka, the single most evil possible circumstance of death]. Well, someone who was there, at the time, composed the song. (Tandó 12 July 1978) ✤

* I have heard the last line given, alternatively, as "Adjáwe boóko ên" ["Adjáwe broke him"]. The last two lines, as printed in 7, are in the esoteric Papá language. I do not have a translation for them.

Fish Story (7)

This *papá* song and its accompanying explanatory fragment are among the least firmly researched in this book. My knowledge of them stems solely from five brief discussions in 1978. Basiá Tandó, a Matjáu *papá* adept, offered the information in 7; Tebíni assured me that Damáwan Creek was indeed across from Plantation Waterland, where Ayakô lived; Peléki offered a similar version of the story; and Asipéi and Otjútju each discussed its significance in daily life. None of these men was certain who Dakúmbe was, what clan he belonged to, or when he lived—a most unusual circumstance, in my experience. Nevertheless, Matjáus seem to believe that the story is somehow about their own slavery-time ancestors.

Today, on the climactic morning of Pikílío funerals, after the *papá* drums that have been playing all night are set aside and people are greeting the daylight by playing *adjú*—to chase the ghost of the deceased, as well as all sorts of evil, out of the village—the *papá* of Dakúmbe is always sung. As Otjútju explained: "Every kind of evil comes out at that moment. If you're there, you have to be afraid! He [Dakúmbe] wanted fish, but they kept coming until his head split open, there were so many." For Matjáus, the *papá* about Dakúmbe is a warning about the consequences of unbridled greed. It is a cautionary song—in its significance, more like a Saramaka folktale (*kóntu*) than a historical fragment—but it seems to have its origin in a faraway incident, remembered from the days of whitefolks' slavery, at Plantation Waterland. ✤

Base Camp at Matjáu Creek

8. After they escaped, they lived for a long while at Matjáu Creek before coming further upriver. The Indians had helped Lánu and Ayakô near there. That whole area, from Matjáu Creek to Balén to the mouth of Sara Creek, has belonged to the Matjáus ever since that period. . . . They lived in the area stretching from Matjáu Creek to Mawasí all the way to Kapasíkèè before they came upriver. (Otjútju 3 August 1976) ✤

The Great Raid

9. From there [Matjáu Creek], Ayakô returned for a second time to their old plantation to liberate people. Lánu again prepared him. There had been a great council meeting in the forest. You see, the white man who had whipped Lánu didn't own just one plantation. They decided to burn a different one of his plantations from the place where he had whipped Lánu because they would find more tools there. This was the Cassewinica plantation, which had many slaves. They knew all about this plantation from slavery times. So

---

Base Camp at Matjáu Creek (8)

Matjáu collective identity, their consciousness of their origins as a group, consistently focuses on their stay at Matjáu Creek. Their residence in this area evidently spanned some two and a half decades, from the late 1680s to about 1715, during which time the group continued to be enlarged by newcomers. Fragments *9–21* describe events that took place while the Matjáus were living in the area of the creek that bears their name. ✤

The Great Raid (9–10)

The great raid from Matjáu Creek, as described in these highly esoteric and "dangerous" Matjáu fragments, represents my very earliest link between the Saramaka vision of their own past and the documentary record. Matjáus have always maintained that this large collective escape, accompanied by violence, was the first such event to take place in Suriname. And more than a decade of research in published, archival, and oral materials has failed to deflate this particular Matjáu claim to glory—in fact, quite the contrary.

Only one written account of what I am now convinced was Ayakô's raid still exists—in an eighteenth-century publication, where David de Ishak Cohen Nassy draws on then-still-extant Portuguese Jewish archives to reconstruct this event, which he describes as Suriname's first slave revolt:

> There was in the year 1690 a revolt on a plantation situated on the Cassewinica Creek, behind Jews Savannah, belonging to a Jew named Imanuël Machado, where, having killed their master, they fled, carrying away with them everything that was there. . . . The Jews . . . in an expedition which they undertook against the rebels, killed many of them and brought back several who were punished by death on the very spot. (Nassy 1788:76)

My own search of the incredibly fragile, decrepit 1689–90 documents in the Algemeen Rijksarchief uncovered no further information, but there is evidence that the apparent official blackout of this event may be explained, at least in part, by Governor van Scherpenhuysen's animosity toward the Jewish community and his efforts to make clear that the incident was their own private

they attacked. It was at night. They killed the head of the plantation, a white man. They took all the things, everything they needed. And then they sacked the plantation, burned the houses, and ran. (Otjútju 12 August 1978)

10. They had called a council meeting, those great men. To go to battle. They didn't go for any other reason! They went and stood watch, patiently, until they saw him [the white man]. Then they killed him. And then they set fire to the plantation. (Otjútju 12 August 1978)

❖

---

affair (see Anon. 1697, Nassy 1788:76, and van Sijpesteijn 1854:22–23).* To my knowledge, the archives of the Suriname Portuguese Jewish community for this period, consulted two hundred years ago by Nassy, are no longer extant (see Bijlsma 1919); those few existing volumes in the Algemeen Rijksarchief that do cover this period are in too fragile a condition to consult, but seem in any case to be concerned solely with internal congregational matters (ibid.).

For Matjáus, the raid was their first great collective act, an act of terrible violence that (given Saramaka notions of vengeance) would forever bind them together. And Matjáus' often-repeated claims that this was the *first* of the great slave escapes continues to serve them in many ways today in matters of political or land tenure precedence. The link between the origins of the Matjáu clan and the Portuguese Jewish planter named Imanuël Machado is my own discovery, made possible, in part, by the richness of the separate fragments about their past that Saramakas remember for use in particular circumstances. Matjáu "folk etymologies" began to be recorded more than two hundred years ago (Schumann 1770, s.v. "Matjaru"), but none implies any knowledge of such a planter, nor has any previous scholar suggested the link. (I believe it quite likely that the knowledge *was* still preserved in the late eighteenth century, but that a conspiracy of silence, ellipsis, and masking [because a particularly "dangerous" murder was involved] permitted the knowledge eventually to be lost.) Nevertheless, esoteric Matjáu oral traditions and rituals regarding the place (Cassewinica Creek), and the order of events (Matjáus as leading Suriname's first violent slave revolt), combine with the names themselves (Machado/Matjáu, pronounced almost identically in Portuguese/Saramaccan) and with other oral materials—Matjáu oral fragments about Ayakô, and Djuka materials about related events—to permit me to make a positive identification. (See, for further discussion, caption to map, p. 57.)

My relationship with Otjútju, the man who finally described this event to me, had been developing for some twelve years. The story's detail—the killing of the white master, the burning of his plantation (later confirmed and enlarged by Tebíni and others)—is in my own experience a unique revelation. That I was later able to match it to documentary materials is one of my greatest satisfactions as a scholar of Saramaka history, and a small way of repaying my Matjáu hosts.

❖

---

* The governor's motives may have been based rather more on practical considerations (his disinclination to commit troops to intervene in individual plantation uprisings at a time when there remained a serious foreign [French] threat to the colony) and less on his feelings toward the Jews than Nassy, writing a century later, anachronistically supposed (G. W. van der Meiden, personal communication, 1982).

Dabí in the Bullrushes

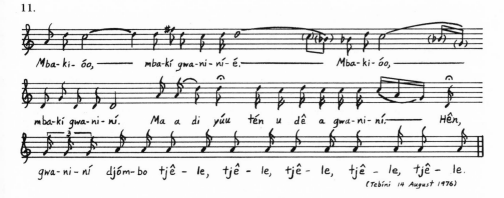

11.

Mba-ki- óo, ——— mba-kí gwa-ni-ní- é.——— Mba-ki- óo, ———

mba-kí gwa-ni-ní. Ma a di yúu tén u dê a gwa-ni-ní.——— Hên,

gwa-ni-ní djóm-bo tjê - le, tjê - le, tjê - le, tjê - le, tjê - le.

(Tebíni 14 August 1976)

This musical transcription, like the others in the book, provides only the barest outline and is not intended as an ethnomusicological document. All songs (except those two with time signatures) are transcribed in free meter; in these cases, the durational value of notes is approximate. In all my transcriptions, pitch values have been transposed for convenience, i.e. they are not absolute. There is considerable variation in Saramaka song performance—in embellishments, in pitch, in rhythm. The transcriptions in this book each represent a *particular* performance segment; indeed, in each of the many repeats that characterize the performance of any song, there is notable variation. For further information on Saramaka music, see Price and Price 1980 and S. Price 1983, and for recorded examples of Saramaka song, Price and Price 1977. Symbols employed in the transcriptions in this book include:

+ = slightly higher than pitch as written;
− = slightly lower than pitch as written;
> = indefinite duration;
( ) = a "ghost note," i.e. a note of uncertain pitch
/ = a glide (portamento).

I am very grateful to Kenneth Bilby for having taken the time to help make the transcriptions in this book as good as they are.

Dabí in the Bullrushes (11–13)

During their earliest years in the forest, Ayakô and his people were constantly on the lookout for enemy troops. These were the days when, as in this story, "going hunting" did not mean for meat, and "whitebird" [*wétifóu*] meant "white man." This story of the infant Dabí's miraculous escape from danger has been preserved for nearly three hundred years in the songs and lore surrounding the great Matjáu war *óbia* called Afíima (sometimes, Kafíima), which has become inactive only during recent decades. According to Tebíni, who sang Ayakô's song for me, "mbakí gwaniní" is the term by which Ayakô addressed the *óbia*. (*Gwaniní* means "eagle" in Saramaccan, and the bird is a key symbol of Afíima *óbia*.)* The song would translate, then, as "Mbakí gwaniní

---

* Afíima gave its adherents invulnerability to bullets and cutlasses (among its many other deeds). I knew, before his recent death, Afoódu—the last man alive to know the Afíima leaves, and the final keeper of its shrine. When the proper leaves were mashed and then allowed to dry in a wad, a three-inch nail would bend if driven into them; and when dropped into cool water, such a wad would immediately set the pot to "boiling." The tribal chief used to like to tell me of seeing the great *óbia* pot, with its twelve large holes, miraculously boiling chickens for a ritual feast and not losing a drop of water. And Peléki told me that when he was young, an eagle would come in the daytime, as a sign. "It would land on the tree behind Afoódu's *óbia* house [in Dángogó]. It would just sit there. And they'd shoot at it [with shotguns] 'gwé, gwé, gwé, gwé'. Until it would open its wings real wide and fly off majestically. That was the true coming of the *óbia*."

12. Ayakô had a wife, Asukúme, in slavery. She traveled with him always. (Tebíni 28 July 1976)

13. One day Ayakô had gone off to scout the forest, "going hunting" as they called it in those days. But this was not hunting for animals; it was to see if the whites were nearby. Ayakô had gone out searching when the whites arrived in Asukúme's garden. She was there with her infant son. Divination told Ayakô that his wife was in danger, that the whites were about to catch her. (In those days, if they came upon you with a child, they would catch you, because the child would cry and give you away.) Ayakô prepared himself ritually and he warned Asukúme. He was far away but he warned her by *óbia*. He sang the *óbia* song that instructed Asukúme to throw the child into the reeds, where it would remain silent, and where it would be unharmed. . . . Well, that child was Dabí! The whites just passed by. She and the child were safe. (Otjútju 3 August 1976)   ✛

The Coming of the Slaves from Wátambíi

14. From the forest the Matjáus sent word to the Wátambíi slaves, saying that they would leave marks, or blazes, on the path, as they continued to walk south, for them to follow; that at such and such a time, they must burn their own plantation; that if they could kill the white man, they should, but if not, just leave. When it got to be late at night and the white man was asleep, the Matjáus prepared their magic [*óbia*] and brought it to them, to give them stout hearts. The *óbia* consisted of . . . [leaves and other ingredients are mentioned, accompanied by a request not to print it in "my book"]. That's what they

---

[term of address for the *óbia*] / In the days we were with the eagle [or, at the time we had the eagle's power] / The eagle would jump *tjêle tjêle tjêle* [the sound of the eagle jumping]."

Dabí, the infant protagonist of this story, was an important mid-eighteenth-century leader. During the final years before the Peace of 1762, he followed in his father's (Ayakô's) footsteps, serving as unofficial tribal chief (see R. Price 1983). There is documentary evidence that Dabí was in fact born on a plantation rather than in the forest; in 1762, a rival chief used the fact that the aged Dabí had been a "bought person" (slave) to argue against his official recognition by the whites (SvS 155, 20 April 1763 [11 November 1762]). Since Tebíni asserts that Ayakô's marriage to Asukúme preceded their escape, Dabí must have been born in slavery ca. 1689, with the infant-in-the-reeds incident occurring a year or two later, soon after they found freedom.   ✛

The Coming of the Slaves from Wátambíi (14–15)

Fragment *14* (as well as *16–19*) serves as charter for the special relationship of the Matjáus and Wátambíis, two clans that have managed to live together intimately for more than two and a half centuries. Until one hundred years ago, they shared a single village, always under Matjáu leadership; since that time the Wátambíis have occupied the village of Akísiamáu, directly across the Pikílío from the village of the Matjáu tribal chief.

Fragment *15*, elicited by a government official in 1888, undoubtedly in a "contact" language, was clearly not intended to be complete and quite possibly not intended to be truthful. It

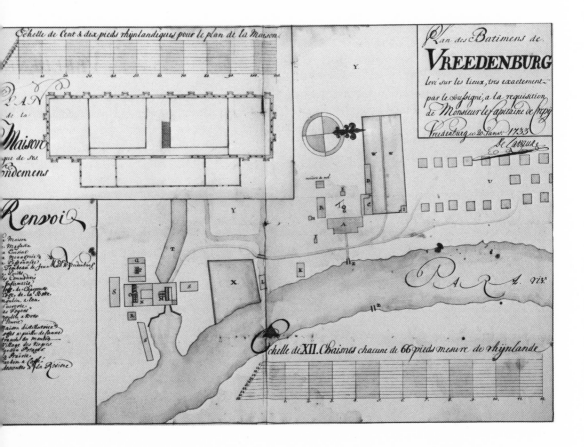

"Plan of the buildings at [Plantation] Vreedenburg ["*Wátambíi*"], drawn on-the-spot with great precision by . . . [Alexander] De Lavaux," 1733.

The key lists *A.* the [great] house, *B.* the store house, *C.* the kitchen, *D.* the barn, *E.* the pigeon-house, *F.* the tomb of the late Mme. Vreedenburg, *G.* the well, *H.* the outhouses, *I.* the hospital, *K.* carpentry shop, *L.* *"Loge de la botte,"* *M.* watermill [*wátambíi*], *N.* boiling house, *O.* fireplaces, *P.* animal-driven mill, *Q.* the stables, *R.* distilling house, *S.* shed for cane trash, *T.* millrace, *U.* Negro village, *W.* kitchen garden, *Y.* grazing land, *X.* coffee grove, *Z.* landing places. (I have been unable to find a translation for *"loge de la botte."* M. Gabriel Debien [personal communication 1982] has kindly suggested that, although he has never before seen this designation on a plantation map, the placement of the structure makes it likely that it served as *la loge du guardien de l'écluse*—the sluice-keeper's quarters.) (*Algemeen Rijksarchief, Collection Vredenburg, No. 14.*)

taught the Wátambíis. They were our kinsmen, something like mother's brother and sister's children. Gúngúúkúsu and Afámbo, the two Wátambíi leaders, and Lánu and Ajakô came from the same place. That's why they went and taught them. (Otjútju 3 August 1976)

15. During the invasion of the "English," Soee [Zóe] and Rosine (both women) and three men (Goengroekoesoe, Sambo [Afámbo], and Dosa) from the sugar plantation Vreedenburg (Watra-miri) in the Para district were secreted at the edge of the forest by their owner, Widow van der Tunk (Ba'ba), and they stayed there ["deserted"]. (Testimony of Wátambíi Captain Elias Kodjo Asikada, 1888, to B. Heyde. Quoted in Morssink n.d., 2:147) ✤

---

apparently refers (like the story in 52, and like various published sources on early Suriname history) to the brief but devastating invasion of the French admiral Jacques Cassard in 1712, during which many slaves were hidden at the edge of the forest by their masters, in hopes of avoiding having to give them up as ransom, and at which time many took the opportunity to escape. It is interesting that an 1829 list of plantations and owners shows that "Vreedenburg" was at that time still in the "van der Tuuk" (their spelling) family (Anon. 1830:61)

I am able, on the basis of both oral and archival materials, to reconstruct a scenario that strongly supports the Matjáu and Wátambíi claims about their shared experience as slaves and their respective rebellions. Because the evidence is at once fragmentary and enormously complex, I merely summarize here, not citing sources, asking the reader to refer at this point to the map on p. 57 and its legend.

By 1690, the slaves on the two Vredenburg plantations (B and D on map) and those on the Machado plantation (A) and Plantation Waterland (E) were in frequent contact because of interlacing ties of ownership and proximity. After the Matjáu rebellion of 1690 (from A [and E?]), while they were living at Matjáu Creek, the Matjáus maintained close relations with the Wátambíi slaves (at D [and B?]). The Matjáus at the creek were joined by some Wátambíis who escaped during the French invasion of 1712, with whom they later returned to liberate others. (A 1729 archival report of a conspiracy between slaves and maroons to liberate the slaves of Plantation Vredenburg may well reflect such an effort [GA 1, 9 March 1729, 12 March 1729, 16 March 1729].) During this same period, the slaves living on or near the former Machado and Vredenburg eastern plantations (A and B)—who by then had become known as "Big" and "Little" *Pinásis*, respectively, as the plantations were now owned by the L'Espinasse family—fled, this time toward Djuka, to the southeast. The related identities remembered and debated when Saramakas and Djukas meet today—that Saramaka Matjáus are somehow of the same plantation origin as Djuka "Big" Pinásis, while Saramaka Wátambíis are the same as Djuka "Little" Pinásis—begin to make sense, in light of this long history of special relations between the set of plantations signaled on the map. ✤

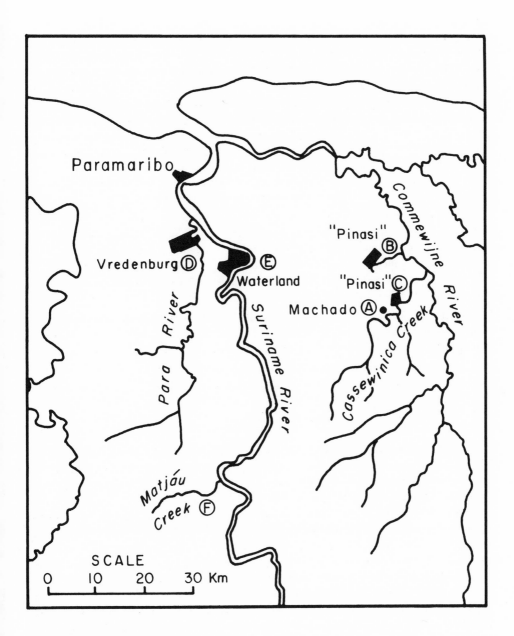

Matjáu and Wátambíi Plantations

A. Machado Plantation, 1690 (approximate site).

B. One of the plantations known by at least 1737 as "Pinasi," owned in 1690 by A. Vredenburg.

C. Another of the 1737 "Pinasi" plantations.

D. Plantation Vredenburg, called in Saramaccan "Wátambíi," owned in 1690 by A. Vredenburg.

E. Plantation Waterland, associated in Matjáu traditions with Ayakô (and Lánu?).

F. Matjáu Creek, the forest area where Matjáus lived for some years following their escape.

The Greeting

16. Now, when he [Ayakô] went off, the first person to follow him was Akísiamáu [the name of the present Wátambíi village, used here metonymically to stand for that clan]. The Akísiamáu great elder followed him all the way. They [the Matjáus] were the first to run away. Now the first people that they met up with again, that was Akísiamáu. No other people greeted other people; it was Akísiamáu and Matjáus who greeted each other. They had parted [on the plantations]; now they met, and they greeted. Other clans may have their stories, man; when a person has *his* thing, he will not tell it to you. But according to what your ancestors recounted, it was Dángogó people [Matjáus] and Akísiamáu, so they greeted one another. (Kála, instructing Abátelí at cock's crow, 1975)

17. When Ayakô was deep in the forest, he called out to the other ones [the Wátambíis] with *óbia*, instructing them to come to him, to do whatever might be necessary to get to him. And he [the Wátambíi] did escape! When they finally met, that first time, the [Wátambíi] man called out, "Awesáánu." The other replied, "Awesáánu." The first said, "Gbégbéde wédjamè." The other answered, "Awandíkbóu." Then they embraced, "djuuwè." (Kála 5 July 1978)

18. When Gúngúúkúsu [the Wátambíi leader] fled to follow Ayakô, divination led him to where Ayakô was living. When he arrived at the edge of the camp, he didn't see Ayakô. But he saw the woman [Ayakô's sister], Sééi. He called out, "Ahúngwadja." She just stared

---

The Greeting (16–19)

These fragments encode two central messages: that the original solidarity of the Matjáus and Wátambíis was based on the experience of suffering slavery together on neighboring plantations; and that the Matjáus' priority in rebellion and the Wátambíis' dependence in having been helped by them to escape is delicately balanced by the volitional aspect of the relationship.

Fragments *16–18*, from Matjáu men, all stress Matjáu temporal priority in the forest—the latter two fragments explicitly using the "greeting" metaphor (see p. 7 above) to underline this basis for Wátambíi dependence. Fragment *19*, however, spoken by the Wátambíi elder Asipéi, depicts the same event from a different slant, ignoring the issue of who greeted whom but adding a key interchange about accepting "fire."* This Wátambíi version, by pointing to their ancestor's potential independence in the forest (as he already possessed fire), neatly insists upon the volitional aspect of their relationship with Matjáus. Although Matjáu and Wátambíi perspectives on this event differ slightly, the crux of the stories concerning the arrival of the slaves from Vredenburg is simple: as perhaps best expressed in *16* (which was recounted in excited whispers by Captain Kála, on tape to his "grandson," not to me), "They [Matjáus and Wátambíis] had parted, now they met, and they greeted." And since that first joyous greeting in the forest between Ayakô and Gúngúúkúsu [also known as Gúngurúku Máitásidágbo, or Mandeésidágua], Matjáus and Wátambíis have lived in a state of harmony quite remarkable relative to Matjáu relations with their other allied clans. These several fragments about the distant past represent, then, the ideological underpinnings for this ongoing political relationship.

* Tebíni once spoke to me with special respect about Asipéi's knowledge: "Your friend Asipéi. He's one of the few who still knows things. At that time [when they were both learning from Captain Bitjénfóu, see above], he was already a full-grown youth."

at him. All she could see was a runaway. He said, "Awángamádesúsu." Because that man had come with a powerful *óbia* and had been living for days at the outskirts of the camp. Every night he would come to see if his friend Ayakô was there, and he had lived by stealing Sééi's chickens. Now, he had finally come by daylight. He knew that if he simply appeared in a strange camp, they would kill him, thinking he was bringing the whites. That's why he called out to her, "Ahúngwadja." Three times he said it. She was silent. Then he said, "Awángamádesúsu. Mi doro ko kadja," which means, "I've arrived. Old woman, put your chickens in their baskets. It's me!" Today [on special occasions] people pour libations using these [secret] words. But it was Gúngúúkúsu who first spoke them. (Otjútju 16 July 1978)

19. The great man [Ayakô] was the first to come. The other one [Gúngúúkúsu] walked behind him. They had made an arrangement to go off together. But the person who's quicker will get started first. And the great man was the quicker of the two. My [Wátambíi] ancestors said that they didn't know if these two were mother's brother and sister's son, two brothers, African countrymen, or simply close friends. But they were something close. . . . When they finally met, they greeted one another. Then the Matjáu invited the other to come and take fire. But he said no thanks, that he carried his own fire. Then he put his hunting sack on the ground, pulled out a flint, rubbed it *kwákwákwá ví!* He'd made fire! In other words, the great man hadn't "caught" him. They'd come as equals. And they remained special friends ever after. (Asipéi 19 July 1978)   ✣

Several other themes that appear fleetingly in these fragments reappear time and again in other oral accounts of the early years in the forest—the great fear of new runaways, who among some early maroon bands were routinely killed; the related use of passwords (usually now-meaningless African-language greetings, which are spoken in retelling a story with considerable phonological variation); and the importance of possessing fire (and, more generally, the extraordinary physical difficulties experienced by the early maroons in the forest).

Fragment *18* neatly illustrates something of the complexity of the process by which Saramakas learn, reshape, and speak about the past. The speaker, Otjútju, claims to have heard this version—with these "African" words—from his "great grandfather," the tribal chief. Meanwhile, Peléki has described to me how he and Captain Kála first heard it from Tebíni and Tebíni's late brother; how a decade later Peléki had "reminded" Kála—who had by then forgotten the words—of it; how Kála had then rehearsed the story to himself for a few days and then told his own brother, the tribal chief; and how years later Otjútju finally learned it from the chief. In fact, however, Otjútju's rendering differs from what the tribal chief has told me, which in turn differs from what Kála recounts (see *17*). And this is far from being simply a consequence of faulty memory. The simplified "chain of transmission" depicted by Peléki ignores the numerous other relevant sources each of these people heard during the period—at rituals, at public meetings, in informal discussion—and the ongoing process in which each man reshapes his understandings to fit his new information. What keeps the Saramaka past alive is not the faithful transmission of "facts" from one man to the next, but rather the active intelligence of a variety of men, each working with all the data at his disposal toward achieving understanding.   ✣

Monkeyshines: Wátambíis Learn the Twin Óbia

20. Ma Zóe was an early Wátambíi runaway. Once in the forest, she gave birth to twins. One day she went to her garden, leaving the infants in a nearby open shed. But when she returned for them, she saw a *kwáta* [large monkey] sitting right next to them. So she hid to watch what would happen. She was afraid that if she startled the animal, it might grab the children and carry them into the trees. She was beside herself and didn't know what to do. So she just kept watch. She saw that the monkey had amassed a large pile of selected leaves. It was breaking them into pieces. Then it put them into an earthenware pot and

---

Monkeyshines: Wátambíis Learn the Twin Óbia (20)

Zóe is a woman of singular importance to Wátambíis, as she was the original priestess of what is still the Saramakas' only twin cult, and the major spiritual possession of the Wátambíi clan, which has always serviced twins and their families from all over Saramaka. The speaker in *20* is Peléki, himself a twin and therefore possessing first-hand and frequent exposure to the rituals and history of this cult. Most historical fragments I have heard depict Zóe as an African-born maroon. There are strong traditions that she was later married to Antamá, whom we will meet below; and this suggests that if she was African-born, and old enough before enslavement to have achieved some knowledge of an African twin cult, her liberation would have taken place ca. 1730, just about the time Plantation Vredenburg was undergoing persistent siege by maroons. (Such a scenario, which is supported by most of the accounts I have heard, does run partly counter to *15*, the "suspect" fragment mentioned above.)

The story of how Zóe founded the twin cult, and the syncretically African content of the cult's rituals (the ritual relations it enforces between twins and monkeys, and a host of other details), suggest a historical process of special note, one that I believe underlies much of the creative culture building effected by the original Saramakas. In a passage written some years ago with Sidney Mintz, I described the significance of this process in general terms and, curiously, used the example of a twin cult to drive home the point:

> We can probably date the beginnings of any new Afro-American religion from the moment that one person in need received ritual assistance from another who belonged to a different [African] cultural group. Once such people had "exchanged" ritual assistance in this fashion, there would already exist a micro-community with a nascent religion that was, in a real sense, its own. We may speculate, for example, that one of the first slaves brought to a particular plantation in a new colony gives birth to twins (or becomes insane, commits suicide, or experiences any one of a number of events which would have required *some* kind of highly specialized ritual attention in almost any society in West [or Central] Africa). It is clear to all that *something* must be done, but our hypothetical mother of twins has no special expertise herself, nor does anyone of her own ethnic background on that plantation. However, another woman, one of whose relatives may have been a priestess of a twin cult in another [African] group, takes charge of the situation, performing the rites as best she can remember them. By dint of this experience, then, this woman becomes *the* local specialist in twin births. In caring ritually for their parents, in performing the special rites should they sicken or die, and so on, she may eventually transmit her specialized knowledge (which may well be a fairly radical selection and elaboration of what her kinsman's cult had been) to other slaves, who thereupon carry this knowledge, and the attached statuses and roles, forward in time. (Mintz and Price 1976:23–24)

placed it on the fire. When the leaves had boiled a while, it removed them and poured the leaves into a calabash. With this it washed the child. Exactly the way a mother washes a child! Then it shook the water off the child and put it down. Then it did the same with the other child. Finally, it took the calabash of leaf water and gave some to each child to drink. The woman saw all this. Then, when it was all finished, the monkey set out on the path. It didn't take the twins with it! And the mother came running to her children. She examined the leaves—which ones it had given them to drink, which had been used for washing. And those are the very leaves that remain with us today for the great Wátambíi twin *óbia*. (Peléki 17 July 1978) ✤

I am suggesting now that the story of Zóe may well represent a Saramaka conceptualization of precisely this historical process. If indeed Zóe may be compared to the hypothetical woman in the above-quoted example, the kind of story Saramakas tell about her today is exactly what one would expect. The story's stress on newness, on the American origin of the cult, is what permits the Wátambíis as a whole to lay exclusive claim to the cult's powers. Yet for any Saramaka, not far behind the belief that "a monkey taught it to her" lies the knowledge that Zóe was an African. The story (and its associated cult) draws heavily on mythological, folkloric, and ritual traditions from Africa *at the same time* that it proclaims the birth of an entirely new cult. This is one example, then, of the ways that Saramaka historical consciousness incorporates the complex processes by which their nascent society was forged. ✤

Saramaka twins

Seven Who Walked Together

21. The Matjáus came as seven. They were seven people plus [the *óbiama*] Kwémayón who walked together. There were [the brothers] Lánu and Ayakô, their eldest sister Sééi, Sééi's daughter and son—Yáya and Adjágbò—Yáya's son Abíni, and a man called Kwasílolá. (Tebíni 28 July 1976)

22. But there is a powerful secret. The most dangerous knowledge about us Matjáus. After Ayakô liberated his sister Sééi and her daughter, he himself raised the daughter. And when she was old enough, he begat with her! This is why no one can say who our collective "father" is. It's as if you had children with your younger sister. You would be at the same time their father and uncle! This is why Matjáus are accountable to no one; we are dependent on nobody but ourselves. (Kála 5 July 1978) ✛

Seven Who Walked Together (21–22)

The core of a number of Matjáu historical fragments is that "seven runaways walked together," but there is some lack of agreement as to which seven and where they were walking. In *21*, Tebíni lists the most commonly cited set of seven, with their putative genealogical ties. Of these individuals, four appear sufficiently often in later documentary sources that I can estimate their birth dates rather closely: Ayakô, b. 1664–1670; Yáya, b. 1674–1690; Abíni, b. 1695–1705; and Adjágbò, b. 1695–1715. Given this information, I believe that the "walk" in question was in fact the long trek from the base camp at Matjáu Creek, around 1715, to the upper reaches of the Suriname River (see *25*). And I would suggest further that these seven names are selectively remembered from what would have been a far larger pool of original runaways at Matjáu Creek because (1) Lánu was in fact the titular head of the group and probably the mastermind of the sack of the Machado plantation in 1690; (2) Ayakô—whether or not his actual brother—was the senior chief of the Saramakas in the years preceding the Peace of 1762; (3) Sééi—again, whether or not she was an actual sister of Ayakô or Lánu—was the genealogical "mother" of a large proportion of Matjáus alive today; (4) Yáya, Adjágbò, and Abíni played critical roles in Saramaka life during the mid-eighteenth century, as will be seen below; and (5) Kwasílolá was responsible for a still ongoing and dangerous ritual relationship between Matjáus and Dómbis, established when his Dómbi wife committed suicide during the 1730s (see *142*). Reasoning backward from the present, then—which follows, after all, the process by which the past is selectively remembered by Saramakas—we may surmise that these seven Matjáus are remembered as the core of the original group (and in three cases quite possibly provided with spurious collateral ties) *because their acts demanded it*; each of these seven (and the mysterious *óbiama* Kwémayón, who walked with them but was never considered part of the group) left a major mark, through his or her acts, on the future course of Matjáu history.

I read *22* as reflecting a central conceptual dilemma: Saramakas, looking backward, must find a way of dealing conceptually with the historical shift in the definition of clan membership from the original nongenealogical criteria (such as common plantation origin and shared early life in the forest) to the later adoption of a strictly matrilineal principle. On the one hand, from a nineteenth- or twentieth-century Saramaka perspective, membership in the Matjáu clan is based exclusively on ties of matriliny (and therefore Ayakô—whom documentary accounts confirm as a great Matjáu war leader—needs to be considered a *brother of* Sééi, who "mothered" so many of the present-day Matjáus). On the other hand, genealogies collected during earlier periods (for

Only Her Name Got This Far: A Second Matjáu Group

23. The oldest daughter of Sééi was Dóti, a woman who was so ugly that the others could hardly bear to look upon her. They gave to her as husband a man called Gúnkamé [or Sakútu], whom they had discovered all alone in a watermelon field, around Báyagádu, on the east bank of the river. No one knows what his origin was; he must have come from the sky. Gúnkamé was a giant of a man, very very large. No one would give him a wife. But he *knew* things, he had possessions . . . not white man's possessions, but *óbia*. So, the Matjáus gave him Dóti. (Otjútju 3 August 1976)

24. The Peace [of 1762] had already come to Baákawáta, and her mother's brother [Ayakô] was already dead before Dóti's people finally arrived upstream [to join the main band of Matjáus]. But Dóti herself [as well as Gúnkamé] died down there. She did not make it to here. Only her name got this far. (Tebíni 6 August 1976)　　　✤

---

example, Morssink n.d.:67) affirm that Ayakô was rather Sééi's *husband* (and therefore, from a modern Matjáu perspective, not definitively a Matjáu at all). I believe that *22* represents an effort by later generations to square what would appear to them to be the contradictory facts of Ayakô's prototypical "Matjáu-ness" and his marriage to Sééi (or her daughter) with current descent group ideology. The "secret," as expressed here, allows modern Matjáus to have their historical cake and eat it (albeit requiring them to posit a case of incest, excusable however because of the circumstances of early life in the forest): Ayakô was not only matrilineally a Matjáu but the father of them all as well. And as in origin stories involving fraternal incest from lineal societies elsewhere in the world, this one serves the additional function—as explicitly stated in Kála's text—of making the descendants of the original pair politically accountable to no one but themselves.　　✤

Only Her Name Got This Far: A Second Matjáu Group (23–24)

Matjáus possess rich historical traditions concerning this tiny group of Matjáus who stayed behind after Ayakô and his followers moved south ca. 1715. Their disproportionate contribution to Matjáu history lies in the political arena, where their descendants have always played leadership roles. The son of Dóti and Gúnkamé, Afadjétosúme, was given one of the original Peace Treaty headman's staffs; their daughter's son, Gbagidí, had the famous god Saa who is given credit for having wrested the office of tribal chief back to the Matjáus in the 1830s; their daughter's daughter's son, Wétiwóyo, in 1835 became the first Matjáu tribal chief since 1767; and for the entire first third of the twentieth century, their matrilineal descendant Djankusó ruled Saramaka as tribal chief. Knowledge about the activities of Dóti and Gúnkamé's descendants between the time of the departure of the main group of Matjáus and their reunion on the upper river is preserved in cryptic fragments, largely in the ritual language known as Papá. It involves dark and obscure historical entanglements surrounding Afadjétosúme's headman's staff and his premature (and highly "dangerous") death, both of which will be treated in the section covering the Peace Treaties, below.

Gúnkamé, of whom it is always said, "He came from the sky,"* exemplifies the image of the

---

* The Herskovitses present a curiously garbled fragment about Gúnkamé in which they (or their Creole interpreter) mistranslate Chief Djankusó's use of this phrase (Sar: "a kumútu gaán-gádu") as "He came from God" (Herskovits and Herskovits 1934:257).

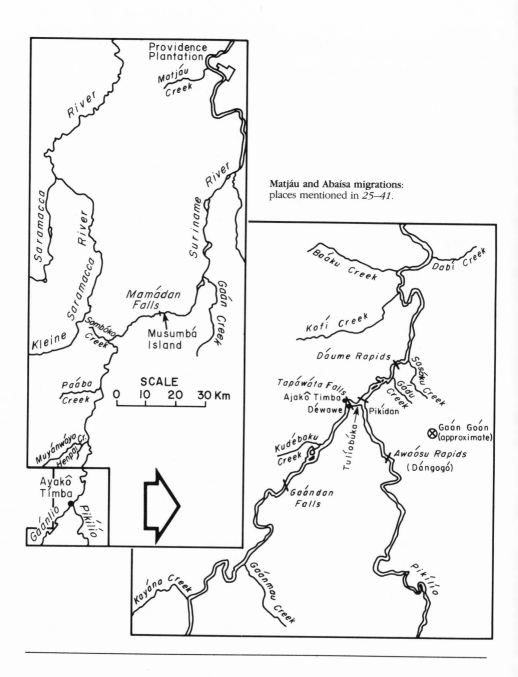

Matjáu and Abaísa migrations:
places mentioned in 25–41.

lone runaway that appears repeatedly in Saramaka traditions about their early years (see, for example, the story of Kúngoóka—125, 166). As mentioned in discussing the arrival of Gúngúúkúsu to Sééi's camp (16–19), these lone men were regarded with genuine ambivalence on the part of the Saramakas and were often simply killed. Both the dangers they posed and the opportunities they offered are expressed in the imagery typically used to describe them: African, physically ugly, supernaturally powerful, but lacking a wife. The groups that today recount taking in such men by the offer of a wife always stress that other groups had previously refused them, and that they themselves took a calculated risk which was, however, richly rewarded in terms of the special ritual knowledge proffered in return.   ✤

THE EVENTS

The Great Southward Trek

25. My "mother's brother" Captain Apeéli [died ca. 1947] used to tell me, "The Matjáus did not walk along the river banks. They walked through the forest itself [in a southerly direction], across the heads of the creeks." Well, the custom was that if you did not pass the creek at its mouth, it was not yours. . . . When he [Ayakô] came to see the river, that area where he came remained Matjáu territory. "Man," he said, "Matjáus were the first to run away to the forest." That's what Captain Gidé [Apeéli] said. He continued, "When they were coming up, the first place they touched the river was at Musumbá Island. When he [Ayakô] went back through the forest, the next place he met the river was at the mouth of Paába Creek. Back in the forest, he crossed the head of Muyánwóyo Creek, and finally, he came to the river again at a place called Tímba, just inside the Gaánlío." I have heard that they walked up in between the Saramacca River and the Suriname, sometimes going to see the one, sometimes the other. "You know," Apeéli said to me, "if Dabítatá [Ayakô] had walked along the [Suriname] river bank, no other clan would have owned any land at all!" (Peléki 22 July 1976)   ✣

The Great Southward Trek (25)

The great migration from Matjáu Creek to Baákawáta, on the upper Pikílío, constitutes a central concern of Matjáu historiography. This set of traditions legitimizes rights to land, establishes political relationships with other clans, and delineates mutual obligations with the gods who dwell in their territory. These traditions (which are most often recounted apropos of land disputes) tend to take on a continuous form: a route will be described, with various points signaled along the way, as if the migration took place as a single event, not extended in time. However, other historical fragments, told in contexts unrelated to land rights, make clear that at least some of the points along the route were village sites involving lengthy residence. (Independent evidence suggests that the trek, begun ca. 1715, ended with the settlement of Baákawáta ca. 1730.) Though Matjáu migration stories incidentally encode considerable information about such diverse subjects as residence history and the initial role of ritual, from a Matjáu perspective their intent is to legitimize claims to territory and the power relations that these imply.

As in many Matjáu accounts, Peléki takes pains (in 25) to explain rather ruefully why Matjáus—in spite of having been the earliest runaways and the first to set out bravely for the deep interior—cannot lay claim to *all* the lands in Saramaka territory. The riverbank sites staked out by Ayakô included Paába and Tímba in all versions I have heard; Musumbá Island is sometimes included (as in 25), but in other versions it is considered to have become Matjáu territory much later, when Musumbá (Ayakô's sister's daughter's son) lived there during the late eighteenth century (see map).   ✣

Making the Upper River Their Own

26. When they got to Tímba, they built a raft. ["Tímba" means raft in Saramaccan.] They poled up the Gaánlío to Gaánmáu [a creek], crossed to the other side, and began descending. (Tebíni 28 July 1976)

27. They heard the roar of Tapáwáta Falls in the distance. [Ayakô's great *óbiama*] Kwémayón did divination, which advised that they continue downstream. At the tiny island right above the falls, [now called] Déwawe, the River "took" a clay pot of Kwémayón, his *tonêpôtò*, devoted to the worship of the river god. (Tebíni 24 July 1976)

28. Kwémayón called out [singing]:

> Déwaweo, Déwawe
> Gánsa, mi yánvaló
> Mi yánvaló nawé o, mi yánvaló nawé
> Déwawe mi yánvaló nawé
> Mi yánvaló nawé o, mi yánvaló nawé
> Gánsa mi yánvaló nawé
> Déwawe, mi yánvaló nawé
> —(Otjútju 3 August 1976)

29. That is how Kwémayón spoke to the River, begging permission to take possession of it, to live there. Then they continued, descending the great falls with their raft, on the side of the *kwamá* reeds. There, at the confluence of the two rivers, Ayakô "cut" the reeds, claiming the Pikílío forever for Matjáus, as Kwémayón "smoked" the whole area continuously with his ritual apparatus. Then, as they crossed the river at Pikídan, just below the falls, the River "took" Ayakô's protective armband [sometimes described as a *kêti*, sometimes a *mongá*]. It fell in the river there. So he swore, he prayed to the Great God, he prayed to the river god. He had "paid," he could now have his way. (Tebíni 24 July 1976)

Making the Upper River Their Own (26–33)

Real richness of detail about Ayakô's travels begins only with his arrival at Tímba (also called "Ayakô Tímba" [Ayakô's Raft], which some Matjáu traditions depict as having been a village or a camp).* Once Ayakô finally arrives in geographical territory that is meaningful to every Matjáu on a daily level, the past comes alive for them in a way the earlier stories cannot match. For me, and I believe for Matjáus as well, there is something eminently dramatic about the central narrative in this set of accounts, in which two men—Ayakô and his inseparable *óbiama* Kwémayón—are the only explicitly mentioned human protagonists, but in which a number of named creeks, islands, and rapids (along with their supernatural inhabitants)—part of the familiar, everyday world of every Matjáu—play a central role and are incorporated, through words, into the Matjáu universe. (Kwémayón was a *nêngèkôndènêngè*—a special class of African who, in Tebíni's words, "did not consort with women, was truly 'ripe' [ritually powerful], could fly whenever he wanted, and if he said 'rain' there would be rain, and if he said 'sun' there would be sun.")

---

* The archives contain numerous references to the early use of rafts rather than canoes by Saramakas. For example, a 1743 military expedition up the Suriname River found "un étalage de bois de cedre ataché avec des lianes en forme de ras," used by maroons to cross the river (SvS 292, 9 July 1753).

30. When Ayakô's armband "went" [into the river], he sang out:

> Wínzu fu Amaíduwe
> Wínzu Amaíduwe
> Hándi kóko djaío
> A goé uou wínzu
> Wenwe yánvaló
> Háni kóko djaí éo
> Winwí yánvaló
> A goéooéééé

which signifies [loosely], "the dearest thing I own you have taken. Finally, I've bested the River. I'll live on this river. I claim it. Because I've paid for it." (Otjútju 3 August 1976)

31. It was then that Kwémayón descended into the river. He slept right there, underwater at the foot of the falls. The African! He slept there at Túlíobúka underwater until he came out and said, "Wherever you can find a suitable place, we can stay there." They rode the raft downstream further, along the west bank, and crossed back at Dáume rapids, starting to pole back up. Divination told them, "Only at Baákawáta will you be able to hide people successfully." And that's the way it finally came to pass. (Tebíni 24 July 1976)

32. Ayakô left his village at Dabí Creek. He crossed over the river and went up Baáku Creek to its head. He crossed the head of Kofí Creek, continued past Kudébaku, and made a new village just above Gaándan Falls. Then he crossed over, made a raft, and came down to the *kwamá* [Túlíobúka]. He was not alone. He was with the man called Kwémayón. His *tonêpôtò* fell into the river. They came down Tapáwáta Falls. He crossed Pikídan on foot. His *mongá*, his *kêti* fell in. As they continued down, he crossed Dáume Rapids on foot, and he claimed the creek called Gádu Creek. Then he went up Gádu Creek and got to Gaán Goón. . . . Then he passed Gaán Goón, and when he came out of the forest he

---

The details of Ayakô's and Kwémayón's wanderings on the raft vary slightly from one teller to the next, but the theme of their *interacting* with the geographical and spiritual environment—and thus being able to claim a relationship with it for Matjáu posterity—animates all versions. Of all the places mentioned in these accounts, Túlíobúka, the spit of land at the confluence of the Pikílío and Gaánlío, remains most sacred. Though today it is desecrated by an airstrip and a bushcamp belonging to the Geological and Mining Service, the shrine that marks the spot where Ayakô cut the reeds is the site of periodic ceremonies, under the direction of the tribal chief, whenever really serious pan-tribal crises occur. It is here, for example, that the tribal chief leads rites to influence the weather in periods of dangerous drought or rain, for—as in the days of Ayakô's and Kwémayón's raft journey—it is here that the Mother of the Waters, Gánsa the *tonê* god, holds sway.*

---

* The historiographical process of "name substitution" was once nicely explained to me using the reed-cutting incident at Túlíobúka as an example. (I transcribe/translate from a 1976 conversation with Otjútju.) "I always used to hear, 'Musumbá and Adjágbò and Gúngúúkúsu cut the reeds at Túlíobúka.' " [RP: "But I don't understand. Didn't Ayakô cut the reeds?"] "No. [I would hear] 'Musumbá and Adjágbò.' " [RP: "Because I've always heard 'Ayakô,' not 'Adjágbò.' "] "But Adjágbò is the name that is called. *Because one wasn't supposed to say 'Ayakô.'* When a libation was poured, they would say, 'the place where Musumbá and Adjágbò cut the reeds.' " [RP: "But Musumbá wasn't even born at that time."] "Musumbá called Adjágbò 'mother's brother'; he called Ayakô 'grandfather.' He wasn't yet alive at that time. But his *name* was always used. That's what confuses people! But it was Musumbá's grandfather who actually cut those reeds."

heard a rapids roaring in the distance, "*wôôôôô.*" So he came to [the site of] Dángogó, the rapids called "Awáosu" [in Papá language]. . . . Ayakô crossed back over the river and through the forest on foot and came to Gaándan. Then he went back upstream to his new village. (Otjútju 3 August 1976)

33. After Ayakô claimed the Pikílío at its mouth, by cutting the reeds, he turned around and ascended the Gaánlío. They did not go directly up the Pikílío, man! According to what my ancestors told me, those people did not ascend the Pikílío. They went up the Gaánlío. They went up as far as Kayána Creek, and "marked" it. Only later did they go on [to Baákawáta]. (Kála, instructing Abáteli at cock's crow, 1975)   ✣

Fragment *32* begins with a reference to the temporary village Ayakô established at the head of Dabí Creek ca. 1720–25, an area that still belongs to Matjáus;* and *32–33* together assert Matjáu claims to the Gaánlío as well as the Pikílío region. The reference to Ayakô's temporary village at Kayána Creek, on the Gaánlío, provides legitimacy to Matjáu claims of their later having "given" the Lángu clan that whole area. Fragment *33*, related on tape by Captain Kála to a younger kinsman (not at my behest), gives some sense of the adversarial flavor of these assertions of priority. Fragment *32* condenses some of the migration stories already cited and combines them with a record of Ayakô's Gaánlío village. It also depicts Ayakô staking out the area of Dángogó, the site of the first Matjáu village after the post-treaty (1770s) move from Baákawáta back downriver and the heartland of Matjáus for the last two centuries. It remains the location of the most sacred of all Matjáu shrines, Awónêngè, devoted to Ayakô and his whole generation of fighting heroes.

Sometime between 1720 and 1740, after years of moving ever southward (as depicted in these various migration fragments), Ayakô and his people finally settled on the upper Pikílío at Baákawáta. And there, as Kwémayón had predicted after his underwater consultation with the river god, they finally found the place that "could hide people [from the whites] successfully."

✣

*Today, Tebíni, Peléki, and Otjútju assert that the Dabí-in-the-bullrushes incident (*11–13*) took place at Dabí Creek, giving it its name. Other clans, however, claim that the creek name derives from Dabí—traveling with his father—having been the first to "see" it. Documentary evidence makes clear that Dabí was an adult at the time of the Matjáus' arrival in the Dabí Creek area, and that the remembered incident must have occurred downriver, while they lived near Matjáu Creek. I now believe that the location of the *óbia* incident must have become shifted in Matjáu memories more than a generation ago, for Tebíni is insistent that he has always heard it said that the infant Dabí was miraculously saved at the creek that bears his name.

THE EVENTS

Shrine at Túlíobúka, 1978

ABAÍSAS, 1693–1748

Mother Kaála

34. Our great ancestor was Kaála. She did not come to the forest with brothers. She came alone [without matrilineal kinsmen]. (Old man, during Abaísa group discussion, Masiákííki, 24 July 1978)

35. Kaála had a brother called Pikípái. They both ran off together, but he turned back. Only Kaála made it up to here. That man fought, but later he went back to slavery. (Lántifáya 24 July 1978)

36. Kaála was the ripest of the ripe! She disputed the Matjáus in land claims. She had an *óbia* that prepared creeks so that no one but her group could safely use them. That's why Abaísas have so much territory, even though Matjáus walked upstream first. (Otjútju 12 July 1978)

37. Ma Kaála had a god that could talk with the water spirits. Her *óbia* could speak to the Mother of Waters. And it knew the forests too! She was very ripe. She and her god were the real warriors of the Abaísa. (Otjútju 3 July 1976)

ABAÍSAS, 1693–1748

Mother Kaála, The Escape, Kaála and her Husband, Abaísas *versus* Matjáus (34–41)

Since the early eighteenth century, the Abaísas have been rivals of the Matjáus, disputing with them over land and leadership and for the favor of the whites.* Because of my own close association with Matjáus, it was not till 1978 that I was finally able to persuade Abaísas to discuss their early years with me, and the fragments recorded in *34–35* and *38–39* stem from these tense and guarded sessions. The Matjáu fragments given here—*36–37* and *40–41*—are also strongly influenced by Abaísa traditions; their remembered source is the late Matjáu Kositán—Tribal Chief Agbagó's "brother" and Otjútju's "great grandfather"—who himself had an Abaísa father with whom he was very close.

Archival evidence places the rebellion of the original Abaísas in 1693 (a scant three years after the Machado rebellion) at Providence Plantation far up the Suriname River. This singular, isolated place was run by the Labadists, a utopian religious community that had already acquired a reputation among the Dutch for unusually cruel treatment of their slaves. During the late 1680s and early 1690s, the Labadists at Providence (which had not turned out to be the "Eden" they had envisioned) suffered multiple setbacks, became prone to severe internecine squabbling, and apparently vented much of their pent-up frustrations quite directly upon their African work force

---

* Initial Abaísa rivalry seems to have been confined to the main group of Matjáus who lived with Ayakô at Baákawáta. There are indications that the Abaísas had solidary relations with the latecoming Matjáu group of Dóti-Gúnkamé-Afadjétosúme during the mid-eighteenth century, before these Matjáus joined their "relations" at Baákawáta.

The Escape

38. In slavery, there was hardly anything to eat. It was at the place called Providence Plantation. They whipped you there till your ass was burning. Then they would give you a bit of plain rice in a calabash. (That's what we've heard.) And the gods told them that this is no way for human beings to live. They would help them. Let each person go where he could. So they ran. (Lántifáya 24 July 1978)

Kaála and Her Husband

39. They were loading the boats to go. It was frantic. There were so many, it looked like a fish-drugging party. Well, the mother of Kaála couldn't get to the river bank fast because she was old. The man who is called Andolé, Kaála's husband, jumped into Kaála's boat and began paddling furiously out to midstream, to get across the river. Finally, the old woman got to the landing. Kaála's mother. Kaála begged her husband, "Look, my mother's there. Let's turn back and get her." But Andolé refused. "How can you say that? Go back! That's my *mother* there," Kaála pleaded. (This is what our ancestors told us. We don't know if it's true or false.) Andolé said he could not go back, and he continued to the other bank, where they fled into the forest. The mother of Kaála had to remain in slavery. . . .

They continued walking upstream. Kaála said [thought to herself] that she herself would not punish her husband for the thing he'd done, but if the gods were her witness, Andolé would surely get his due. They kept going upstream. They passed the mouth of Gaánkiíki,

---

(Dittelbach 1692:54–57, passim; Wolbers 1861: 67–70; Knappert 1926/27). By 1712, the maroons from the 1693 rebellion at Providence were living in the forests to the southwest (Hof 612, 27 May 1712). Abaísa-Matjáu disputes over precedence are nothing new; in 1772 a group of Saramakas "known among Bush Negroes as Labadissa Negroes . . . from the plantation La Providence" insisted to a government official that "they belonged to the oldest family in the forest" (Hof 87, 26 February 1773 [12 February 1772]).

Of the women who figure as original maroons in the Saramaka stories I have heard, the Abaísa ancestress Kaála stands out as the single strongest leader. Precisely because she was a woman, however, I am unable to enlarge on Abaísa traditions by means of documents, which for the early years are concerned almost exclusively with men. In contrast, Samsám—who at least one Matjáu historian insists was Kaála's son—repeatedly appears in archival sources and seems to have emerged as a leader of the group as early as the 1730s; the documents make clear that from the 1750s until his death in 1777, Samsám was among the most powerful Saramaka chiefs.

These fragments about the Abaísa rebellion and escape testify vividly to the importance of the family in slavery—the ambiguous reference to Kaála's brother (who may well have been recaptured by the whites), the heartrending abandoning of Kaála's aged mother to continued bondage, and the ambivalent conjugal relationship between Kaála and Andolé. Their traditions of migration, only touched on in these fragments, depict them moving ever southward, never far from the banks of the Suriname River toward the upper Gaánlío; major village sites along the way include the head of Sombóko Creek, where it reaches toward the Kleine Saramacca River, and

passed Mamádan, and passed Musumbá Island. But they hadn't gotten up to here yet. Then, she left him because of what he'd done to her. She left him on the way upstream. And she took a new husband from the Nasí clan.

Kaála had her divination. No one could measure themselves against the likes of that woman. She was the ripest person alive! She would take her divining stick, and they would all walk in the direction it indicated. That's what told her to leave Andolé. (Lántifáya 24 July 1978)

40. Kaála tricked her husband so he died on the way up. They came to the forest together and traveled much, but she killed him. Andolé, of the Lángu clan. At a certain time, the man no longer had any strength [speaker motions to genitals]. He just couldn't [get it up] anymore. Well, the woman would not take this after a while, and in desperation she abandoned the old man. They say he died. (Agbagó 8 July 1978)

Abaísas *versus* Matjáus

41. Matjáus were the first to get away, but Abaísas came right behind them. When Ayakô and his people came upstream, the Abaísas were following, trying to best them, to take possession of land. As the Matjáus walked up, through the forest, the Abaísas claimed the creeks at their mouths. Samsám [a leader of the Abaísas] was trying to pass Ayakô. But Ayakô got him! . . . He finally caught Samsám at Kudébaku Creek. Ayakô had crossed the river at Dabí Creek and had gone up Baáku Creek. Samsám saw his tracks, but he marked [claimed] the creek mouth. Samsám claimed Kofí Creek. Then he continued upstream. He marked Sasásu Creek. Then he crossed back to the other side and continued up. Ayakô was coming down the creek [Kudébaku] by then. They met there, at its mouth. Samsám would have taken this creek too, but Ayakô was already standing there. Ayakô asked Samsám what he thought he was doing there. They almost fought. But Samsám was obviously no match for Ayakô. Ayakô said, "I have caught you, because I already have a village here." [He meant his village just above Gaándan.] Ayakô told Samsám that he would make him his village watchman (for he did not want Samsám going off on his own). And that is how the famous "sinking" incident [of 1750, see *158–61*] was set up. (Otjútju 3 August 1976) ✛

---

inside Muyánwóyo Creek, on its first southern tributary, Henpái. The documentary evidence—too complex even to introduce in this book—reveals the Abaísas from the first to have possessed unusually large villages (known to outsiders as the Papa Dorpen, see 167C–168C) as well as fierce warriors, and they seem to have constituted a major force within the nascent Saramaka nation.

Fragment *41* describes from a Matjáu perspective the symbolic subordination of the Abaísas. It also sets the stage for one of the critical events in Saramaka history—the betrayal of the whites in 1750 (see *158–61*). The four creeks which, in this fragment, are described as having been given by Ayakô to Samsám, all lie in territory that, in pan-tribal tradition, is owned by Matjáus. This fragment (like several others), then, asserts Matjáu temporal priority in the area, grudgingly acknowledges what Matjáus view as legalistic Abaísa claims to several creeks, and affirms the general subordination of Samsám (and the Abaísas) to Ayakô (and the Matjáus). ✛

Allegorical representation of the naturalist Maria Sibylla Merian, who arrived at Providence Plantation (seen through "window") in 1699. Though scientifically productive, her stay proved personally unpleasant, "ce Climat étant d'une chaleur qui ne convenoit pas à mon temperament," and she returned to Europe in 1701. Engraved frontispiece of Merian's *Dissertation sur la generation et les transformations des insectes de Suriname,* The Hague, Pierre Gosse, 1726 (3d edition, orig. 1705).

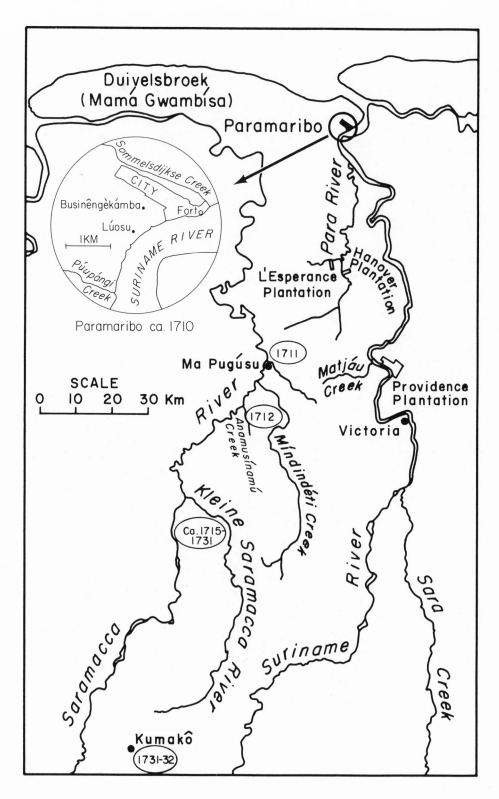

Early Lángu Migrations: places mentioned in *42–58*

THE EVENTS

LÁNGU, 1690s–1731

Abortive Escape to the North

42. They brought these [Lángu] slaves to the city, to put them to work. They kept them in a room called "Búsinêngèkámba" [Bush Negro room]. This was at [present] Zwarthoven-brugstraat, just above Kersten's [Department Store] in the direction of the hospital. That's where they escaped from to go behind the city [to the north]. (Tebíni 28 July 1976)

43. They went to the pool called Mamá Gwambísa. They were behind the swamp there when the whites found them. The place could not protect them any longer. There was no place to go. They were surrounded by the sea, the Saramacca River, and the Suriname River. (Tebíni 24 July 1976) ❖

LÁNGU, 1690s–1731

The important Lángu clan now lives along the Gaánlío, above the daunting barriers of Tapáwáta and Gaándan falls. Their name derives from Loango, the African region near the mouth of the Congo where their two most famous leaders (Kaási and Wíi) were born. My accounts of their earliest years come from Lángu men as well as Matjáus. Living in relative proximity, and linked by rituals that date from the eighteenth century and are crucial to the prosperity of the Matjáu tribal chief's office, Lángus and Matjáus relate to each other as equals, and this has helped me to find Lángu men willing to share some of their historical knowledge.

Taken as a whole, this set of Lángu traditions recounts the separate early histories of the two main segments of the clan, Kaapátus and Kadósus; it chronicles their eventual consolidation and their fierce fighting against the whites; and it describes the sites of their main villages between their initial escape in the 1690s and their arrival at the great village of Kumakô, which they shared briefly with the Nasí, Biítu, Dómbi, and Awaná clans during the early 1730s.

Abortive Escape to the North (42–43)

These two fragments preserve my only known Saramaka link to the runaway camps that dotted the mangrove swamps to the north-northwest of Paramaribo, in the area known to whites as Duivelsbroek (Devil's Marsh). I have discovered documentary confirmation of military expeditions against maroon villages in the area from as early as 1711 (when six whites, eight Arawaks, and eighteen slaves marched against such a group [Hof 612, 28 December 1711]) and 1718 (SvS 130, 31 January 1718), and these sorties continued sporadically into the mid-nineteenth century (see also Hartsinck 1770:813 and Hoogbergen 1978:17). Although most of the earlier archives are too fragile to examine, I strongly suspect that such villages date from the initial years of colonization.

The Saramaka name for the pool (or swamp), Mamá Gwambísa, commemorates the name of the *apúku* (forest spirit) who dwelled there and protected them for a time. (Saramakas believe, in general, that the Lángu clan has an especially intimate relationship with *apúku*s.) I have heard other versions of how these runaways initially crossed Mamá Gwambísa and the means by which she protected them there; these draw on a formula that frequently appears in Saramaka folktales

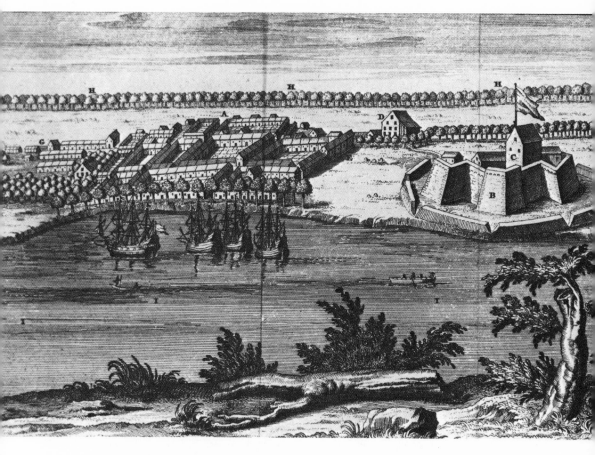

Paramaribo soon after 1700. The engraving is from J. D. Herlein, *Beschryvinge van de Volk-plantinge Zuriname* (Leeuwarden, Meindert Injema, 1718), and is labeled as follows: *A,* the city of Paramaribo; *B,* the Fort or Castle Zelandia; *C,* the Magazine of the Fort; *D,* the Governor's House; *E,* the House of the Commander; *F,* the Church and Town Hall; *G,* the New Area [*uitlegging*]; *H,* the Great Forest; *I,* the Suriname River.

(*kóntu*): a cayman (alligator) agrees, in return for a magical payment or password, to carry people across—unless, as in the case of a military expedition, they come to do evil.

I suspect that the barracks in *42* preserves the memory of a place used temporarily to house slaves requisitioned by the colony from individual planters to provide labor for public works projects. (There are frequent edicts ordering planters to "lend" slaves to the government, beginning with the very first days of Dutch settlement; in 1669, for example, the commander of the colony wrote that "the slaves of the planters are now busy digging out and broadening the canal" [Fontaine 1972:41, and see Schiltkamp and de Smidt 1973 for others].) The beginning of this fragment represents a fine example of the characteristic Saramaka use of geographical detail to breathe reality into historical accounts; in this case, for more than ten generations Lángu elders have taught youths precisely where these barracks stood, pointing out the site when they went to the city together, in order to insure that the building, for example, of a department store would not obliterate their collective memories. ✤

THE EVENTS

Kaási's Flight: Kaapátus

44. After the whites caught them, they were put back in the Búsinêngèkámba. But soon the whites decided to move them in the direction of the forest, so it would be harder to run away to the first place they had run to. They moved them to a new barracks called Lúósu. It was a great long house, right where the gas company is today. At that time the whole city was right around the governor's house [that is, the Lúósu was, in those terms, isolated and distant]. From the Lúósu they sent the slaves out to work near Púupángi Creek. (Tebíni 28 July 1976)

45. When they were at Púupángi, the slaves were kept in a big house, a long one called Lúósu. We used to sleep on banana leaves. That was our hammock! They'd cut a banana leaf, throw it on the ground, and sleep on it! Well, in that house they boiled rice for them in a single pot. Often the rice was not cooked through. The slaves wouldn't know whether the rice would be cooked through or not. But they had a special way of talking about it so

---

Kaási's Flight: Kaapátus (44–47)

This set of fragments describes the escape of the great Lángu leader Kaásipúmbu (Kaási from Púmbu), who is the Lángu counterpart of the Matjáus' Lánu (though his name and exploits are not held secret in the same way).* In condensed form, they trace the path of Kaási and his burgeoning group from their Paramaribo (nonplantation) escape to their first real village at Ma Pugúsu pool, and their subsequent settlements along the Míndindéti ("Midnight") Creek. (See map, p. 74.)

Lángu traditions agree that the escape took place during gang labor near Púupángi Creek (Poelepanje or Dominee Creek on official maps), which by 1700 was still some two kilometers

* Saramakas preserve *explicit* memories of at least the following names of places where their ancestors came from in Africa:

Aladá, also called *Papá-kôndè* (from the names of the major slave-shipping ports of Allada/Ardra—the coastal kingdom of seventeenth-century Dahomey—and Grand and Little Popo, in neighboring Togo);

Anagó (the Ewe word for Nigerian Yorubas);

Asóba-áyni (location uncertain, possibly the Agni [Ayni] in the Ivory Coast);

Asantí, also called *Komantí* (from the name of the central Gold Coast kingdom—the Dutch shipped Fantis, Ashantis, and members of other interior Gold Coast peoples through their fort at Koromantin);

Awanwí (probably the interior Gold Coast people known in colonial literature as Wanway/Wanwie—see Oldendorp 1777:279);

Bíian, also *Gbían* (location uncertain, but possibly the Bieng who live along the Kasai River in the Congo Basin);

Dáume (from the name of the expanding seventeenth-century kingdom of Dahomey);

Kwáo (location uncertain because there are several African homonyms);

Luángo (from the name of the kingdom and port near the mouth of the Congo [Zaire], through which large numbers of Bantu-speaking slaves were shipped to Suriname);

Púmbu (from Mpumbu, the Kongo word for Malebo [Stanley] Pool, on the Congo River, and used in colonial accounts to refer to a large region in the interior of the Kongo);

Tjámba (location uncertain, since there exist both interior Gold Coast and Bantu-speaking peoples with similar names, but historical traditions about the Lángu clan (see, for example, *192*) make the Tsamba, to the southeast of Stanley Pool, the more likely source);

Zóko (location uncertain for identical reasons as for *Tjámba*).

A large number of other African place names, names of kingdoms, or names of ethnic groups (for example, Kongo, Yombe, etc.) are preserved in aspects of Saramaka speech, but they are not to my knowledge explicitly remembered as African homelands.

only they would understand. One person would call the other one, "Aladí-o." The other would answer, "Aladí." The first would say, "Aladí kúku bandási," which meant, "the rice is boiled: if it's cooked through we must eat it; if it's not cooked through we must eat it." (Otjútju 18 July 1978)

46. There, they decided to escape. They crossed Púupángi. One person said to the other, "Brother, I can't make it across." The other said, "Take off your cloth [*púu i pángi*], and you'll make it." And they crossed. Divination told them, "Just keep right on going." And they went straight on. . . . Finally, they reached Ma Pugúsu [a large pool], but could not get across. Kaási used his "god" [*sóói-gádu*] at this great swamp. And they were able to pass! It was Kaási who brought them across. Then, once they crossed over, they split up into different groups. (Tebíni 28 July 1976)

47. At the pool, one man said to another, "Gwínzu." The second one answered, "Gwínzu." The first said, "Gwínzu, the whites are getting close. When I *tjulú* you should *tjalá*." The other answered, "No way, Gwínzu, I simply can't make it." The first said, "Gwínzu, just keep at it, and you'll succeed." Later, the second said, "I can't go on." The first said, "Just keep going, and little by little you'll win." And thus they passed the swamp. [The late famous] Captain Maáku of Kámpu used to tell us boys, "Gwínzu, keep at it and you'll succeed." (Tebíni 10 August 1976) ✣

---

from the inhabited area of Paramaribo. (The folk etymology of the creek's name included in this account is part of generalized [coastal] Suriname folklore, and is not usually associated with escape from slavery.) The tradition that Kaási's people were slaves recaptured from an earlier collective escape suggests a possible reason for their having been isolated as a gang; an eighteenth-century writer reported that during the early years of Saramaka history, "large numbers of unruly slaves were herded together and kept under military surveillance in the forests and outlying areas of Paramaribo" (Riemer [1780] in Staehelin 1913–19, 3:ii:253–54). The barracks story in *45* is characteristic of fragments of the past preserved through bits of remembered speech patterns; however, I heard it only once, from Otjútju, in circumstances that make me suspicious of its authenticity as a tradition. I have no indication of the time it took for the "walk" to the swamp or pool called Ma Pugúsu (after the *apúku* who holds sway there), but this site is the first I have heard mentioned by Saramakas as a true village for Kaási's people.

Documentary evidence confirms Saramaka traditions about Kaási's presence at Ma Pugúsu, in a village nestled between the swamp and the large creek that feeds it. In 1711, an expedition was sent out to destroy the village of the maroon leader known to whites as "Claas," but it returned without success (Hof 612, 17 January 1712). The two reluctant "guides"—recaptured members of Kaási's group named Diamant and Bassot, later burned alive by the whites "as an example to others"—did, however, provide sufficient geographical intelligence for a large attack to be mounted (and this geographical information, with its details of march routes, permits me to locate the village quite precisely). In 1712, an expeditionary force led by Diamant and Bassot, and consisting of forty-eight slaves, sixty-two Indians and seventeen whites, marched through some abandoned Para plantations toward Kaási's village. After several days, they discovered the site, which had twenty-five houses and was protected on one side by a swamp and on the other by a deep creek. The inhabitants, apparently warned by their scouts, had fled a few days before, leaving a quantity of goats, turkeys, and other fowls, a great deal of food (bananas, taro, corn, manioc, yams, sugar cane, oranges), some cotton, and other supplies. After plundering and burning the houses and ruining the surrounding gardens, the troops abandoned the site (Hof 612, 23 January 1712–4 March 1712).

"Family of Negro Slaves from Loango."
Engraving by William Blake, after a
drawing by John Gabriel Stedman
(1796:Plate 68). Stedman's deliberately
idealized drawing, from the 1770s, was
intended to depict "a Negro family in
that State of Tranquil Happiness to which
they [slaves] are all entitled When they
are Well treated by their Owners"
(Stedman 1790:Chapter 26).

The protected location of this precipitously abandoned village, between a swamp and deep creek, confirms Lángu traditions about Ma Pugúsu. The emotionally intense crossing of the swamp, described in the oral fragment, links suggestively with the events described in the archives for 1712. Preserved in esoteric language at rituals at the Dángogó shrine of Awónêngè, as well as in proverbial form ("Gwínzu [said to be obsolete for 'Man'], just keep at it"), the condensed story of how Kaási led his people across Ma Pugúsu, moments before the arrival of the enemy, remains a high point of early Lángu history. This account also provides first mention of Kaási's god which, as we will see, plays a key role not only in subsequent Lángu history but in the history of the Saramaka nation as a whole.

The original plantation affiliation of Kaási remains obscure, though I have heard several relevant oral fragments. A half-century ago, a Kaapátu descendant of Kaási told a government official that Kaási's original plantation was called L'Espérance (Junker 1922/23:477). And Tebíni consistently claimed to me that Kaási left the other half of his group behind when he escaped, at the Para River plantation of Hanover (which allegedly still has a branch of the same sóói-gádu— the Loángo god—that Kaási brought with him to the upper river). Given this information, the most likely plantation called L'Espérance—there were several at the time—would seem to be the one that lay on the Coropina Creek (see Lavaux 1737) within an hour's walk of present-day Hanover. During the 1760s and 1770s, these self-styled "Kaapátus" inhabited, among other villages, two that they called (according to the orthography of white officials) "Cabriata." I do not yet know the origins of this name, which may derive from their initial plantation experience.*

✢

* I would note, however, as a possibility, that when Kaási's earliest known village was abandoned in 1712, the troops found left behind many of what they called "cabriaten" (goats) (Hof 612, 4 March 1712). And to my knowledge, Kaási and his people are the only Saramakas known to have raised this animal.

Kaási's Adultery

48. Kaási ran away with two wives. There was the one he brought from Africa, called Amímba. And there was the Indian one, Piyái's sister. (Tebíni 28 July 1976)

49. The Indian wife of Kaási was called Talí. (Djógilési to Otjútju 1977 or 1978)

50. Amímba's descendants are called "Gaán Kaapátu," the Indian's descendants, "Pikí Kaapátu." (That's why those people are so "red" to this day. Just like Indians. Their skin is red!) Piyái was Kaási's *óbiama*. Indian *óbia* is the strongest of all *óbia*s! He was the one who carried the basket [*pakáa*] of Kaási's god. At some time, Kaási adultered with the Indian wife of Piyái. Piyái then left Kaási. And when Piyái died, he became an avenging spirit (*kúnu*) for the Kaapátus. (Mètisên 31 July 1978)

51. They had arrived at a certain place in the forest. Kaási saw an Indian woman there. And he caught her and presented her to his brother-in-law, Piyái. This was the first wife Piyái ever had. (He was the younger brother of Kaási's wife.) Then they all stayed together for a long time, until . . . one day, Kaási adultered with his brother-in-law's wife, the one he had given him. This affair finally became a very big thing and led to the splitting up of the group. Kaási's own Indian wife left him, since he had taken her brother's wife, and she went with Piyái. And finally, when the brother died, he became *kúnu* for Kaási's people. (Mètisên 2 July 1976) ❖

Kaási's Adultery (48–51)

Today, that segment of the Lángu clan that traces its descent from Kaási is divided into "Big" Kaapátus and "Little" Kaapátus. These historical fragments explain the origin of this division and reinforce it through the idiom of ritual. The intimacy of Indians and Africans in early Suriname society, whether as fellow toilers on the plantations, hunters of runaway slaves, or co-conspirators in rebellion, is confirmed again in the matter-of-fact report that Kaási had two wives in slavery— one Indian, one African. And like Ayakô, Kaási always traveled with his personal *óbiama*, in his case the Indian Piyái (whose name means "shaman" in the Indian languages of Suriname). Kaási's brother-in-law Piyái was entrusted with the knowledge of Kaási's most sacred possession, his Loángo god; and Piyái is said to have taught Kaási *dángara óbia*, the magic that permits invisibility. The catching and marrying of an Indian woman, as in fragment *51*, is a theme that occurs in the traditions of other clans as well, and must have happened a number of times. But the crux of these fragments about Kaási's adultery is that his act caused an irrevocable division; his descendants, even today, continue to be plagued by the avenging spirit (*kúnu*) of Piyái, which serves as a constant reminder of these domestic events that took place more than two and a half centuries ago. ❖

Wíi's Escape: Kadósus

52. We were brought to the colony during a war. A man named Kardoso had purchased the whole shipload of Africans. Afraid that since the colony was under attack by large ships we would fall into enemy hands, he sent us into hiding in the forest near Púupángi, to await the departure of the enemy. Among us was a man named Wíi, who had been a chief in Africa. In the forest he had contact with runaway slaves who told him about the terrible things that awaited him on the plantations. Wíi spoke with his sister Abêti, and they both decided to run off with any others that wished to join them. Wíi had decided that the safest route would be to follow the Saramacca River and settle far upstream. Under Wíi's leadership, they begin the trip. Arriving at the Saramacca River, they found no unoccupied territory fit for newcomers, so they continued upstream. My ancestors settled there and planted manioc gardens. But the manioc was not yet ripe before new runaways arrived with the news that patrols were following close on their heels. They had to move higher and higher up, and things continued this way for many years. Many other people had followed the Kleine Saramacca River upstream before our ancestors arrived. When Wíi got to the mouth of this river, he realized that there would be no room there for his sizable group, and he continued farther and farther up the Saramacca River, until it became quite small. ("Disiforo," to government official Junker ca. 1918, quoted in Junker 1922/23: 461–62)

53. Wíi came very very late. He "walked" way after the other Lángu leaders. But he was responsible for the escape of a whole group. At that period they were digging a canal from the Suriname River to the Saramacca River. The work was too much to take. So the slaves held a secret meeting. One day, while the overseer was walking along, inspecting the work

---

Wíi's Escape: Kadósus (52–54)

A rather consistent set of traditions surrounds the early years of Wíi, another of the Lángu founding fathers, who lived to play a decisive role in the peacemaking events of the 1760s. They agree that he had been the slave of a certain Cardoso; that he fled significantly later than Kaási's group from the area of Púupángi, accompanied by his sister Abêti Kadósu; and that his group migrated up the banks of the Saramacca—not the Suriname—River. Several fragments suggest as well that Wíi and his group escaped during an invasion of the country, pointing to the aftermath of Cassard's attack in 1712.

Fragment 52 was published in 1922–23 by L. Junker, the much-hated government official in charge of Saramaka affairs during the early twentieth century, who claimed to have taken it down verbatim from a Kadósu descendant of Wíi (Junker 1922/23:461–62). Though clearly embellished for Junker's ears, that part of the account describing Wíi's escape and initial migrations confirms much that is contained in the fragments I heard a half-century later. Fragment 53 was told to me by Mètisên, a Kaapátu descendant of Kaási on his mother's side who was raised in his Kadósu father's village, Bundjitapá, where the descendants of Wíi hold sway; its choppy style stems from my having recorded it, uncharacteristically, by handwriting rather than on tape. The flight of Kofí, and his famous jump across the ditch, seems to allude to the early history of the Kwintí maroons; by the mid-eighteenth century, they were led by a certain "Coffij," whose escape is said to have been commemorated in the placename Kofídjómpo, not far from Paramaribo (SvS 206, 6 December

further down the canal, they ran off. Wíi told them, "You go. I'll follow later." The whites arrived in the afternoon and saw only two people, Wíi and a man called Kofí. Wíi said the others had deserted. When the whites asked when, Wíi replied, "Since those *kánkan* [black birds] cried out in the forest" [that is, since morning]. Kofí became frightened and fled . . . all the way to a ditch that he jumped over, and the whites couldn't follow. This was Kofídjómbo ["Kofi jumped"]. Wíi continued to play the role of the faithful slave and advised the whites against trying to follow the runaways. Later, Wíi escaped with his sister's son Antamá, and they were reunited with the others, including Wíi's sister, Abêti Kadósu. He had wanted to give them time to get safely away. (Mètisên 2 July 1976)

54. It was near [present-day] Kwakúgoón that Wíi met those who had escaped earlier. At the big pool there they all met. Wíi, Kaásipúmbu, Bákisipámbo, Agósudanyéi. There was a giant cayman who lived in this pool. It was just waiting to eat them. But Kaási "smoked" it with his special pipe. (There's a leaf called "*makóko* tobacco." Well, Makóko is Kaási's other name!) With the *makóko* leaf he smoked the whole pool. The cayman was so drunk it didn't know where it was. And they successfully crossed the pool. (Mètisên 31 July 1978) ✤

1769; Bakhuis 1902:725). This fragment also introduces Antamá, Wíi's sister's son who becomes an important Lángu leader later in the century.

Fragment *54* focuses on the meeting, almost certainly apocryphal, of four great Lángu leaders at the pool of Ma Pugúsu—Kaási, Wíi, Bákisipámbo, and the much younger Agósudanyéi, all of whom play major roles in later events of Lángu history. (There is a general Saramaka tendency to transform later-eighteenth-century figures who were actually born in the forest, like Agósudanyéi, into original African maroons—see, for a similar Nasí case, 80C.) This crossing of the pool, which we already encountered in *46–47* and can tentatively date to 1712, seems somehow to set the stage for the many subsequent years of battles, fought jointly by these men and their companions. Kaási's pipe and *makóko* tobacco are prototypical *apúku* paraphernalia, reaffirming Kaási's—and Lángus'—special relationship with the forest spirits. ✤

Cuffi see Wood.

Battle Fragments

55. In those days [after passing the pool of Ma Pugúsu] they would meet by day, then by nightfall they'd be dispersed. They might meet the next day. Meeting and separating, fighting intermittent battles with the following troops. (Mètisên 31 July 1978)

56. Once there was a really big battle near Victoria. They completely finished off the whites! Bákisi, Antamá—his warrior name was Odínko Kánkánkán!—and Kaásipúmbu. Those were real men! Antamá and his younger brother Makambí. Men's men! (Djógilési to Otjútju 1977 or 1978)

57. They were on the run. They got to the creek [now] called Anamusínamú. Tatá Bákisipámbo and Kaásipúmbu killed a *namú* [bushfowl]. Kaási's wife cooked it, but she served them something else to eat. So the man said, "Sister, what will you do with the *namú*?" She said that since it was already boiled, it would keep till the next day. He agreed. Then,

---

Battle Fragments (55–58)

These diverse traditions about constant attacks and movement (protected throughout by the gods and *óbia*s) condense a tumultuous twenty-five years of lived experience. Within months of the destruction of Kaási's just-abandoned village at Ma Pugúsu, an expedition tracked him to his new village several miles south on the Míndindéti Creek, took four women and eight children prisoner, and burned and plundered his houses (Hof 612, 27 May 1712). (Ironically, one of the two leaders of this expedition was Jacob Cardoso, who may be the very same "Kadósu" who was about to come into the ownership of a new shipment of Africans that included Wíi.)

Lángu people, looking backward today, tend to envision Kaási and his companions during this period as a relatively homogeneous and isolated group. Archival reports suggest otherwise: two captives from Kaási's village gave as their place of origin two different Jewish plantations on the upper Suriname River, and the Abaísa village (mentioned in 34C–41C) was located very close by and included not only maroons from Providence Plantation but Dómbi maroons (from the plantation of Dominee Basseliers, see 93C–95C) as well. This was a period of constant harassing of outlying plantations by Saramakas; for example, the administrator of Providence complained that the maroons were freely visiting and "corrupting" his slaves, and that they had become "much more numerous" since the recent French invasion (Hof 612, 16 September 1713).

It seems likely that Kaási moved his people south from Míndindéti Creek soon after 1712, for large expeditions were being prepared to come against him during the second half of that year, and it could no longer have been a very hospitable stretch of territory. Anamusínamú Creek is just south of Míndindéti, and the incident commemorated in the historical fragment about its naming would seem to date from this time. (It was presumably also during this period that the battle near Victoria took place; Antamá's younger brother Makambí is known to have been killed in battle soon after, as the group moved south—see 85.) The next place they settled was along the Kleine Saramacca River, where they were not discovered by the colonists until 1730, at which time several absolutely massive expeditions were sent to destroy their villages.

The growth of Kaási's population is suggested by comparing the 1712 archival report of his 25 houses to those of 1730–31, which described five "Claas" villages, the first three of which alone included some 440 houses (see, for example, SvS 132, 25 October 1730). The remarkable diversity of Kaási's people, in terms of their plantation origins, is indicated by a document listing the "owners" of twelve of the adult captives brought back to Paramaribo by two 1730 expeditions

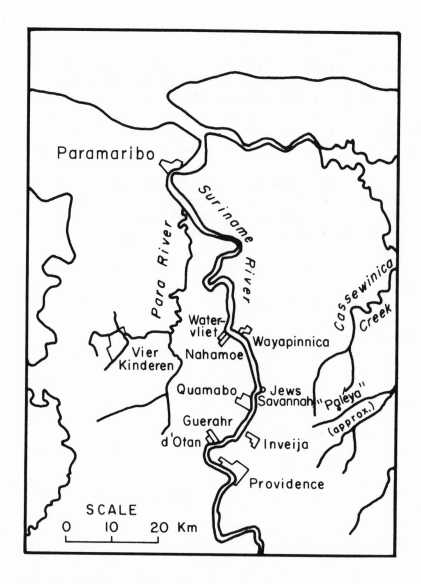

Plantations of 11 Maroons Captured at Kaási's Villages by Military Expeditions, 1730. (*Sources:* Lavaux 1737; SvS 132, 14 December 1730.)

Slave	Owner	Plantation
Joosie	Jan Beeks	Watervliet
Wierrie	Samuel Nassy, Sr.	Inveija
Manbote	Abr. de Britto	Guerahr
Lucretia	Jacob Messias Penso	Wayapinnica
Ambira	Miss Peyreyra	"Paleya"
Aga	Benjamin Henriques Granada	Nahamoe
Flora	Isaac de Meza	d'Otan
Gomba	"La Providence"	La Providence
Marie	Wid. Papot	Vier Kinderen
Victoria	David Mendes Meza	Quamabo
Christina	Jan Beeks	Watervliet

during the night, *óbia* told them that the whites were hot on their trail. They jumped up and prepared to flee. The woman asked, "What should we do with the *namú?*" He said. . . [words are indistinct on the tape]. So she threw out the *namú* broth and ran, carrying the pot. That woman was Anamusí. The creek where she threw out the broth is known as "Anamusí's Bushfowl," Anamusínamú Creek. (Mètisên 31 July 1978)

58. In those days, they might just be sitting down to eat a meal when . . . "Hurry! The whites are coming. Run for your lives." They would find a night's campsite and be ready to sleep when divination advised that the whites would surely find them if they stayed. So they'd trek onwards. Until, finally, they got to that hill [Kumakô], where they found "a couple of days" of rest (Mètisên 31 July 1978)   ✛

(SvS 132, 14 December 1730); I show the locations of these plantations on the facing page (except for one case, which I could not find). Note that only two of the maroons—Joosie and Christina—came from the same plantation, and that at least seven of the twelve maroons had been owned by Portuguese Jews. In December 1730, eleven of these twelve captives from Kaási's villages were "brought to justice . . . in the hope that it would provide an Example and deterrent to their associates, and reduce the propensity of slaves to escape" (Hartsinck 1770:763). Their sentence, administered by the Court of Policy and Criminal Justice in Paramaribo, read as follows:

> The Negro Joosie shall be hanged from the gibbet by an Iron Hook through his ribs, until dead; his head shall then be severed and displayed on a stake by the riverbank, remaining to be picked over by birds of prey. As for the Negroes Wierrie and Manbote, they shall be bound to a stake and roasted alive over a slow fire, while being tortured with glowing Tongs. The Negro girls, Lucretia, Ambira, Aga, Gomba, Marie and Victoria will be tied to a Cross, to be broken alive, and then their heads severed, to be exposed by the riverbank on stakes. The Negro girls Diana and Christina shall be beheaded with an axe, and their heads exposed on poles by the riverbank. (SvS 132, 14 December 1730; Hartsinck 1770:764–65)

The abandoning of Kaási's villages on the Kleine Saramacca River occurred in the wake of the terrible battles of 1730–31.* A rare edition of Lavaux's famous map of Suriname—drawn by a man who was actually present at some of these great battles—depicts the wounded Kaási himself, being borne from the battlefield southwards, in a hammock, toward his new home (see illustration). By 1732, after decades of wanderings and battles, Kaási and his followers seem finally to have settled comfortably, in the hilltop village of Kumakô, between the Saramacca and Suriname Rivers. There they finally found, as they put it, "a few days of rest." But within a couple of years, the always-restless Kaási pushed southward again, seeking greater security for his people, just as other clans began flocking to Kumakô.   ✛

---

* Hartsinck (1770: 760–66) describes these expeditions, which numbered at least seven, drawing on documents now in sealed volumes. Among the more useful archival fragments that are still available are SvS 132, 4 August 1730, 25 October 1730, 14 December 1730, 30 January 1731, 21 April 1731, 16 September 1731; SvS 259, 24 January 1732; GA 1, 29 March 1731, 22 April 1731, 16 May 1731, 27 September 1731, passim. See now, for a summary, also de Groot 1982.

"A Negro hung alive by the Ribs to a Gallows." Engraving by William Blake after a drawing by John Gabriel Stedman, based on a 1773 eyewitness description, confirmed by a second eyewitness: "Not long ago . . . I saw a black man hang'd alive by the ribs, between which with a knife was first made an insision, and then clinch'd an Iron hook with a Chain—in this manner he kept living three days hanging with his head and feet downwards and catching with his tongue the drops of water (it being in the rainy season) that were flowing down his bloated breast while the vultures were picking in the putred wound" (Stedman 1988:103–5). This engraving, then—though illustrating the kind of execution meted out to the captured Saramaka Joosie in 1730—in fact depicts a much later execution (*pace* de Groot 1982:30).

THE EVENTS

"The Execution of Breaking on the Rack." Engraving by William Blake after a drawing by John Gabriel Stedman, who himself witnessed the depicted scene in 1776 (1988:546–50).

G

Lavaux's eyewitness depiction of the 1730–1731 destruction of Kaási's villages. This detail includes the final battle, showing at *G* "the Flight of Claas and most of his Negroes," and at *K* "Claas fleeing," apparently wounded, in a hammock. The map also clearly depicts wooden palisades ringing the villages; white soldiers marching in parade position, while their slaves struggle with enormous vats of gunpowder and attack dogs leap at fleeing Maroons; the use of bows-and-arrows and spears by Maroon defenders, some of whom are being fired upon by black colonial troops; and the destruction of Maroon gardens and the flight of Maroon women carrying various goods in their arms (see also de Groot 1982). (Alexander de Lavaux, *Generale Caart van de Provintie Suriname,* 1737, Universiteitsbibliotheek Amsterdam.)

MATAWÁIS: FROM PLANTATIONS TO THE TUKUMÚTU CREEK, 1700–1740s

Version 1

headings ←

59. <u>And the Matawáis escaped into the forest.</u> Sometimes they returned to the plantation at night to get machetes, axes, and other things to take away. In the forest they made gardens, burning the fields and planting <u>rice from seeds</u> that they had carried in their hair. After a few months, once the crop was harvested, they'd trek farther and make new gardens. They kept on going. There were older people with them who knew all kinds of *óbia*. For example, there was one that prevented defeat, and another that let them go for long periods without food. Three brothers led them in the forest—Bekú-Musínga, Okó, and Akwali. When they got near Djibi Creek, they crossed the [Saramacca] river to the east. They went up the creek and made a large village near its headwaters. When they left there [moving south], they next met the Saramacca River at Yawe Creek. They made several villages there, where there are still almond trees standing today, and where people still find all kinds of old things.

One group of people went further up Yawe Creek and, by walking along a small connecting creek, reached Muyánwóyo Creek. They followed it to the Suriname River where they remained. The others came down Yawe Creek and followed the Saramacca River to its head, where it looks like a small creek, at the foot of the mountain [Tafelberg]. There, on the mountain, they made the village of Hánsesipó. They stayed there for some time and finally decided to follow the creek on the other side of the mountain, which led to the Tukumútu Creek. They made various villages there, but Tuído was the largest. Farther up the Tukumútu there was Tupinêngè village . . . and a bit downstream, Tukumútukapéè. (Leo Emanuel to Chris de Beet and Miriam Sterman, 1976)

MATAWÁIS: FROM PLANTATIONS TO THE TUKUMÚTU CREEK, 1700–1740s

Versions 1 and 2 (59–60)

The Matawáis, now one of the six independent maroon "tribes" of Suriname, live along the Saramacca River. They did not formally separate from the Saramakas until the mid-1760s, after serious intergroup violence (see Price n.d.). Events of the subsequent years have pushed the groups still further apart, especially the mass conversion of the Matawáis to Christianity one hundred years ago. Matawáis provide a fascinating perspective on the years of their shared history with Saramakas. Though I have not had the opportunity to work with them at first hand, I am privileged to have access to accounts gathered from them during recent years by other scholars (especially through the kindness of Chris de Beet and Miriam Sterman, who have generously allowed me to translate and use their materials here).

The plantation origin of Matawáis is peculiarly obscured in all accounts known to me. Plantations Hamburg and Uitkijk are consistently mentioned by Matawáis, but the indicated locations on the lower Saramacca River do not seem to have been used as plantations during the relevant period. In contrast, Matawái migration routes seem relatively clear: south along the west bank of the Saramacca River to Djibi Creek on the east, where they crossed over and established a village by the early 1730s; on to Yawe Creek where they lived for a time; then, splitting from the

Version 2

60. The Matawáis could no longer take slave life, so they escaped from the plantations, from Uitkijk and the one right across the [Saramacca] river from it, Hamborgubuka or Sukugoon. They fled in two groups, one under the leadership of Tatá Akwali and Mamá Tjówa, which fled along the west bank of the river, the other under the leadership of Apétipeébi and Ba Ando, which fled along the other bank. At first when they fled, they didn't know the location of the others. But they had brought with them from the plantation an *óbia* called "Loángo kómiki" that protected against weapons. This *óbia*, which they carried on their heads, would, for example, warn them when whites were approaching and render them invisible. They could watch the whites pass by without being seen. It was this *óbia* that told them that their "brothers" were on the other side of the river.

With Apétipeébi's group there were also Saramakas. When Tatá Akwali was bitten by a snake and couldn't go on, they made a camp, burned some fields, and planted rice and maize, which Mamá Tjówa had bound into her hair before escaping. That's why women, right up to the present, must not cut their hair.

After the harvest, they trekked much farther [south] until they again met the [Saramacca] river at the mouth of Djibi Creek. There the two groups came together. They had been able to communicate with each other previously with the help of *óbias*. They crossed the river to Apétipeébi's side [the east] and had a big meeting. Because they felt the whites would soon be after them, they decided to move further upstream. The Saramakas were still with them.

When they got to Yawe Creek, the Saramakas continued up it, toward the Suriname River. They left many things behind there—jugs, guns—which we still find when we go there to cut timber. The others went further [west] to Tafelberg, where they sought refuge on the heights. (Paulus Andoma to Miriam Sterman, 1973) ✛

Saramaka contingent (which went down Muyánwóyo Creek), southwest along the Saramacca River in the late 1730s, all the way to the great mountain of Tafelberg where they established the village of Hánsesipó; and finally, by about 1740, back down into the interior of Tukumútu Creek, where they lived in the very large village of Tuído, which they remember as being so large that it had six separate landing places.*

I can say little about the individuals mentioned in these Matawái traditions, as only three of them are known to me from Saramaka accounts—the important mid-eighteenth-century chiefs Musínga and Bekú (whom many modern Matawáis seem to merge into a single identity, but whom archives confirm to be separate people) and the Nasí leader Kwakú Étja. Curiously, Matawáis seem to recall Kwakú Étja casually, using a name that is considered highly dangerous in Saramaka—Apétipeébi, his horn name, used in the wars (see 92).

According to Saramaka traditions (as well as my readings of the many documents concerning Saramaka-Matawái interaction in the 1760s and 1770s), the Saramaka group closest to the Matawáis were those Lángus under Kaási. This meshes well with the Matawái tradition (in 60) about the Loángo *óbia* that accompanied their march. Indeed, it is possible that the man Matawáis refer to as Ando was in fact Alándo, Kaási's famous son, who played an important role in later-eighteenth-century Saramaka history. According to Saramakas, Étja also traveled with the Matawáis from time to time, but only because his sister was married to a Matawái man (see 92). ✛

* Toledo was the name of a Suriname River plantation, which was used several times in the naming of Saramaka villages as well. My tentative dating of these Matawái migrations is based on the corresponding activities of non-Matawái Saramakas, whom their general travels paralleled.

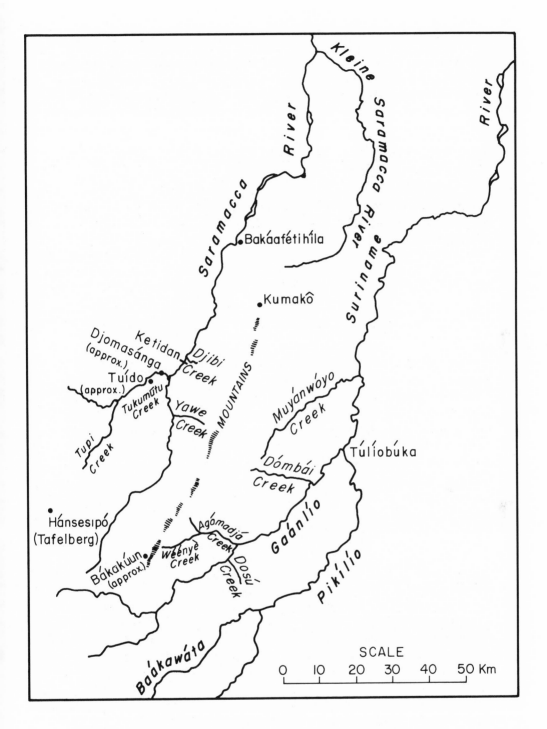

Matawái and Lángu Migrations: places mentioned in *59–79*

LÁNGU: FROM THE KLEINE SARAMACCA RIVER TO BÁKAKÚUN, 1732–1749

With the Matawáis at Tukumútu Creek

61.

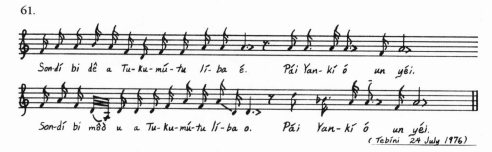

Translation: Something happened at the Upper Tukumútu/Son-in-law Yánki, do you hear?/Things were too much for us at the Upper Tukumútu/Son-in-Law Yánki, do you hear?

LÁNGU: FROM THE KLEINE SARAMACCA RIVER TO BÁKAKÚUN, 1732–1749

With the Matawáis at Tukumútu Creek (61–65)

In the wake of the bloody battles of 1730–31 on the Kleine Saramacca, Kaási led his group south, first living briefly at Kumakô, then traveling south along the Saramacca River where he lived with the future Matawáis at Djibi and Yawe Creeks. Saramaka traditions are clear that for some time during the 1740s, Kaási and his people lived in the great village of Tuído, inside the Tukumútu Creek; Matawái and Saramaka accounts seem to agree that his group was never at Tafelberg.

Saramaka memories of Tuído are preserved in several beautiful *apúku* (forest spirit) songs, one of which is reproduced as *61*. Fragment *63* formulaicly mentions names that no longer have identities attached to them for this Saramaka teller; what they do preserve for him is that Tuído's size and importance were not something to be taken lightly.

Matawáis preserve more specific fighting traditions from their time in Tuído. Fragments *64* and *65* point to three battles and two abortive attempts by the whites to make peace—none, judging by the location of the sites, predating the 1740s. The frustratingly poor state of the relevant archival pages permits only tantalizing glimpses of these events from a colonial perspective. For example, in 1743, the expeditionary force that sacked the village of Kumakô (*107–20*) also reported finding a village called "Seremeca," which was probably the village at Djibi Creek; the follow-up expeditions that criss-crossed the area during the next year may well have fought at that site or at nearby Keti Rapids, as Matawáis report today—we simply cannot be sure. We do, however, know rather more from the archives about the battle at Tuído itself, the shed at Djomasánga, and the ambush (and the goods left behind) along the river near Bakáafétihíla.*

---

* The central document—the official report of Captain Brouwer's 1747 expedition to "Loangodorp" [Tuído]—is in a sealed volume and is unavailable for consultation. The two best alternative sources are an account written in French in 1753 by a man who had before him as he wrote another account of the expedition

62. Tuído was the largest of all villages. All kinds of clans were there. (Tebíni 24 July 1976)

63. Gabídesé was over on that side. Tjatjáátja was over there. Ahúnmasámba was there. So we recount their names. (Agbagó 8 July 1978)

64. While they [the Matawáis] were living in Tuído, they regularly scouted the whites downriver. There were battles at two places—near Tuído and near Ketidan. At Ketidan they had hidden in the forest [at the riverbank], and they knew how to shoot the man steering the boat so that it sank. An *óbia* called *akuti* warned them whenever the whites were coming. . . .

On various occasions, whites were sent out to them to try to make peace. For example, there was Djo, who made a large camp where he unloaded all sorts of goods—pots, guns, almost anything that people needed. He let them know that the governor had sent him to make peace, that the fighting should end, and that they would be free. The elders told the others that no one should touch anything [of the goods]. They did not want peace. So, the whites went back, leaving those things behind, where they just lay there until not much

---

The story, as pieced together from the archives, begins with a foiled Saramaka raid on the Coutier plantation (apparently in the Para ` region, possibly plantation Vier Kinderen, see 179C–182C). In April 1747, some one hundred Saramaka raiders were repelled, with losses, when a "faithful" slave named Iakje warned Coutier, who was able to lock up many of his own slaves and fight off the maroons. (Four months later, Iakje was rewarded by the Council in Paramaribo with a silver bracelet inscribed with the word "getrouwheid" ["fidelity"].) Several weeks after this raid, a white bounty hunter who was combing the area with his slaves captured a wounded Saramaka who had been left behind near a large swamp when the raiders retreated. The governor rewarded this white man with a special prize of 100 guilders, as the captured Saramaka—called variously in the documents "Akako," "Ajappoe," "Accapo," "Accape," and "Acabo," but known to Saramakas as their great Matjáu ancestor Adjágbò—agreed, upon "interrogation," to lead an expedition up the Saramacca River to the previously unlocated "Loangodorp" (Tuído). Captain Evarardus Brouwer commanded this 1747 expedition, which included nearly 250 men, traveling in three large and twenty-two smaller canoes. The day before the troops reached Tuído, they are reported to have established a large "magazijn" (storehouse for matériel)—the "Djomasánga" described in *64* and *65*. Their attack on Tuído resulted only in the capture of one Saramaka, as everyone else had escaped just moments before the arrival of the troops (who found pots filled with food cooking on fires in houses throughout the village). After several quiet days in the area, exploring the very fine and extensive Saramaka gardens that surrounded the village, Brouwer decided to make a peace overture. (For complex political reasons, Brouwer tried to keep this initiative secret from all but two members of his massive expedition.) Toward this end, he clandestinely released Adjágbò—who had apparently been bound and restrained during the whole journey—giving him a new suit of clothes and a "cachet"-ed letter for the Saramaka tribal chief (Ayakô), who lived in a different village over the mountains to the southeast. (Adjágbò had told Brouwer that there were three mulattoes who could read and write in the so-called "Criole-dorp"—probably at that time the group of villages located at the headwaters of Agámadjá Creek.) When Adjágbò—"in

by a participant, and several official testimonies by participants in the expedition, relating to the conduct in office of Governor Mauricius. I draw directly on nearly two dozen archival fragments in reconstructing the story of Brouwer's expedition. Among the more important of these sources are SvS 139, 15 February 1747, 24 May 1747, 24 August 1747; GA 553, 26 April 1747, 2 May 1747, 19 December 1747; SvS 201, 11 December 1749; SvS 285, 11 December 1749; SvS 292, 9 July 1753; SvS 155, 3 October 1763; Anon. 1752, 2:556–60.

was left. That was at [the place now called] Djomasánga ["Djo's shed"]. (Leo Emanuel to Chris de Beet and Miriam Sterman, 1976)

65. [When they lived at Tuído] the whites came after them to fight many times. The Maroons would be warned of the whites' arrival by their *óbias*, and they had developed a special strategy. They would hide near a rapids and wait till the boats arrived. The white man would usually be sitting on a stool in the middle of the boat, and the Indian who served as guide normally sat up front. As the boat began ascending the rapids, they would first shoot the steersman at the stern so that the boat would go out of control. They [the whites] always had a parrot with them who would fly back to the coast and report how many people had been killed and at what place. There were battles like this in three places—near the mouth of Djibi Creek, then at Ketidan, and finally just below Tuído.

The whites still wanted to make peace with them, and they made various attempts. The first time, they made a camp near [what is now called] Bakáafétihíla . . . where they

---

spite of the promises he had made to be faithful to the whites" and to return with an answer in three days—failed to come back on schedule, Brouwer realized that he had been betrayed, and he and his troops departed downstream in great haste (apparently leaving behind considerable matériel at the storehouse at Djomasánga, just as Matawáis remember). Two days later, the fleeing expedition was caught by the Saramakas in a massive ambush, receiving vicious cross-fire from the two sides of the river, and were thoroughly defeated. (The probable location of this battle, as I reconstruct it from the documents, is Bakáafétihíla.) Destroying their own remaining canoes, abandoning supplies, and throwing their heavy metal tools into the river, the troops were forced to continue their flight on foot.* The expeditionary force finally arrived on the coast, a beaten and badly depleted group—an unusually large number of slaves had deserted from the expedition, and the troops had suffered many casualties, including a serious gunshot wound to Brouwer's own son—where Brouwer was subjected to particularly harsh criticism for this military disaster.†

It is not surprising that Saramakas (at least to my knowledge) do not preserve memories of Adjágbò's capture, his involuntary service as a guide, or the letter he delivered, though they remember a good deal else about the man (see *143–46*); for in these incidents Adjágbò was uncharacteristically the victim—at least in part. What is remembered most vividly by the Matawái descendants of the mid-eighteenth-century principals seem to be the piles of "whitefolks' goods" abandoned at Djomasánga as well as at Bakáafétihíla (see *65*), and their great riverside battle victories. And the archives, though not permitting me to flesh out the oral fragments as fully as in some other cases, contain enough supplementary data to confirm that what Matawáis do remember were, indeed, among their finest wartime moments.   ✛

---

* There is evidence that the Saramakas recovered some of the sunken goods. Two years later, during an expedition up the same river, one of the whites recognized a particularly fine Saramaka musket that had been lost overboard by Ensign Labadie during this ambush.

† This botched expedition, like that of Picolet in 1750 (see *158–61*), continued to preoccupy the whites for years as they squabbled among themselves to assign blame for its failure. In 1749, during Creutz's "peacemaking" expedition to Saramaka (see *147–51*), the whites specifically asked the Saramaka chief about Adjágbò's letter, which he said they had indeed received "with four seals upon it"; during this same expedition, Adjágbò himself was also interviewed by Creutz and claimed that his reason for not having returned on time to Brouwer was that the men who could read happened to be absent from the village when he arrived with the letter; and many years later, after the final Peace of 1762, the new governor of Suriname was still expressing eagerness to discuss with Adjágbò, now visiting Paramaribo as a free man, exactly what had happened in 1747!

unloaded all their goods. They called the Matawái to meet them there to make peace, but the Matawái were frightened that it was a trick—just as they had been tricked in Africa—and they didn't come. They stayed at Tuído. The whites left the goods there and returned to the coast.

The next time, they went farther, to the Tukumútu, to the place now called Djo-masánga. The man who wanted to make peace was Masra [Master] Djon. He made a large camp on an island and built a big shed where the whole cargo was placed. But again, the people of Tuído didn't come to him and left everything lying there. (Paulus Andoma to Miriam Sterman, 1973) ✛

Kaási's Redoubt at Bákakúun

66. All streamheads meet at Bákakúun. (Faánsisónu 24 July 1976)

67. If you follow Wéényè Creek all the way to its head, you'll arrive at the mountain. You see it looming up, almost touching the sky, pitch black. They lived on the other side, facing Matawái. An arm of the Saramacca River called Nyawí Creek comes right to its base. (Agbagó 8 July 1978)

68. Wéényè Creek is the arm of Agamadjá Creek that goes to Bákakúun. Wéényèntèn was a woman who was buried there. Today, when we say "I'm going as far as Wéényè," it just means "I'm going very far." From the Gaánlío, the peaks of Wéényè appear to be clouds, they are so distant. (Tebíni 24 July 1976)

69. Bákakúun has three levels. Kaási built his village on the first one, facing toward the west. (Mètisên 2 July 1976)

70. There wasn't just one village at Bákakúun. Kaási had his, others had theirs. (Agbagó 8 July 1978)

71. Kaási lived long enough to set eyes on the [Upper] Suriname River. He came over to explore the Gaánlío, but then he went back to Bákakúun Wéényè. That's where he lived and where he died. (Tebíni 24 July 1976) ✛

Kaási's Redoubt at Bákakúun (66–71)

Kaási's final village was at Bákakúun ("Behind the Hills"), far to the south of Tuído. This village—or as one Saramaka fragment recounts, and as documentary sources confirm, this cluster of villages—was home for the Lángus, Dómbis, Awanás, and probably the Nasís and Biítus, during the 1740s. Saramaka accounts (and the proverbial expression, "I'm going to Wéényè") consistently stress its enormous distance from the territory today considered familiar; archival accounts combined with oral fragments permit me to locate it, within a margin of a few kilometers, just behind the distant mountains that appear as clouds on the horizon from the Gaánlío territory the Lángus today call home. (No site in Saramaka oral traditions was more difficult for me to locate exactly; more precise information awaits either the discovery of new expeditionary maps or surface archaeology conducted in the region itself.) The name of the creek that reached to Bákakúun Wéényè was apparently carried forward after the abandonment of the site: in 1762, Ayakô's son Dabí called the name of the Saramaka capital for the whites, who wrote it as "Woendjee" or "Wannie." ✛

The Dispute Between Abámpapá and Ayakô

72.

A fí a na kwonú
Kwanákwa
Kwanákwa adjú
Kwanákwa*
—(Tebíni 28 July 1976)

73. [While the Lángu people lived at Bákakúun] Ayakô took Abámpapá's wife. When he found out, he decided to go fight him. He was going to kill him. One of them would surely die. In those days, people walked on footpaths. Abámpapá got ready. He prepared himself [ritually] for two whole days, smoking his [specially prepared] pipe while he readied himself, and saying out loud, "Ayakô, you and I are going to meet. You won't be left in peace." Alúbutu [Abámpapá's grandson, whom he had raised from childhood] said, "Don't go. Leave him be." But Abámpapá answered, "I can't be dissuaded." They had more words together, but Alúbutu saw that he was continuing with his preparations for the fight. The day arrived and Abámpapá set off. Alúbutu warned him in every possible way he knew. Abámpapá took the footpath. He was finally prepared. Alúbutu pleaded with him: "Grandfather, I have warned you until I don't know what more to do." But Abámpapá was gone.

Alúbutu entered the forest. He didn't take the path, where he would be seen following. He ran through the forest, the way a young man can, and he cut off Abámpapá at a bend in the path, blocking his way. He said, "Grandfather, don't go." Abámpapá asked, "And who is this?" He said, "Grandfather, it's me. I've come to speak with you. Don't go. Don't go

* I have heard this rendered also as *a fí a na kwonú/kwanákwa adjú/kwá kwá kwanákwa/kwanákwa adjú/kwanákwa.* This is a *nòngô*, a semantically compressed proverb, the meaning of which is not derivable (at least in the twentieth century) from the words themselves. Its meaning would be expressed in everyday Saramaccan as *disá ná a táki sábi sô* ("not doing something can avoid 'I told you so'"), not committing a rash act insures that you will not later say, "If only I had known. . . . "

The Dispute Between Abámpapá and Ayakô (72–73)

Matjáus remember Abámpapá (also known as Folú) as a special friend of Ayakô and one of the earliest men to take to the forest. Alúbutu—whom Matjáus depict as Abámpapá's grandson, but his own descendants as his sister's son—was an enormously well-liked man, described in various historical fragments as a friend of the Lángu leader Wíi, the Awaná leader Alábi, and many others. Brought up by Abámpapá, Alúbutu took on the older man's name (Folú) after his death and served as an important captain in the post-treaty period. The adultery incident, which ruptured the long friendship, must have occurred when the two principals were in their late sixties—old but still active—dating it to about 1740.

Today, Folú's descendants, usually known as the Kwamá clan, live just south of the Abaísas in the village of Túmaipá (or Maipá). During their early years they traveled with Kaási's group, but they are remembered as the first to establish a village inside Agámadjá Creek (ca. 1740), where Kaási's people joined them after the battle of Bákakúun. Matjáus are still able to point out the footpath that led from Agámadjá Creek, whence Folú set out, to Baákawáta, where Ayakô held sway.

Behind such incidental themes as abused friendship and the tenderness between Alúbutu and Abámpapá, this Matjáu version preserves a specific memory of a partial transfer of political

fight with Ayakô." Abámpapá replied, "You and I will soon have something to fight about!" Alúbutu said, "Fine, grandfather. Let *us* fight then, but leave Ayakô." The old man turned suddenly and sat down. He struck a flint and lit his pipe. Alúbutu said, "I've come to speak with you." He answered, "I don't have time. I'm on my way to Ayakô." Alúbutu said, "But I have something to talk to you about." He answered, "Talk fast, then. I am in a hurry," and he lit his pipe. Alúbutu said, "Don't go to Ayakô and fight." "That's what you came to tell me?" "Yes." He got up and strode off.

Alúbutu entered the forest and cut him off again. "Who is this blocking my way? Where do you think you're going?" "There's still one thing I want to talk to you about. Because, the way you're going, maybe you'll win the fight, maybe the fight will win you. Perhaps you'll come back alive, perhaps you won't. Well, I want to talk with you. I still have something I want you to hear." The older man sat down and lit up his pipe. "What do you want to say?" He replied, "Don't go to fight Ayakô." "That's all you wanted to say?" "Yes, don't go. Leave it alone." The man got up and continued on his way.

Alúbutu entered the forest and cut him off for the third time. The man said, "Who is this? You and I will have something to fight about! I will forget Ayakô and attack you, because *we* have a grudge now." Alúbutu said [mournfully], "Yes, grandfather. But there is still something I wish to say to you. Because, the way you're going, maybe you'll return, maybe you won't return." "Well, sit down." And they did. Alúbutu said, "Don't go to fight Ayakô." He said, "*A fí a na kwonú/Kwanákwa/Kwanákwa adjú/Kwanákwa.*" The man spun around and said, "Child, is that the way it really is? Then I give in."

Alúbutu went and told Ayakô what had happened. He said, "My grandfather was coming to kill you. He got up to a certain place on the trail and I finally turned him back." He described the whole thing. Finally, Ayakô spoke. "Child, the thing you've done here . . . I don't know what to say to you. Because I would not have been able to handle Abámpapá. Well, don't you see, you've saved my life." Then Ayakô took his stool and gave it to Alúbutu. (Peléki 22 July 1976) ✤

---

authority. Before the Peace with the whites, Ayakô was considered to be the preeminent Saramaka chief. In the closing lines of this story, he gives his stool, symbol of office, to Alúbutu, in return for saving his life. This is why, Matjáus claim, Alúbutu is often referred to today as *"mátu"* ['forest,' as opposed to government-appointed] tribal chief." And indeed, Alúbutu—at that time called "Adoe" by the whites—seems to have been the chief Saramaka negotiator with the whites in 1749 (see 147C–151C below). By means of this story, Matjáus stress that Alúbutu had no other (that is, dynastic) claims to the office, and therefore no rights to pass on later; he was chief, or deputy, purely by the grace of Ayakô. The only other mention I know of Alúbutu's "enstoolment" occurs in fragments relating to the aftermath of the death of Tribal Chief Abíni in 1767. According to these narratives, three lines of pressure were brought to bear upon Abíni's reluctant son Alábi to persuade him to accept the office in lieu of seeking revenge against his father's killers, the Matawáis: one coming from the Matjáus, one from the Nasís, and one from the "Kwamás," who offered Alúbutu's stool (see Price n.d.). ✤

Purifying the River

74. Kaási came upstream after Ayakô. They met in the forest, near the mouth of Dómbái Creek. Ayakô said, "You've come?" He answered, "Yes." Kaási asked, "Is this the river?" "Yes." "Well, how is the water?" Ayakô said, "It's all right except for one thing. It couldn't be clearer to drink, but one can't wash in it. There are these little things in it that attach to your skin if you wash in it. They make you sick; they'll kill one without fail. But otherwise, it's all right." ([To me:] Some say it was a kind of fish, some say snakes, some say it was a thing that swallowed people. But Captain Apeéli did not tell me those! He said "worms" [*bítju*], that's what was in the water. As soon as you went into the river, they covered your body, stuck on fast, killed you.) Ayakô said, "Well, if you know anything to do, you'd better do it." And Kaási, who already had his *sóói-gádu*, took it and threw it in the water, killing all the worms. ([To me:] He did not throw in the god itself. It was something the god knew how to make. Because the Lángu people still do that sometimes, I've seen it with my own eyes. They say "we are drugging fish" [*fón ndekú*]. But it's not really *ndekú* [the vines used for fish drugging]. But it's other vines and things they know how to make to "prepare" the river.) Well, the worms were all dead! That is what Lángu did to the river. That's what Captain Apeéli taught me. (Peléki 22 July 1976)

75. Long before, Kaási had accompanied Ayakô in battle, and when they returned, they remained friends forever. That's why he fixed up the river for Ayakô. They hadn't been able to drink the water. A woman was pregnant, and she drank the river water. Well, her pregnancy "dried up." At that time, if you dove into the water, you were as good as dead. You wouldn't come back up! Friend, that [Kaási] was a man! (Djógilési to Otjútju 1977 or 1978)

Purifying the River (74–79)

I have heard various fragments about meetings between Kaási and Ayakô, near the head of Dómbái Creek (at whose mouth Kaási's descendants live today at Béndiwáta on the Gaánlío) or at Túlíobúka (the confluence of the Pikílío and Gaánlío). Some are clearly about priority in the area, with Matjáus for example depicting Ayakô as telling a surprised Kaási that there is a great river at the mouth of the creek. Others describe Ayakô capturing a fleeing Indian woman at Túlíobúka and giving her as a gift to Kaási. Still others show Kaási coming down to Ayakô's camp at Túlíobúka to fight at his side against the whites. But by far the most famous story from Kaási's period of residence at Bákakúun involves the purification of the river.

I present here six fragments. The first (74) is a rather rich Matjáu fragment, referring for authority to the teller's "mother's brother," Dángogó Captain Apeéli (Gidé), who died a generation ago. Fragment 75 is taken from a tape recording made (possibly surreptitiously) by Otjútju, being instructed by the man said to be the oldest living descendant of Kaási. Fragment 76 is a clarifying statement from Tebíni, who has spent much time with Lángu ritual specialists. It insists that the formulaic "Kaási fixed up the river," often heard in ritual discourse, is a rhetorical device, with "Kaási" simply standing for the Lángu clan. (However, there remains the alternative possibility that "Alándo" is today used by some Lángu people as a less "dangerous" substitute for the name of his father [as happens for example with other younger-older pairs such as Ayakô and Lánu].) Fragment 77—probably the most interesting of this set—comes from a tape recording of a senior Matjáu captain instructing his potential successor at cock's crow; Abátelí, the younger man, kindly

76. Kaási's oldest son was Alándo. It was he, not Kaási, who came down and purified the river. (Tebíni 28 July 1976)

77. Now the way things are changing, the way you younger fellows think you're learning things, never let anyone tell you that some other clan has rights on the Upper River. Lángu, they do have claims on the Gaánlío, but not because they arrived at the same time as us [Matjáus]. The thing that was here. When they arrived they had a solution for it. And since they did, well, we gave them their little place to move around in for themselves. . . . Because they *helped* us. . . . Others can talk all the nonsense they like, but they [Lángus] did not walk with [at the same time as] us. It's because they helped that they have their lands. (Kála, instructing Abáteli at cock's crow, 1975)

78. The names of the three people who first went to the Suriname River were Pámbo, Sámbo, and Alábi. They carried with them a bottle filled with Saramacca River water which they mixed into the Suriname River to make it fit to drink. (Captain of Haarlem to Chris de Beet, 1976)

79. Two of Tjowa's sons were Sambo and Pambo. While Sambo stayed in Tukumutu . . . Pambo explored the eastern branch of the Upper Saramacca, Tupi Creek, and Njanwe Creek. One day he discovered the Suriname River. He found a fish there, called *supali* [stingray], that was not in the Saramacca River. He brought the fish back to the Saramacca River and put it in the water, in the presence of Sambo. The fish died immediately and Pambo took this as a sign that he should take his people and go settle on the Suriname River.* (Matawái traditions collected by Green, who presented them in "composite summary form . . . (a) homogenization of . . . several versions" [1974:39])   ✤

* In fact, the stingray (Saramaccan *sipái*) lives in the Suriname River and Pikílío, but not in the Gaánlío or the Saramacca River.

---

permitted me to transcribe it here. Note Captain Kála's deliberate vagueness about the central event—"The thing that was here . . . they [Lángus] had a solution for it." Nevertheless, Kála effectively communicates to Abáteli the central meaning of the event for Matjáus.

From a Matjáu perspective, this story of the river purification serves as a twofold charter. First, it permits them to stress their temporal priority in the area (essential in questions of land tenure). And second, it lies at the core of the Matjáu ritual dependence upon Kaási's descendants in the village of Béndiwáta, the people who control Kaási's "Loángo *óbia*," or "*gádu*," known as Ávogádu, the most powerful of all *sóói-gádu* in Saramaka. Matjáus are quite explicit that this god's having made the river usable placed them in a permanent position of clientage toward Kaási's people. And to this day, whenever the Matjáu tribal chief consults Ávogádu at Béndiwáta, the story is invoked to underline the special relationship.

Fragments 78 and 79 come from Matawáis. They provide a dim and distant trace, seen from a Matawái perspective, of the departure of part of their group for the Suriname River, where they became "Saramakas." These fragments also associate the departing group that fixed up the river with Pámbo, the Lángu leader Saramakas know as Bákisipámbo, who always traveled with Kaási (see 54).   ✤

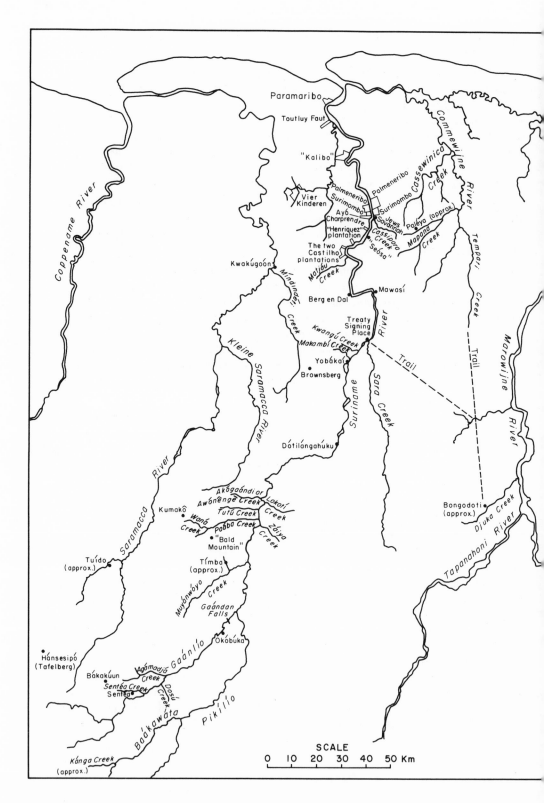

Places Mentioned in *80–202*

THE EVENTS

NASÍS, 1690s–1743

The Family

80. There were the great warriors Kwakú Kwádjaní and his older brother Kwakú Étja. They had one mother and one father, Bíatiísi and Yebá. . . . Bíatiísi had another son, Kofíkióo, and three daughters, Ambeezú, Mimí, and Babái. (Bakáa 28 July 1978)

NASÍS, 1690s–1743

The Nasís, another of the original great clans, today inhabit the Middle River portion of the Suriname River, around Muyánwóyo Creek. Their own traditions, as well as those of other clans, characterize their first ancestors as the premier warriors of the Saramaka. From the 1720s to the 1750s, they seem to have been the most aggressive raiders of plantations and to have been in the forefront of the action whenever military expeditions entered Saramaka territory.

Nasís and Matjáus have been sworn enemies since 1835, when the whites deposed the Nasí tribal chief in favor of a Matjáu. For some time, because of my Matjáu connections, my own knowledge of the Nasís' early years depended on stories I heard from others, whether their allies such as Awanás and Dómbis, or their rivals such as Matjáus. In 1978, however, I was able to persuade a group of Nasí elders, in an emotionally tense setting, to discuss their early years with me; some of these materials are included here.

This set of traditions about the Nasís moves them through space and time from their plantations near Jews Savannah (where they were slaves of the Nassys, the colony's most prominent Jewish family, in the 1690s) to Kaási's village near the Míndindéti Creek (which was abandoned ca. 1712), and on up the Suriname River, past the village of Yobákaí (Yebákaí, where Yebá "met" the river, walking upstream) all the way to Kumakô, where they had become the dominant clan by the mid-1730s.

The Family (80)

As in the early genealogies of other clans, Nasís tend to preserve the memory of men because of their deeds, and women because of their progeny. Yebá, who was a peer of Kaási, was killed in the battle of Kumakô in 1743 (107–20); Étja and his younger brother Kwádjaní served, respectively, as tribal chief and captain during the 1770s; Kofíkióo was also active in mid-eighteenth-century politics; and Bíatiísi's three daughters "mothered" the main descent groups of the modern Nasí clan. The current Saramaka tendency to conceptualize all of their eighteenth-century heroes as original escaped slaves, even when they were actually born later (see 54C), receives confirmation in a chance utterance written down in 1773, from the mouth of Étja. He is reported to have asked a white official, in anger, how he could claim to know whether the Abaísa leader Samsám was or was not lying: "I was born in the forest and you think you know Samsám better than I!" (SvS 165, 17 May 1773 [15 April 1773].) The general Saramaka tendency to conceptualize early maroons as family groups is matched, then, by this tendency to transform conceptually the creole forest-born leaders of the mid- and late eighteenth century into late-seventeenth-century runaways.

The Escape

81. The Nasís were famous fighters. They killed the whites near Seósa, at the creek we call "Red Creek" because of all their blood. That's why Nasí people have a taboo on going to that place, until today. Kwádjaní and his brother Étja. That is where they fought it out with the whites, alongside their father, Yebá. (Améiká 21 July 1978)

82. Bíatiísi had a younger sister who worked at the master's house at Jews Savannah. When the Nasí slaves had made an escape plan, Bíatiísi told a male slave named Záiya to go tell her sister to come to her. But she told him when he went that he should be careful not to say "kiníngosu." Instead, he should talk *akoopína* ["play-" or "disguised language"], because if he said "kiníngosu" the white man would pick it up and forbid her sister to go out. Záiya went to the sister, but what do you think he said? "Kiníngosu!" He forgot to talk *akoopína*. The white man caught on and didn't let her come. Then Záiya returned to Bíatiísi to say the white man wouldn't let her sister come. She understood that he hadn't followed her instructions and told him that he would have to stay with her ever after, until the death. Bíatiísi with her husband Yebá with this man, until the death. Years later, in the forest they were desperately searching for water, and Záiya finally found the river. At the place now called Záiya Creek. (Bakáa 28 July 1978)

83. While living at Míndindéti Creek, Kaási returned to the plantation to liberate his friend Yebá, and his family. They lived together thereafter. ("Anonymous," by choice, 1976) ✜

The Escape (81–83)

The powerful Nassy family owned several plantations in the area of Jews Savannah, but Nasí oral traditions combine with information on a 1687 map to suggest that Bíatiísi's plantation lay on the Cassipora Creek, just north of Suhoza ("Seósa"), where they fought the battle described in *81*. The Nasí prohibition on visiting the site of their ancestors' bloodly battle with the whites (apparently fought in the immediate aftermath of their escape) vividly preserves its memory, as does the name of the creek itself.

During the 1690s, the prosperous community at Jews Savannah was already flourishing, with a population of nearly six hundred whites, and more than nine thousand black slaves who worked some forty sugar plantations (Nassy 1788:48–49). What is said to have been the first synagogue in the Americas, built of wood, was consecrated in 1671 next to the Cassipora Creek, the site of Bíatiísi and Yebá's plantation (Fontaine 1980:33).

The theme of family-left-behind-in-slavery, already encountered in Abaísa traditions, appears again, touchingly, in *82*. Just as Andolé, the offender of Ma Kaála, received poetic justice years later (*39–40*), so Záiya, who incurs a debt to Bíatiísi for failing to bring along her sister, must pay her back years later by finding for her and her Nasí kinsmen precious water.*

The information in fragment *83*, which I have been told matter-of-factly by Matjáus and Lángus, may or may not be accepted by Nasís. (It was vigorously denied by the Nasís during my group discussion at Kambalóa in 1978.) Just the same, my reading of archival materials discloses an absolutely staggering amount of maroon-slave contact during the relevant period, and it seems likely that very few large rebellions or collective escapes did not involve some participation or encouragement from those who were already free in the forests. ✜

---

* The principles of delayed compensation and its negative counterpart, delayed retribution, are central to Saramaka notions about social life. As Saramakas are fond of saying, proverbially, "When a leaf falls into the water, it's not the same day it will rot." (For discussion, see Price 1975:36–37 and S. Price 1978.)

"View of the Settlement called the Jew's Savannah," 1770s. Anonymous engraving after a drawing by John Gabriel Stedman (1796: Plate 70). Although this depiction dates from eight decades after the first Nasí escapes, the Savannah had not really developed during the period, rather having suffered a gradual decline.

Fighting Their Way South

84. Once in the forest, the Nasís walked for years with Kaási's people. But Kaási slept at night, while our man [Kwádjaní] didn't. That's why we found more land than Kaási. Wherever Kaási went, the Nasís had already been there. Because Kaási used to sleep at night, but our man didn't. (Aláfo 22 July 1978)

85. The Nasís battled the whites in many places. Kwakú Kwádjaní carried the fight to the area of Ayó, to those savannahs behind Ayó. They fought all around there, right on up to the head of Makambí Creek. . . . They had a big battle there with the whites, they and Makambí. He was one of Wíi's people, but he was fighting alongside the Nasís. They fought until the battle was too much for him. The whites bested [*wíni*] him. They killed him. Afterward, the Kwádjanís [that is, the Nasís] kept coming up and finally "met" the river again at Yobákaí. Then Kwádjaní went back for Makambí. He went and gave him a proper burial there, at the head of [the place now called] Makambí Creek. (Tebíni 24 July 1976)

✤

Fighting Their Way South (84–85)

Whether or not Kaási helped the Nasís escape, their own traditions clearly place them as traveling with his group during their early years in the forest. Fragment *84* provides a neat Nasí explanation of their superior landholdings in the Middle River region. Fragment *85* refers to raids and battles that probably took place soon after the abandoning of Kaási's village at Míndindéti Creek in 1712. The "savannahs behind Ayó" are just across the river from Jews Savannah and suggest early Nasí raids in their old plantation territory—a practice they were to continue into the early 1760s (see 185C–196C). The name of Makambí Creek commemorates for all Saramakas the cooperation in battle of the Nasís and Wíi's sister's son and the courageous return of the Nasís to bury him as a hero. Yobákaí, where the Nasis "met" the river, was probably a village site (just as were the places where Ayakô "met" the river on his way south; see *25*). Though surrounded by lands belonging to other clans, the creek called Yobákaí has always been considered the property of the Nasís.

The First Canoe

86. From Yobákaí they continued upstream on foot. Coming from the coast, everyone had walked on foot. But the Nasís, they were the first to use paddles [canoes]. At Dóti-lángahúku, divination (*fíi*) told them to build a canoe. Kwakú [Étja] and his brother Kwádjaní, they felled the silk-cotton tree and built the canoe. They felled a *bóóánti* tree, split it, and made the paddle. My father and [famous Captain] Bitjénfóu and I were on our way to the city once. They showed it to me. Right there, at Dótilángahúku, they had split the *bóóánti* to make the paddle. Just recently the stump finally rotted all the way through and disappeared. Well, those Nasís continued upstream to Kumakô by canoe. The silk-cotton tree canoe. Baaad! [*ogi!*] They split the *bóóánti* to make paddles! (Tebíni 24 July 1976) ❖

The First Canoe (86)

I have heard this story about the Nasís from members of three clans and know no rival claims to priority in canoe building. We know that early maroon canoes were very crudely constructed, compared to modern craft. (Indeed, there has been notable technical refinement in canoe making, even within the past century—Price 1970.) In 1747, a military expedition used this common knowledge to confirm that their Saramaka enemies were close by: five days up the Saramaka River they saw a canoe "so gross and badly fashioned that it could not have been made by Indians" (SvS 292, 9 July 1753). The original construction materials mentioned by Saramakas are noteworthy as well. There has always been a blanket prohibition on felling silk-cotton trees (which house *apúku*s) in Saramaka. And the use of *bóóánti* for paddles would today be equally bizarre, as would the use of the similar hardwood *giánti* or of *múkumúku* reeds (mentioned to me as the paddle source by the Dómbi Améiká and the Nasís of Kambalóa, respectively). I do not know quite what to make of these assertions, except that modern Saramakas see them as confirming both the remembered ignorance of their early forefathers in the lore of the forest and, at the same time, their superior supernatural powers. ❖

A modern Saramaka canoe

The Village of Kumakô

87. After much hard traveling, they ascended Akógaándi Creek [Awónêngè Creek] until they got to the great mountain called Kumakô. That's where they built the village. (Aseedu 22 July 1978)

88. On the upper course of the Awónêngè Creek we found some years of rest, and many earlier runaways joined us there. . . . The Nasí Yebá was chosen chief. ("Grandompie" to government official Junker, 1917, quoted in Junker 1922/23:473)

89. [During this period] women, weapons, and ammunition were our most pressing needs. And the Nasís were especially masterful bush scouts. ("Grandompie" to government official Junker, 1917, quoted in Junker 1922/23:474)

"A Rebel Negro armed & on his guard." Engraving by Francesco Bartolozzi, after a drawing by John Gabriel Stedman (1796:Plate 53).

90. Once Kwádjaní and his son Gáu—the one he had with the Lángu woman Amímba—were preparing themselves to go raid Paléya, to test their manhood [*poobá sinkíi*]. But then Ma Gúmbi, Gáu's Dómbi wife, saw that she was pregnant, so they didn't go on the raid. That child was Tatá Akeesu. (Bakáa 28 July 1978)

91. [Using Kumakô as a base] they raided the plantations, fighting great battles at Kalíbo, then at Paléya. When they left Paléya they fought in the savannahs across from Ayó. (Tebíni 28 July 1976)

92. Apétipeébi is the *gaán nén* [great name] of Kwakú Étja, the one they'd play on the wooden trumpet, in battle. When that name is spoken, it means war! One could live in a Nasí village for a full year and never once hear that name. Apétipeébi went with the Matawáis to Tafelberg. The Nasís had family there. One of Bíatiísi's daughters had a Matawái husband. She went to live with him and made lots of children. (Bakáa 28 July 1978)

⬥

The Village of Kumakô (87–92)

According to the combined accounts of many clans, the population of the village of Kumakô consisted of Nasís, Dómbis, Biítus, Awanás, and a few Papútus. (Kaási and his Lángu group lived there for its first two or three years, but then moved on southwards; see 55C–58C.) Combining oral fragments with documentary materials, I date the Nasí move into the general area of Awónêngè Creek to 1715–20, and the establishment of the large village to the aftermath of the attacks of 1730–31, when refugees from the Kleine Saramacca flooded the region. The famous village of Kumakô, then, would have had a lifetime of some thirteen years, from ca. 1731 until its destruction in 1743 (see 107–20).

Fragment 90 was related by a Dómbi; it is remembered by that clan because of the role later played by Akeesu in legitimizing their land claims in the area of Kwangú. Incidentally, it preserves as well a memory of the intent to raid Paléya, a raid that a separate historical fragment (91) relates as actually having taken place.

Many of the Nasí raids on plantations, carried out from the area of Kumakô and preserved in the memory of their descendants, can be confirmed from documentary sources. For example, archives for 1738–39 report a major revolt by the slaves of Manuel Pareyra, in which they killed their master, as well as the direct involvement of Saramakas in the violence at this "Paléya" plantation (SvS 134, 21 December 1739 [8 December 1739]; SvS 266, 8 December 1739; Nassy 1788:91–92). (A Jewish expedition spent six weeks following these Saramaka raiders and returned home with forty-seven prisoners and six hands of dead maroons—a striking indication of the size of the raid and the fierceness of the fighting; a "faithful" slave claimed that the raiders had come from the village of "Pongoe," almost certainly the former Dómbi village of Kwangú, at the time probably used mainly as an advance camp for raids—see 94 [Nassy 1788:91–92].)* And other archival reports from this period indicate fierce raiding and fighting behind Jews Savannah, precisely "across from Ayó," as Nasís report today. I have not as yet found direct confirmation of the reported battle at Kalíbo (Plantation Accaribo, in the Para region), but there is suggestive evidence: in 1730, Saramakas were reported to be readying a new garden for a group of slaves they were preparing to liberate on a future raid on the plantation adjoining Kalíbo (Hartsinck 1770:761).

⬥

* The phoneme "oe" in Dutch orthography is English "u"; "kw" and "kp" are allophones in Saramaccan. Thus, "Kwangú" may be pronounced "Kpangú"—which a Dutch speaker might well write as "Pongoe."

DÓMBIS, 1710–1743

From Slavery to Kumakô

93. The Dómbis escaped from Plantation Palmeneribo. The silk-cotton tree with the large iron ring where our forefathers were attached for punishment is still standing there ("Grandompie" to government official Junker, 1917, quoted in Junker 1922/23:473)

94. There was a [man who later became a] Djuka called Búsima. He was married to Polína, one of Ma Momói's daughters. When he ran off with Polína, they ascended the Sara Creek. They bore a daughter called Sála there, which is what gave the creek its name. Polína's [matrilineal] relatives parted with Búsima at the mouth of Sara Creek. They crossed the river there [to the west side]. He went on, with Polína, to join his Djuka relatives. The others continued up on this [west] side. They went up Kwangú Creek and lived there. Then they went up Míndindéti Creek, all the way to [the present site of] Kwakúgoón. There they saw Kaási, who had been living there, and joined him. (Bakáa 28 July 1978)

95. After a short while living together, Kaási said he'd leave them, that the whites would surely follow their escape route, and he was not yet ready to make peace. So he walked up Míndindéti Creek, then up the Kleine Saramacca River, and on to Agámadjá Creek. Meanwhile, the Dómbis went to the headwaters of Akógaándi and Tutú Creeks. Everyone met there—Nasís, Biítus, Awanás, Papútus. That was Kumakô. There were seven battles at that village before it was finally taken [by the whites]. They lived there a long time. (Bakáa 28 July 1978) ✣

DÓMBIS, 1710–1743

Today, the large Dómbi clan is the downstream neighbor of the Nasís, on the middle Suriname River. Though their traditions hold that they escaped somewhat later than the Nasís, they traveled fairly closely with them for their first four decades in the forest.

From Slavery to Kumakô (93–95)

All Dómbi accounts trace their origin to the large adjoining plantations of Palmeneribo-Surimombo, just below Jews Savannah. "Dómbi" derives from Dutch "Dominee" ("Minister"), which is how their name was often written in past centuries; during the 1670s and 1680s, Surimombo was the center of the sugar empire of the colony's chief cleric, Calvinist Dominee Johannes Basseliers, and his slaves were known as "Dominee negers" (van der Linde 1966; see also Staehelin 1913–19, 3: ii:139).* In 1702, upon the death of Basseliers's daughter, ownership of Surimombo and Palmeneribo passed to her husband, Jonas Witsen, who lived in Europe. He soon sent the artist Dirk Valkenburg to Suriname to serve as bookkeeper for his plantations, with special instructions to record for Witsen—in sketches and paintings—as much of what he saw as

---

* As with the names of other Saramaka clans, the "historical" literature on Saramakas contains various spurious "Dómbi" etymologies (e.g., Kahn 1931:93; Jozefzoon 1959:10).

Slave "play" on the Dómbi Plantation, 1707. Painting by Dirk Valkenburg. (*Danish Royal Museum of Fine Arts, Copenhagen.*)

he could (van Eeghen 1946, van der Linde 1966:127). Thanks to this circumstance, we have excellent pictures of the plantations from which the Dómbis soon afterwards escaped. Indeed, perhaps the finest of Valkenburg's plantation paintings, of a slave "play" in 1707, almost certainly depicts some of the very people who just a few years later become the original Dómbi maroons.

Many Saramaka Dómbis also call themselves "Mísidján," a name that refers to an important Djuka group as well. The Mísidjáns seem to be later maroons from the same two plantations, named after one or another of the widows who exploited them. Johannes Basseliers's widow—in 1690 the sixth largest sugar exporter in the colony—was known to the Dutch as "Juffrouw Basseliers," and would probably have been called in slave speech "Missie Djon." Likewise, the widow of Jonas Witsen, who owned the plantations until 1760, would probably have been called "Missie Djon." Fifty years ago the government official L. Junker stopped at Palmeneribo and claims to have seen the iron ring referred to in 93, still fixed in the tree; he also reports in a non-Dómbi story that I have been unable in any way to confirm that the female plantation owner, "Missie Jans," was killed by her slaves and hung from that very ring (1922/23:473). In 1978, Basiá Bakáa, a Dómbi, told me simply that "Mísi Djon was the wife of Masa Dómbi." In any case, the Dómbi plantation, whose Saramaka name derived from Dominee Basseliers, became known after his death also as Mísidján, after one of the widows who carried on its affairs.

Modern Dómbis insist on conceptualizing the very large group of original Dómbis as a single matrilineal family. Their genealogies tend to show Ma Momóimítji as apical ancestress with various daughters—Húnkwade (whose daughter is later captured by the whites at the battle of Kumakô), Kilambí (whose daughter Ahágbò marries the Matjáu Kwasílolá, and whose son Dóndo Ainsá is an important late-eighteenth-century captain), Polína (whose progeny become one segment of the Djuka Mísidjáns), and Asukúme (who was married to Ayakô and is the "mother" of the village of Soolán)—each of whom founded what is today a major matrilineal segment. And there seems to be agreement that Momóimítji's "sister" (said actually to have been her mother's sister's daughter), Sêsi, is the apical ancestress of the village of Dáume. The precise genealogical connections of the original men in the group are less well agreed upon (as they are of less consequence in the later determination of group affiliation), but they are usually said to include the brothers Dóndo Kasá and Maśiála (both of whom later served as captain), Adímbula, Kimóko, Asentéa (another late-eighteenth-century captain), and Mutífata.

Fragment 94 encodes the splitting of the Djuka Mísidjáns from the Saramaka Dómbis, at the mouth of the Sara Creek, and the subsequent Dómbi settlement at Kwangú Creek. From here, they probably joined Kaási in the Míndindéti Creek area about 1712 and then went their separate ways, with the Dómbis traveling south closer to the Suriname River, always to the east of Kaási and his group. Around 1731 they would have participated in the founding of Kumakô, where their memories preserve "seven battles" before it was finally destroyed.

Dómbis do not seem to preserve a memory of Kaási at Kumakô, depicting him and his group as traveling directly from the Kleine Saramacca to the Gaánlío. The absence of such a tradition fits well with what Lángus themselves remember; that Kaási's stay at Kumakô was brief, and that he and his group departed before the great battles that so strongly etched themselves in the memory of the groups that did participate. ✤

Sugar-making Facilities at the Dómbi Plantation, 1708. The drawing, by Dirk Valkenburg, is labeled, "No. 1. The mill at Surimombo. 2. the boiling house there. 3. the distillery. 4. the Kaentras Hill. 5. the pasture." (*Rijksmuseum Amsterdam, Rijksprentenkabinet.*)

The Planter's House at the Dómbi Plantation, 1708. The drawing, by Dirk Valkenburg, is labeled, "This view of Palmeniribo is seen by standing before the alley of Negro houses and looking between the houses and orange trees. 1. the kitchen. 2. the rear gallery of the plantation house. 3. the front gallery. 4. the storehouse. 5. the smithy. 6. orange trees. 7. lemon trees. 8. grapefruit trees. 9. the well." (*Rijksmuseum Amsterdam, Rijksprentenkabinet.*)

Africa Remembered

96. Friend, listen well. Vumá came out from Africa. He and his [pregnant] sister Tjazímbe. Akoomí was born here, on the [Lower] Suriname River. No one knows who her father was. He never left Africa. But when they came [to Suriname], and the child was born, Vumá said, "She has become mine" [*A kó u mi*], and that's how Akoomí got her name.

They had left Africa during a war. Vumá's African wife had a great *óbia* called Madánfo. . . . When Vumá and Tjazímbe were loaded onto the ship, it wouldn't move. Vumá's wife didn't want him to depart. Well, she was the one who kept the *óbia*. She was very ripe. But women can't use *óbia*s like men. Men are the ones who wander, the ones who go to battle. Vumá was really ripe! With Madánfo he could walk in a wink from here to the river [200 yards], and walk right across it as if it were solid ground. He couldn't be followed. They say that Vumá could fly like a bird. But he was a human being. He'd prepare the *óbia* till it was just right, push that ring onto the tip of his thumb, *súúú*, like this [motions]. That's what let him walk on water. Well, his parrot feather, specially prepared. He'd tie it to his belt like this—*sááá*. And he'd fly, *vauu píít!* Until he alit. Then he'd remove the feather and put it into his sack, *tjó*.

AWANÁS, 1690s–1743

Some of my most pleasant days discussing early history were passed with the Awaná Captain Góme, only months short of his eightieth birthday when I was his guest in Tutúbúka in 1978. A descendant of Alábi, the first Moravian convert and tribal chief during the late eighteenth and early nineteenth century, Góme combines a deep respect for book learning with a keen understanding of traditional Saramaka ways. Nearly blind and quite frail, Góme seemed to find genuine pleasure in the opportunity to talk with someone who cared about these long-ago people and places as much as he. At one point, he interrupted a story he was telling to comment excitedly to a friend who was listening in on our conversation: "It's just like a woman who has cicatrizations. She hasn't 'wakened' [recut] them in a long time. Then he [indicating me] comes to visit. It's as if the cicatrizations were suddenly 'wakened.' No way you'll be able to sleep that night! It's like a new new thing for me, a true pleasure." And Góme also explained his willingness to be open with me about usually hidden subjects: "It was only because of the Pikílío [that is, Matjáus] that an Awaná became tribal chief. Because of Abíni [a Matjáu]. He begat Alábi with Akoomí for the Awanás. And we are still eating [benefiting from] that wonderful deed today." Rationalized by our mutually strong, if different, relationship to Matjáus, and spurred on by the happiness of remembering stories that he had not considered for a very long time, Góme shared with me some of the earliest recollections of the Awanás.

Africa Remembered (96)

This tortured departure from Africa, with the slave ship mysteriously becalmed off the coast, is the only such detailed story I know about leaving the motherland nearly three hundred years ago. The great *óbia*, Madánfo, was the collective possession of the Awaná clan, and it was Madánfo that Alábi tried to shoot and destroy, in a documented incident later in the eighteenth century, as a demonstration to his fellows of the powers of his newly embraced Christianity (see Price n.d.).

❖

He told his sister, "Go. Go with these people. Don't be afraid. But expect me back. I shall return." Tjazímbe was very frightened. She didn't want to be without him. But he said, "Don't worry. I'll be back. I'm just going to take proper leave of my wife." Because they were running off. So he didn't get on the ship.

Well, the ship was finally ready to sail. But the wind wouldn't blow! It just sat there. Then, the wind blew them out to sea but later blew them right back again. Right back to Africa. It was Vumá who did all this. Then he killed his wife. If he hadn't killed her, he couldn't have come to rejoin his sister. His wife was ripe. She had "tied" him [to Africa] with the óbia. It's not that he knocked her with a stick or anything like that, but he managed to kill her somehow [with óbia]. That's what allowed him to come to Saramaka [Suriname].

So he went right to the place where the ship had left from, and it was still there. Then he walked right across the water onto the ship. He said, "Sister, I'm here." (But this is a secret. What I am telling you. The people here no longer know it.) He had taken the óbia from his wife, and he brought it with him. He'd prepared it just the way he wished, before he came. (Góme 20 July 1978) ✠

Plantations

97. They landed us at Paátaboóki; that's the wharf where we came ashore. Our first plantation was small, almost hidden. The landing place of the plantation was hidden, not opened up. I think it was somewhere near Domburg; when you get old and can't travel you forget so many things! That's the place where they broke their backs [with work]. (Góme 20 July 1978)

98. The white man was called Tobiási. They were called "Tobiási slaves." But I can't pin down its exact location. (Bakáa 28 July 1978)

99. The Awanás and Bákapáus were close friends. The Awanás were Tobiási slaves, the Bákapáus were Tíifou slaves. They came from Tíifou plantation, below Domburg at a creek on the west, just below the mouth of the Para. Awanás and Bákapáus have stayed together ever since that time, Tobiási slaves and Tíifou slaves. (Bakáa 29 July 1978) ✠

Plantations (97–99)

Though it was apparently on the tip of his tongue, Góme could no longer recall the name—which he once knew—of his ancestors' plantation. Nevertheless, geographical detail is striking in his stories: for example, the precise location of the wharf at which his slave ancestors first set foot in the New World, and the "hiddenness" of the landing place at their small plantation. Given Akoomí's liasons with both Ayakô and Abíni (see *100, 105*), we can date the arrival in Suriname of Vumá and his sister to just before 1700. (There are hardly any archives and maps for this period that are available for consultation, and the only contemporary "Tobias" I have encountered was a newlywed from Guadeloupe, Catarina Tobias, whose marriage to Adrianus Wiltens—a man who became a prominent planter—was celebrated at Plantation Waterland in 1698–99 [van der Linde 1966:120]; whether she had slaves of her own, I do not know.) In any case, Awanás and Bákapáus, who have always traveled together (and whom other clans for most purposes simply consider "Awanás"), apparently came from neighboring plantations just south of the capital. And one of them I can positively identify: "Tíifóu" is Plantation Toutluy Faut, which was located exactly where Góme describes it, on the west bank of the Suriname River, below the mouth of the Para River (see map, p. 16). ✠

"**Group of Negros, as imported to be sold for Slaves.**" Engraving by William Blake, after a drawing by John Gabriel Stedman (1796: Plate 22).

114

In-law Troubles

100. When he was already middle-aged, Ayakô [the Matjáu leader] took the young Akoomí as his wife. Ayakô did not get along with Vumá [the girl's mother's brother], accusing him of being a witch. There was a big palaver in the forest at Mawasí. The Matjáus decided that those people were witches, and that they would not walk south with them. (Otjútju 3 August 1976)

101. Abíni [Ayakô's older sister's daughter's son] had been sleeping with Akoomí, and they had run off to the east, toward the Tempati, to hide from Ayakô. [Vumá may have sided with Abíni, thus causing the rift with Ayakô.] Akoomí told Abíni that she was pregnant with Ayakô's child, and as the pregnancy progressed, he became afraid that the whites would find them, so they crossed the Suriname River and settled across from the mouth of the Sara Creek, where a daughter was born. (Otjútju 1 July 1976)

102. Some Dómbis lived nearby at Kwangú, and when Abíni and his wife left the area, it remained Dómbi territory. (Otjútju 3 August 1976)

103. Once, when Abíni was living near the Sara Creek, he decided to return to the Cassewinica area to raid the plantation for supplies. He and his wife needed all sorts of things, as they were no longer with Ayakô. When he went to the plantation, they saw him and

---

In-law Troubles (100–105)

This set of stories explains why Abíni, the Matjáu who became the first post-peace treaty tribal chief, went to live with the Awanás, with whom he stayed throughout his life. The first four fragments were told to me by the Matjáu Otjútju, the final two by the Awaná Góme. The first (*100*) describes the difficulties between Ayakô and his young wife's uncle and the decision not to bring Awanás along on the Matjáu trek south. The second (*101*) implies that Abíni adultered with his "grandfather" Ayakô's wife, a fact more explicitly recorded by Góme (*105*), and reports his temporary residence "hiding out" near the mouth of the Sara Creek. Other Matjáu fragments concur that Abíni lived for years on the Lower River: "Abíni was a wanderer; he lived as far away as the mouth of the Sara Creek; he went from place to place; he lived at Kumakô; but always with the Awanás." Fragment *103* describes an unsuccessful raid attempted by Abíni on the old Machado plantation, revealing incidentally how little romanticism Saramakas possess concernng slave-maroon relations, which in fact were always a matter of great delicacy, danger, and unpredictability.

Góme's vision of the Awaná past clarifies the many related but often-contradictory fragments I have heard from Matjáus and other Awanás. (Characteristically, too, it is laced with personal details that keep the past alive in an especially vivid way, for example, the fact that Ayakô, in spite of his prestige and power, could no longer sexually satisfy his youthful wife.) Góme envisions the major Awaná matrilineages as descended from Akoomí's daughters, with one of these fathered not by Abíni but by Ayakô; the Awanás as harboring the young Abíni after he adultered with his grandfather's wife; and Abíni, in return for this kindness, as sharing with them the luster of the office of tribal chief and being ultimately responsible for his Awaná son, Alábi, himself succeeding to the position. There are, however, other Awaná versions that insist that Bôsi was the child of Tjazímbe (whom some Saramakas call Tjasíngbe) rather than of Akoomí. It now seems clear to me that these rival versions—whether distinguishing Bôsi as the child of a different father or a different mother from her four "sisters"—are the reflection of nineteenth-century Awaná political maneuvering, attempts of descendants to jostle for relative genealogical closeness to Abíni and Alábi, the wellsprings of whatever claims to tribal authority the Awaná clan possesses. ❖

almost killed him, but he got away. He had thought it would be easy to return to the plantation that the Matjáus had already burned, to find things. But the slaves began asking him who he was, and when they realized that he was a Matjáu, they tried to get him. But he ran away. If they had caught him, they'd have killed him. (Otjútju 12 July 1978)

104. My elders said that Yoyó, Máiya, Bébi, Alíwò, and Bôsi were the daughters of Akoomí and Abíni. Yoyóme was the real name, but her children couldn't pronounce it, and Yoyó stuck. Abíni "made" the Awaná clan with Akoomí. Five daughters. (Góme 20 July 1978)

105. There is a deep secret. Bôsi was not Abíni's child! Her father was Ayakô. Listen carefully. Abíni was a famous man [*nênma*, a man of reputation]. So the Awanás gave the child to Abíni to bring up. Only the other four sisters are Abíni's children. It is not true that Abíni took the woman when she was pregnant. But he did take her from Ayakô. She had borne the child first. Abíni raised it. She always called him "father." You'd never guess it wasn't his child. Her lineage gave her to him to raise. This is very secret! Ayakô was a man's man! Abíni was a real man too. Ayakô was powerful. He was Abíni's elder. Both were very powerful, with *óbia*s. But Akoomí loved Abíni more than Ayakô. Ayakô was already getting old when he took Akoomí. You yourself must have heard this: the bell doesn't ring so loudly any more, not loudly enough to go to church! My mother's brother didn't hide this from me, but he told me it was secret. If I speak it, my ancestors may kill me. Ayakô was a real man. When all this happened, Abíni's wife's people, the Awanás, didn't throw him out. They held him close. That's why Ayakô couldn't get the better of him. That's why Abíni came to live with the Awanás. While his kinsmen went upstream, he stayed down with the Awanás. (Góme 20 July 1978) ❖

To Kumakô

106. Coming upstream, the Nasís, Dómbis, and Awanás walked together. They had no problems with one another. The Nasís and Dómbis went up Akógaándi Creek. The Awanás went up Tutú Creek. And they met where these creek heads arise, at the great hill called Kumakô. (Góme 21 July 1978) ❖

To Kumakô (106)

The Awanás seem to have escaped in the early years of the eighteenth century, and Ayakô was apparently with Akoomí just before his trek southward ca. 1715. For some thirty years the Awanás must have lived in the area southeast of Míndindéti Creek, near the Nasís and Dómbis, and moved slowly up the Suriname River basin. This historical fragment, from Góme, suggests that the Awanás lived alone for a time on the Tutú Creek, near where he took me to bathe in the cool of one summer's evening, two and a half centuries later. From there, in the early 1730s, they joined the other clans at Kumakô, in what is remembered as the largest Saramaka village yet created. (And it was only decades later, long after the Peace, that the Awanás again moved down to the area of Tutú Creek.) ❖

THE BATTLE OF KUMAKÔ, OCTOBER 1743

Surprise Attack

107. There are certain days when you can't go to Kunákúun ["Kuná's hill"=Kumakô]. If you go, there's no telling what evil things you'll meet. (Améiká 22 July 1978)

108. The war came to Kumakô seven times before the village was finally destroyed. (Bakáa 28 July 1978)

109. An old woman foresaw the battle. She was lying in her hammock. She said, "The whites are coming, they're already on the way." And it was true, it happened that way. (Bayo 22 July 1978)

110. Kaási and the Lángu people had already moved south. By the time of the final battle, the people who lived there were the Nasís and Biítus, the Dómbis, the Awanás, and some Papútus. (Améiká 21 July 1978)

111. The attack on Kumakô occurred while a corpse was laid out [preparatory to burial]. The men had gone off hunting for the funeral rites. Papá Kuná was the dead man. They had to flee at night, leaving the corpse unburied. But the whites buried him after the battle. (Améiká 21 July 1978)

112. It was the Long Dryseason. All of the men had gone to the Kleine Saramacca River. It was the tenth moon [ca. September/October], and water was gone from the forest floor. The men had gone to hunt fish in the pools left in the dry creekbeds. That's when the battle began. (Bakáa 28 July 1978)

THE BATTLE OF KUMAKÔ, OCTOBER 1743

Surprise Attack (107–20)

Detailed memories of the battle of Kumakô are preserved with considerable drama—the old woman's "prediction"; the absence of the hunters who were seeking game for Papá Kuná's funeral; the unusual ambush laid by the enemy and their use of an especially devastating gun; the perfidious killing of the chief, Yebá, and the capture of a Dómbi girl; Étja's journey to the whites to seek her return and their pacification of him with a gift "jacket"; and the eventual dispersal of Kumakô's inhabitants, with the final romantic reunion of a husband and wife who had been parted by the battle (this last is treated in *122*).

At the time of its destruction, Kumakô's inhabitants included the Nasís and their close allies the Biítus (see *128*), the Awanás, the Dómbis, and some Papútus. (Papútus trace their origin to a single massive escape from their Para plantation; their own traditions combine with archival sources to permit me to localize this event at Plantation Vier Kinderen in 1729, when a maroon raid liberated practically the whole slave force of the Widow Papot. Though a few of these Papútus traveled with the Nasí group, the bulk of them remained in the Para area, far downstream, until 1758 [see 179C–182C].)

There is some irony that the destroyer of Kumakô was probably David Cohen Nassy, the aging but indomitable leader of the Jewish militia, whose relatives had kept Yebá and his fellows as slaves decades before. In 1743 Captain Nassy, although very old, left in the month of August

113. The slave who brought the whites, who showed them the way, must have known Maroon customs. He told the soldiers to line up on either side of the path outside of the village, and he called out at the top of his voice, "Fóódênde. Fóódênde" [this is the call when wild boars have been killed]. The young people came running out of the village, thinking pigs had been killed. And the soldiers tried to grab them [to return them to slavery]. The children who were in the lead shouted, "Wóóó, white people! Kids, run for your lives!" But the soldiers caught a young Dómbi woman, Kokóóko. (Bakáa 29 July 1978)

114. The whites used the gun called "kwantákwalá" at Kumakô. If it's shot here, it lands across the river [400 yards]! Its shot is spread over a broad area. (Góme 21 July 1978)

115. The "great *óbia*" brought from Africa and the great drum were kept at this place [Kumakô]. By treachery [betrayal], the whites learned the location of our village and made an attack. But there was sufficient time to bury the great drum there before fleeing with the great *óbia* toward the Gaánlío. Everyone who was not wounded or captured by the whites fled. ("Grandompie" to government official Junker, 1917, quoted in Junker 1922/23:473–74)

116. Yebá, the leader of Kumakô and the father of Kwakú Étja and Kwakú Kwádjaní, was killed in the battle. Some people say he was captured, but he was really killed. We don't like to say it. It was only because the able-bodied men were all absent when the whites attacked. They'd gone to the Pikísaamáka [Kleine Saramacca River] to hunt. The old man was resting up against a tree when the whites started shooting at him. The hail of bullets was so intense, it actually felled the tree. Just think, the father of Kwádjaní and Étja! (Bakáa 28 July 1978)

---

with 27 civilians, 12 soldiers, 15 Indians, 165 slaves and 60 canoes, following a plan he had formed and presented to the Council on July 1, 1743. After having followed the Suriname River and having passed several cataracts . . . he began his march, and the enemies were attacked on the day of *Kippur, or of Atonement of the Jews*; and without any regard for this sacred day, he pursued the enemies, put their cabins to the torch, utterly ruined the village, tore their crops from the ground by their roots, took fourteen prisoners, and killed a large number. (Nassy 1788:93)

I have found the following letter, written by Nassy at Jews Savannah on 9 October, addressed to the Governor and Council:

We have destroyed the Criole Village but did not damage the gardens. We located as well the Papa village and the village Seremeca. It being my Holy Days, I have not yet been able to come [to the city] but on Monday I shall come with the corporal bringing the spoils as well as the journal of the journey. (SvS 272, 9 October 1743)

Unfortunately, Nassy's own long report of the expedition is not available for examination, but Governor Mauricius's journal entry for 10 October noted that Nassy had just returned from his expedition and that, in addition to captives, he had returned with the head of the maroon chief (SvS 199, 10 October 1743).

The identification of the battle of Kumakô with Nassy's expedition cannot be considered definitive, given the number of lacunae in the currently available archival materials. Nevertheless, the combined use of canoes and marching (which fits the information in *118*), the governor's report of the taking of the chief's head (which fits the usually secret story in *116*), the September-October dating of the attack (which fits Saramaka traditions—*112*), and the march routes described for this and related expeditions in the archives all make the case highly probable.

117. In the battle of Kumakô, the whites captured Kwakú's father. He was old and couldn't go out to do battle any longer. (Tebíni 24 July 1976)

118. The whites arrived and took him [Kwakú's father] suddenly, carried him away. Then Kwakú swore to the Supreme God. He said, "If night doesn't fall too quickly, there is no way I and those whites shall not meet." And they did meet, at the large mountain [Brownsberg] just above Afobáka. He caught up to them, but the whites continued to flee till they arrived across from the mouth of the Sara Creek. Then he began to travel with them. They didn't know it! He snuck right into their boat [which they began using at the level of the Sara Creek, to return to the city]. The whites just saw a bunch of blacks [slaves] and didn't notice him. Later, he began fighting with them again. (Tebíni 28 July 1976)

119. The very oldest of all Momóimítji's daughters, Húnkwade, was the mother of the girl who the whites caught at Kumakô. Kwakú Étja or Kwakú Kwádjaní was the father, but he was not the woman's husband. He had slept with another man's wife. . . . When the men returned from hunting, the battle was over. The Dómbis made trouble with Kwakú Étja, saying that since he was so ripe, and the whites had caught the child he'd fathered with the Dómbi woman, he had better know what to do to get her back for them (Bakáa 28 July 1978)

120. So he [Étja] went to the city, right to the government people. He didn't go to fight; he went to reason with them. I don't know if it's true, but they told him they'd already sent her to another country, and they pleaded with him to end the fighting. That's when they gave him the famous "jacket" to compensate him, to cool his heart and to beg him to make peace. (Bakáa 29 July 1978)   ✤

In spite of the specificity of detail in the Saramaka fragments, the selectively of these stories—as of all Saramaka history—must be stressed: the capture of one woman (not coincidentally the woman of Kwakú) stands in this story for the capture of some fourteen; and the killing of the chief is preserved, while that of the "large number" of others is forgotten. The story of Kwakú receiving a "jacket" from the whites is remembered because of the role it plays in 1767, after the death of Tribal Chief Abíni, when Kwakú uses it to placate Abíni's son Alábi and thus prevent a war against the Matawáis (see Price n.d.). My efforts to link this jacket-giving tradition to a particular act recorded in the archives have so far proved fruitless, though I have found several similar cases of gift giving during the two decades preceding the Peace Treaty of 1762.   ✤

The Village at Tímba

121. From Kumakô they came down Waná Creek. (They saw a *waná* [edible rodent] there as they were fleeing the battle.) They crossed Paába Creek and walked along Gaánbakáapási ["Big White Man's Path"], past the big bald mountain where I often go hunting, just a couple of hours from here, and on to Tímba Creek. That creek is an arm of Muyánwóyo Creek, coming downstream. There's a big hill there; that's where the village was. (Bayo 22 July 1978)

122. After the battle, people fled in different directions. The Awanás went to Tímba, in Muyánwóyo Creek. The soldiers stayed a long time at Kumakô, but when they finally left, people came back to get their belongings. A man called Pítajánfaasú, a Papútu, was the

---

FROM KUMAKÔ TO THE GAÁNLÍO, 1743–1749

After the destruction of Kumakô, its inhabitants moved quickly into the area of the great creek called Muyánwóyo ("Wet Eye")—the Awanás and Dómbis establishing a village at Tímba Creek, a branch of Muyánwóyo, and the Nasís and Biítus living along the mother creek itself. It was not long before the soldiers found them in their new location, probably during the expeditions of 1744–45 (led by Visser, Hildebrand, and others), after which they again moved south—the Awanás and Dómbis to join Kaási at his mountain redoubt of Bákakúun, the Nasís and Biítus to Dosú Creek on the Gaánlío. Incidents from the brief Muyánwóyo period are remembered by each of the groups that lived there, as are events from the earliest years along the Gaánlío, later in the 1740s.

The Village at Tímba (121–24)

Fragment *121* was spoken to me by a Dómbi captain for whom the relevant geography is part of everyday reality, his own village being quite near the sites in question. It describes matter-of-factly the route that the fleeing Dómbis and Awanás took to the new village of Tímba.

Fragments *122–23* record the circumstances surrounding the birth of Djánti, a late-eighteenth-century Dómbi captain.* Incidentally, they attest—like so many Saramaka stories—to the strength of romantic love among the early maroons. What Saramakas today refer to as "husband and wife things"—the relations between the sexes—are portrayed as being just as central in slavery and early runaway times as they are today. Saramaka stories, like Saramaka life, are infused with the warmth and the jealousies that characterize their vision of sexual relations. Romantic reunions, such as that depicted here or in the story of Paánza (*143–46*), help Saramakas preserve the essential humanity of their earliest ancestors.

Fragment *124* records the single most famous event that occurred during the brief stay at Tímba—the birth of future Tribal Chief Alábi, the son of Abíni (the first post-treaty tribal chief) and his Awaná wife Akoomí. ✥

---

* Neither my tape recording nor my notes of Basiá Bakáa's discussion of this incident make it absolutely clear that fragments *122* and *123* are related. But I *think* they are referring to a single incident.

husband of the woman whose daughter was captured at Kumakô. He was returning from Tímba to the old village to get his belongings. His wife had been separated from him in the battle and had run in the direction of Matawái [west]. Later, she saw that she was pregnant, and she set out for the old village of Kumakô, in search of her husband. And they were reunited there, at the ruined, abandoned village. Together they came to the new village at Tímba. (Bakáa 28 July 1978)

123. That is where [the future Dómbi Captain] Djánti was born. But the war caught up with them there and they had to flee—all the way to Bákakúun. (Bakáa 28 July 1978)

124. She [Akoomí] carried Alábi in her belly all the way from Kumakô to Tímba. That's where Alábi was born. (Góme 20 July 1978) ✜

The Dómbis Harbor a Stranger: Kúngoóka's Story, Part 1

125. Kúngoóka was a lone runaway. The first group he met up with were the Biítus, and he tried to find a wife there. But they said that he was too ugly, and they denied him a wife. [To me: "He was *really* ugly, man!"] Then he went to the Mísidjáns, the Dómbis. At the other place they'd made fun of him, taunted him. But the Dómbis gave him a wife. Well, they had been so generous with him that he said, "Brother-in-law, catch a chicken and bring it to me." He did. "Now break its leg and put it under that basket there. Then go bring . . . [leaves and other secret ingredients]." He also went and gathered ingredients himself. Then he prepared it all until he was satisfied. He said, "Brother-in-law, watch carefully." And he applied the medicine to the chicken. Every day for seven days. Then they lifted the basket. The chicken ran off *tjá tjá tjá tjá*! It didn't run *tíngo tíngo tíngo*! Then he said, "To express my thanks for your generosity, this *óbia* is now yours." (Peléki 27 July 1976) ✜

The Dómbis Harbor a Stranger: Kúngoóka's Story, Part 1 (125)

For Sarakamas, Kúngoóka's fame is simple: he gave that group of Dómbis who eventually settled in Dáume (which they named after Kúngoóka's African birthplace, Dahomey) their great *óbia*, which sets broken bones as if they were new, which cures gunshot wounds, and which helped engineer their battle victories over the whites. As of 1980, the mission hospital at Djumú had never seen a broken bone or gunshot wound, though they had treated tens of thousands of cases of illness and accident, and though many such cases occur each year in upper river Saramaka; all continue to be handled by the keepers of Kúngoóka's *óbia* at Dáume (or by the functionally similar but historically separate *óbia* at Kapasíkèè).*

Kúngoóka's story is also about the assimilation of individual male maroons into the nascent society, a problem broached above in the discussion of Gúnkamé (23C–24C). Spies and counterspies were common during this period; indeed, few expeditions ever made it to Saramaka territory without at least one Saramaka "turncoat" as a guide. Any newcomers were therefore suspect, and as already mentioned, some groups at certain periods simply killed them.

* The sole "exception" occurred in late 1979, when Dr. Alex van Waalwijk van Doorn, then practicing at Djumú Mission, was summoned to the site of a tree-felling accident, not to set the multiple complex leg fracture but to administer anesthesia while the patient awaited the arrival of the *óbiama* from downriver.

Inside "Wet Eye" Creek

126. It's called "Wet Eye" Creek because long ago when the whites came after them, the creek was so high they couldn't ford it. They would try, until all you could see were their eyes, but they couldn't make it across! (Group interview by government officials with Nasís at Lafánti, 17 March 1978)*

127. The whites were coming through the forest, looking for the runaways. They finally got to the [Muyánwóyo] creek and saw the people on the other side. So they waded in to get across the creek. They got in deeper and deeper until they said, "I can't go further because my eyes are getting wet." That's why it's called Muyánwóyo ["Wet Eye"] Creek. (Group interview by government officials with Nasís at Kambalóa, 18 March 1978) ✤

* This fragment and *127* were translated from tapes kindly lent me by Dr. J. B. Ch. Wekker, Centraal Bureau Luchtkartering, Paramaribo.

Lone male runaways often became desperadoes, too fearful to try to join a group yet relying on its crops to live, hoping someday to make contact with a person they had once known on a plantation. Nevertheless, from the perspective of the settled groups, finding a new runaway who could add something special to the group brought great prestige, and the fame of certain early Saramakas is today closely linked with the people whom they "brought" (and whose descendants help preserve their memory, as part of the ongoing relationship between the groups).

I cannot yet definitively date Kúngoóka's arrival in Saramaka, but provisionally place it during the mid-1740s, when the Dómbis lived at Tímba (on the basis of Saramaka traditions about his later history, and post-Peace Treaty Moravian documents). I have heard vague historical fragments that suggest that Kúngoóka may have passed through Matawái, where he learned the bone-setting part of his *óbia*, before coming to Saramaka, but I cannot confirm these. Most Saramaka accounts claim simply that he came from Dahomey—and all agree that his war *óbia* originated there—and that he simply showed up (in some versions "flew over from Africa") in Saramaka territory. Today, Dómbis remember the wife they gave him as Dína, a daughter of Momóimítji's "sister" Sêsi, and a brother of Adugwéungu, the unnamed "brother-in-law" in this account of Kúngoóka's story. ✤

Inside "Wet Eye" Creek (126–27)

Saramaka memories of their brief residence inside Muyánwóyo Creek focus on terrible battles fought in the midst of heavy rains. The very name of the creek is said to derive from the difficulties the colonial troops had fording it; and contemporary documents present numerous reports attesting to similar difficulties (for example, "Having seen the tracks of the runaways and having heard the drums they use in their celebrations, the heavy rains did not permit us to advance to discover whence they came" [SvS 199, 2 February 1743]).* An engraving made a half-century after the events in Muyánwóyo nevertheless gives some sense of what it must have been like. ✤

* These battles inside Muyánwóyo seem to have been against troops led by Visser (who in 1744 fought at a new village above the recently discovered "Crioledorp" [Kumakô]), L'espinasse (who commanded for a time in 1744 the troops indefinitely stationed at Kumakô), and Hildebrand (who traveled far up the Suriname River in 1745). None of the full expedition reports from this period are available for consultation, and my information comes only from archival fragments—for example, SvS 199, 25 March 1744, 26 March 1744; SvS 200, 20 March 1745; SvS 275, 1 March 1745.

"**March thro' a swamp or Marsh in Terra firma**." Engraving by William Blake, after a drawing by John Gabriel Stedman (1976: Plate 55).

Bringing Down the Rains

128. Wherever the Akwádjanís [Nasís] had walked, the Biítus walked with them. *Máti ku máti* [friends with friends]. The Akwádjanís had been battling all over the forest. The Biítus just stood to one side [supported them]. Finally, they all got to Muyánwóyo. . . . The whites followed them to there. Then the Biítu man called Gweúnga said to them, "Now it's your turn to stand aside. I will help you fight." And he brought down the rains! He brought them down until . . . the whites were completely encircled by rain. They were stuck right in the middle. It sunk those soldiers, finished them off completely! He did that thing, Gweúnga. And it's still there, deep inside Muyánwóyo. Not many people know about it. It's called Vunguyáapási, an arm of Muyánwóyo. The whites, where their feet marched, it made a creekbed. That's called Vúnguyáapási. [Peléki to Tebíni:] Isn't that the thing you revealed to the Nasís at the time of the big tribal council, that astounded them? [Tebíni, continuing:] Yes. And they went to look for it. And they found it right where I said! (Tebíni 28 July 1976)

129. There was a great battle at Gaánbakáapási ["Big White Man's Path] inside Muyánwóyo. Today, if you happen to swamp your canoe in Muyánwóyo, you're as good as dead. The creek has been used to killing since early times. (Améiká 22 July 1978)

130. That creek [Muyánwóyo] has no taboo against drowning people! (Tembái 23 July 1978) ✤

Bringing Down the Rains (128–30)

The Nasís, almost from the first, traveled with the smaller group known as Biítus. Like the "Tobiási" and Toutluy Faut slaves, or those of the Machado and "Wátambíi" plantations, the slaves of the Nassy and Britto families lived on neighboring plantations and forged ties that have lasted to this day. (Britto was a common Portuguese Jewish name in Suriname; the precise plantation from which the Saramaka Biítus escaped is given variously as Beaumont [see also Morssink n.d.:45] or along the nearby Matjáu Creek [see also Junker 1922/23:473]: both places are quite close to the Nassy plantation at Cassipora Creek and to the several other upriver plantations that belonged in the early eighteenth century to the Nassy family.)

Fragment *128* is vintage Tebíni. In its direct but dramatic style, it encodes two main messages for Saramakas: that the two groups had come as equals, and that it was the African Gweúnga who brought the great Biítu water *óbia, tonê* (which controls the rains and dwells in the rivers, and for which Biítus remain the major Saramaka priests).* ✤

---

* It was *tonê óbia* that Kwémayón, Ayakô's mysterious companion, possessed as well; a small clan of obscure origin that today lives in Asáubásu on the Pikílío also has special *tonê* knowledge; see *169*.

Folú Fired Agbáila

131. Folú e, Agbáila e, Adáumêni o

Folú tutú Agbáila
Adáumêni, i o yéi

Folú [man's name], Agbáila [gun's name],
Adáumêni [woman's name]
[When] Folú fires Agbáila
Adáumêni, you will hear [it]
—(Bakáa 29 July 1978)

132. There were three sisters. The one the whites captured, that was Dáume [Adáumêni]. Then Folú went and caught up with them. He shot the whites. It was when the whites were crossing Muyánwóyo Creek. They had felled a tree to make a bridge and were on it, crossing. Then he fired the shot. He fired Agbáila! (Tembái 23 July 1978)

133. They had captured his child or something like that. Adáumêni was his sister. Folú told her he would go after the girl, but that when he fired the shot from his gun, Agbáila [when "Folú tutú Agbáila"], she [Adáumêni] would hear. And he did it! (Bakáa 29 July 1978)

134. He had said to her, "My sister, Adáumêni, I'm off. But when Folú shoots Agbáila [his gun] you will know it!" Here, among the Dómbi clan, when we sing *papá* [at a funeral], in

---

Folú Fired Agbáila (131–35)

This famous incident is preserved in the ritual language of Papá, sung on the final night of funeral celebrations. I have collected relevant fragments from Matjáus, Dómbis, and Abaísas, and from Folú's Kwamá descendants themselves. The lack of agreement about the precise relationship of Adáumêni (or Dáume) to Folú stems from the cryptic medium of preservation (Papá); even those Saramakas most interested in the past are not certain of the details of the story. Matjáus tend to claim that Folú fought at this battle alongside Ayakô; I even once heard it said that he fired the gun at Gaándan Falls, with the soldiers' bodies being found at Maátasándu (confounding the incident with the famous "Sinking"; see *158–61*). In any case, almost all speakers agree on its powerful kernel: the great warrior Folú, leader of the Kwamá group, came down Muyánwóyo from his village inside Agámadjá Creek and simply blew away the whites with one shot from his famous gun named Agbáila.

Many of the named guns, the prized possessions of those First-Time warriors who owned them, were ordinary muskets, but some of the more famous were undoubtedly heavier arms—blunderbusses or muscatoons captured in battle. Captain John Gabriel Stedman, an anti-maroon soldier in late-eighteenth-century Suriname, describes his own first experience with one of these heavier guns.

> I met with a Small accident viz, by firing myself one of the blunderbusses which having placed like a Musquet against my Shoulder I received such a violent Stroke by its repulsion as through me backw.ds over a large hogshead with Irish beef, and had nearly dislocated by right Arm—this it seems was owing to my Ignorance of the Manoeuvre, as being since told that all such Weapons ought to be fired under the hand (especially when they are heavily charged) and when by swinging round the body at once with the Arm the force of the Repulsion is broke without effect. . . . [This] is only to show in what manner heavy loaded Muscatoons ought always to be fired, especially since without any Aim the execution of their wide Mouth is equally fatal. (1988:131)

It seems likely that Folú's Agbáila—which blew away a whole column of soldiers with a single blast—was a gun of this general type. ❖

the early morning, we sing this song. It is the signal to fire the funeral salutes. (Bakáa 29 July 1978)

135. They say that Folú had not been present. And the whites killed his father, or something like that. He arrived to find the village in an uproar. They told him that there had been a fierce battle. So he said to his sister, "Adáume, I'm going. But when you hear Folú shooting Agbáila, you'll know. You'll hear it, I guarantee." So he went. He passed by the whites and tied his gun, resting it right on the edge of the fallen tree [bridge]. The whites passed by and mounted the log. Some had even begun to get off at the other side. The others were right on top of the log. That's when he fired! He shot every one of them right off the log, into the water. The people back in the village said, "Folú fired Agbáila." They *had* heard! (Bakáa 29 July 1978) ❖

To the Gaánlío

136. Kaási was the first to leave Tuído, to go to Bákakúun. Later, the others [Lángu people] followed him to there and came to live at Bákakúun. Still later, they came down from the mountain and made villages at the head of Agámadjá Creek (Tebíni 11 July 1978)

137. From Tímba, the Awanás followed Kaási to Bákakúun. They helped roll those tree stumps down on the whites there! (Góme 20 July 1978)

138. After the battle at Tímba, inside Muyánwóyo Creek, the Dómbis fled all the way to Bákakúun. (Bakáa 28 July 1978)

139. [Our Nasí ancestors] fled to the Upper River, and only much later, after the conclusion of the Peace with the whites, did they come back down [to the Middle River, around the mouth of Muyánwóyo Creek]. ("Grandompie" to government official Junker, 1917, quoted in Junker 1922/23:474)

140. The Nasís went to live at Dosú Creek, on the Upper Gaánlío. Well, that *óbia*. That's where they found it. Dosú. That's where it first "caught" them, while they were traveling. That's why they call the place Dosú Creek. (Góme 21 July 1978) ❖

To the Gáanlío (136–40)

Following the battles inside Muyánwóyo, probably around 1745, the Awanás and Dómbis abandoned Tímba and moved into Kaási's village at Bákakúun. We know also that even earlier, Folú had moved down from the mountain to make his village beside Agámadjá Creek, and that by 1749 there were several small villages spread along this creek that ran east from Bákakúun. Meanwhile, the Nasís and Biítus, after leaving Muyánwóyo, settled on Dosú Creek on the opposite side of the Gaánlío, where they were to live until the 1770s. ❖

THE MATJÁUS AT BAÁKAWÁTA

The Place That Could Hide People

141. Well, they [the Matjáus] lived there [Baákawáta]. And they hid. All kinds of people came to live with them there. It hid them all! Well, the god [Wámba] that was in Mamá Yáya's head. It hid them so well. The *apúku*. [At first] if you went to get water at the river there, it was not fit to drink. You could not eat the food from the forest [without getting sick]. As soon as newcomers arrived, the forest [gods] would trouble them. But Yáya's god fixed that! So everyone decided to make Ayakô tribal chief, to put him above all other people. And then they cut footpaths, from Bákakúun to Agámadjá, from Agámadjá to Sentéa Creek, and from Sentéa across the river to Baákawáta. (Tebíni 28 July 1976)   ✣

THE MATJÁUS AT BAÁKAWÁTA

The Place That Could Hide People (141)

This minor fragment, spoken in passing once by Tebíni, introduces the region Matjáus consider their true homeland—Baákawáta, a large tributary of the Pikílío. There, they hosted not only the Wátambíis, but also the Kasitús and Papútus, and the ancestors of the people who live in Asáubásu (see *169*), as well as countless individual newcomers. It was in Baákawáta that the Matjáus celebrated the Peace of 1762, and from Baákawáta that Ayakô held sway over all of Saramaka, as "forest" [unrecognized by the government] tribal chief.   ✣

Tribal Chief Agbagó (Abóikóni), matrilineal heir to Ayakô's legacy of leadership.

Kwasílolá's Dómbi Wife

142. Kwasílolá [an original Matjáu runaway] was married to Ahágbò, a Dómbi woman. While he was married to her, Kwasílolá was caught with the Dómbi wife of another man, himself a Dómbi. The Dómbis refused to allow Kwasílolá to keep the second woman, saying that Ayakô's case [he was married to both Asukúme and Kilambí, two Dómbi women] did not constitute precedent. During the ensuing palavers, this disappointed second woman killed herself to wreak vengence (as a *kúnu*) on her own [Dómbi] people. The Dómbis then abducted a Matjáu woman as compensation for their own woman; her death, they claimed, had been caused by the Matjáus. This Matjáu captive had two children by Dómbis, one a woman who was infertile, the other a man who remained with the Dómbis. He helped, through his offspring, to increase the strength of the village. (Abáteli 31 July 1976) ✤

Kwasílolá's Dómbi Wife (142)

I know little about this event, having heard only a single fragment from Abáteli, a Matjáu with a Dómbi father. Its peculiar style stems from my having written it down as rough notes (without recording it on tape) and reconstructing the version in *142* only several hours later.

Matjáu relations with Dómbis were severely strained by this incident that seems to date from the 1730s. Its background includes the fact that Ayakô is known to have had two Dómbi wives, Asukúme (Dabí's mother) and Kilambí. (Although having two closely related wives runs against Saramaka notions of proper marriage, Ayakô's prestige is said to have persuaded Dómbis to permit it in that case.) The protagonist of this story, the Matjáu Kwasílolá, is usually counted among the original seven who walked south together (see *21–22*), and in some accounts he is considered to have been a "sister's son" of Ayakô.

From a presentist perspective this is an unremarkable story, suggesting that interclan relations in the eighteenth century had a tone quite similar to those of today, and it is remembered largely because of the *kúnu* (avenging spirit) relations it established. Today, Saramaka men are commonly caught with other men's wives, and the prior affinal relations in this case make the transgression more serious legally, but hardly unique. Nor are suicides to punish one's own lineage uncommon; and they are threatened rather often, as part of the standard rhetoric of anger. The abduction of a woman as compensation, though it appears in several historical accounts about the eighteenth century, does, however, indicate the gravity of the case. It attests quite clearly to the heightened value of women during the early years in the forest, when there was a severe female shortage, and when the loss of a single woman could mean a serious blow to the collective capacity of the descent group to maintain itself through time. ✤

Paánza's Story

143. The sister's son of the most important Matjáu runaway stole Paánza. He knew her from slavery since she was on the neighboring Kasitú plantation. They had seen each other while working in the fields near each other. When he was in the forest, he ached to see her again. So he went back and stole her from a field where she was cutting rice. She stuffed the rice seeds into her hair and they fled, escaping to Baákawáta. (Peléki 18 April 1968)

144. Now the people of Kasitú, Paánza's people, they were the first people besides Akísiamáu [Wátambíis] that we [Matjáus] brought to the Pikílío. The sister's son of the man grew up until he was causing real difficulties with other men's wives. So he told him to stop it, that he would create a *kúnu* [avenging spirit] if he didn't watch out. And he answered, "Mother's brother, if you want me to stop it, you'll have to go get me a certain wife. Then I'll stay put." Then the older man went back to get her for him. His very own mother's brother went to take her for him. After this happened, he did stay put. And he had children with her. (Kála, instructing Abátelí at cock's crow, 1975)

145. Avó Ayakô had been in the forest for a very long time. He'd been living at Baákawáta, he and his brother Lánu. They had brought Adjágbò there as a youth [*kióo miíi*]. Well,

---

Paánza's Story (143–46)

The story of Paánza, in its simplest form, is a moving love story; but on closer inspection, it may be seen also to reflect conflicting claims about interclan relations, as well as being a vehicle for the preservation of some fascinating glimpses of early plantation and maroon life. Paánza's descendants became the Kasitú clan, today centered in the Pikílío village of Bêndêkôndè and its lower-river offshoot, Kapasíkèè. Because their collective "father" is the Matjáu Adjágbò, they possess their lands, ritual prerogatives, and other rights as clients of the Matjáus. However, relations between the groups have long been delicate. Late-eighteenth-century Matjáus believed that the elderly Adjágbò was favoring his own children (the Kasitús) over his sisters' children (the Matjáus), and many of his most valuable possessions (inherited from Ayakô, Lánu, and others)—in particular, his *óbias*—were in fact passed on exclusively to his Kasitú sons. The bitterness engendered by this conflict is reflected in the ways in which Paánza's story is told today.

Fragment *143* represents one of my first hearings of any First-Time narrative, told me spontaneously by Peléki in 1968. Its essence: the slave Adjágbò (though not mentioned by name) loves Paánza and escapes to the forest; he later returns to liberate her. She leaves with him, carrying rice seeds in her hair; and they live happily ever after.* Comparison to later fuller versions I heard—some of which also came from Peléki—reveals what was here omitted, masked, or conflated: there is nothing in *143* about Paánza's ancestry or siblings. Adjágbò (the

---

* I remain unsure about the meaning of the bringing of rice seeds in a woman's hair, today attributed by Saramakas to Paánza, and by Matawáis to Tjówa (see *59–60*). (One visitor to the Maroons claimed that it was "widely believed" that their female ancestors had hidden rice in their hair in Africa and thus transported it all the way to Suriname—Vaillant 1948:522.) Saramakas, extrapolating from the tradition that Paánza brought rice seeds, claim that before her arrival, their only rice was *mátu alísi* ("forest-," or "wild-rice"), which they grow today solely for ritual use. And at the shrine of Awónêngè, when special meals are prepared for the First-Time people, it is always *mátu alísi* that is used. I suspect that the raiders who liberated Paánza returned with an important new variety of rice, but that cultivated hillside (nonwild) rice had already been present in Saramaka; however, I cannot be sure.

they lived there until he took someone's wife [*toóbi sèmbè*], Maáku said. Then they [the people of the wronged husband] came to try to kill them [the Matjáus]. Well they lived . . . until he once again took someone's wife, and those people came to try to kill them. By then, Ayakô was ready to kill him too! But before he could, Lánu said, "Don't kill him. Leave the child to me." He called him over and said [gently], "What's wrong? What is doing this to you? You go to one woman, you screw her, then you go to the next, you screw her, but you stay with none. If you don't stop this, Ayakô will really kill you." Adjágbò said, "Mother's brother, it's because I had someone I loved, when we were on the coast, in the savannahs at Djúgoón." "What do they call her?" "Paánza." "Paánza, huh? You and she loved each other?" "Yes. That's the problem. I keep thinking of her. I can't see another woman without thinking of her." "Is that what's really bothering you, then?" Lánu asked.

Lanú called his brother [Ayakô] and spoke with him. He said, "So that's what he said?" Ayakô asked [sarcastically], "Well, does he think he is going to be able to get her himself?" Lánu said that he would do it. Lánu called a council meeting. He prepared everyone [ritually] as fully as he wished. In those days they didn't travel by canoe. Then he set out . . . all the way to the Kasitú plantation, on foot. (My father used to raise his hand when we were on our way downstream to the city to point out the plantation, right there upstream from Lamá [Rama].) There they were cutting rice in the great field, the savannah field, just cutting and cutting that rice. . . . He kept watching for Paánza until suddenly he saw her clearly. He "took" her. He called her. The woman was bending over, arranging the

---

"sister's son") acts completely alone; and there is nothing supernatural implied in this fragment. This is, I think, rather typical of the "sterilized" versions of early history given by Saramakas to a *bakáa*, even one who speaks their language well and lives among them.

In contrast, fragment *144* bears witness to some of the ways that Saramakas typically withhold, mask, and condense historical information *among themselves*. This transcription comes from a tape recording (in which I played no part) of Captain Kála giving a careful lesson in First-Time history to his potential successor at cock's crow. Again, comparison with fuller versions reveals key omissions: Paánza's ancestry and siblings are not mentioned; her plantation is not named (though this may be understood by the younger man because of the "Kasitú" reference); neither Ayakô-Lánu nor Adjágbò is mentioned by name; and nothing is said about the raid/liberation itself. Such a fragment makes clear, I think, why "learning" a historical "story" may take a full lifetime in this society, and why any person's information takes on the fragmented form that it does. (It also makes all the more remarkable the richness of information about the distant past that is in fact collectively preserved by Saramakas.)

The information in *145*, told me by Tebíni, was given to him a half-century ago by Maáku, the famed female Matjáu captain of Kámpu. In terms of its inclusions and omissions, it represents the accepted Matjáu version today. The technique of "boiling" a person, mentioned here incidentally by Tebíni, was one of a number of ways used by Saramakas to gain control over their enemies. As Peléki explained to me (in fact revealing very little about it): "They prepare the *óbia* [ingredients], call your name, put the *óbia* pot on the fire. [Said in the tone used for praying:] 'You see now, Lisáti [RP]. You're the one we've put in the pot here. You're who we're boiling. As we boil you here, you're dizzy, you're so confused you can't walk. Your strength is sapped. You're who we're boiling here.' " He then described boiling a plantation manager to put him to sleep during the whole time a group was raiding and taking supplies. "The watchman would be boiled too. He'd leave the door of the plantation house wide open."

THE EVENTS

harvested rice. He had "boiled" her. In a flash he was standing next to her. She exclaimed, "What's this?" "I have come to take you away, to give you to that lover of yours called Adjágbò. He's not dead. He's in the forest. Let's you and I go together." She hesitated, "What am I to do?" He said, "Let's get going." She was acting as if she didn't know how she could just pick up and leave. He said, "What's this? We're leaving!" She consented. Then she turned around, picked up the rice in one motion, and they were off. The others were eating. When they returned, they didn't see her. They searched high and low for Paánza. The white man's daughter! The whites entered the forest, for they heard she had been taken away. They searched and searched. But Paánza was already in Baákawáta. Avó Adjágbò took her in an instant. (Tebíni 10 August 1976)

146. This story. Matjáus don't know [admit] it. The tribal chief doesn't acknowledge it. Tebíni doesn't acknowledge it. Kála doesn't acknowledge it. But my grandfather Kositán told it to me! These others refuse to hear it.

Mama Paánza . . . was not only Adjágbò's wife. She was his "sister"! [his mother's mother's sister's daughter's daughter] They were both Matjáus. The very same lineage. The white man, he took Paánza's mother and got her pregnant. He took her to live with him. Paánza did not look like a black person. She was light-skinned. But her mother came from Africa. When they saw the mulatto child, the blacks were angry. They didn't want to accept Paánza or her mother as theirs any more, and they no longer treated them well. The whites, too, treated Paánza and her mother badly. The white man couldn't bear to see Paánza, but she was very attractive to him. So he sold her to another white man. She was

---

In *146*, the Matjáu-Kasitú conflict, mentioned above, comes to the fore. This highly "dangerous" version was insisted upon by the Matjáu elder Kositán, who was urging greater generosity toward the Kasitús, at a major 1950s (?) council meeting; his death almost immediately afterwards was attributed to his having told this story in public. (The man from whom I heard it, Otjútju, is Kositán's "great grandson," who is in a privileged position to have heard relevant fragments at many points in his life. As mentioned above [1C], Otjútju is intimately linked to Paánza through his *néséki*, whose own *néséki* was the child of Adjágbò and Paánza.) The details of Paánza's privileged plantation life are not disputed by other Saramakas; I have heard many fragments concerning her special position as one "white man's daughter" and another's preferred mistress. (For Matjáus, this version is dangerous simply because if Adjágbò and Paánza had in fact been consanguines, the Kasitús would really be Matjáus-by-another-name, and would therefore have as their birthright the lands, offices, and privileges they now enjoy by the grace of Matjáu largesse.) I suspect that this consanguineal claim is relatively recent (ca. 1900), and that it was designed as a foil to heavy-handed Matjáu handling of Kasitú rights. To my knowledge, it is not even widely known among Kasitús, but represents a powerful and threatening answer, useful in certain circumstances, to Matjáu pressure on Kasitú rights, particularly rights to land.

Our understanding of Paánza's story can be enriched by combining oral fragments with documentary materials. Paánza would seem to have been born very close to 1705—with Adjágbò knowing her when he was a boy at Matjáu Creek (where Saramakas remained in close contact with the nearby plantations)—and she died between 1775 and 1780 (the inclusive dates of the Pikílío village where she is known to have been buried). Paánza's liberation must have taken place sometime between 1730 (the approximate date of the Matjáu arrival at Baákawáta) and 1740 (when she would have been 35 years old), since Paánza was still young enough when liberated to bear several children with Adjágbò. The location of Paánza's plantation is well known to Saramakas, and her Kasitú descendants are named after it. Just above Rama on the Suriname River

"A Surinam Planter in his Morning Dress." Engraving by William Blake, after a drawing by John Gabriel Stedman (1796: Plate 49). This eighteenth-century Suriname planter is being attended by a quadroon house slave whose position was probably not unlike Paánza's at a similar age.

still a child. Paánza had a brother, Tjapánda. They sold him too. Paánza's mother was Lukéinsi. Her first child, Paánza's older sister, was also called Lukéinsi. The white man would only sell all these people together—Paánza, her mother, her sister, and her brother. That's how the other white man bought them and brought them to work at Kasitú. He took Tjapánda and made him "watchman" for Paánza. He made Lukéinsi, the older sister, Paánza's personal maid. Because Paánza was like a *bakáa*! The man who bought her kept her as if she was his wife.

Once they were sold, these people were off on their own. The Matjáus said, "She took a *bakáa*, broke the rules. She's no longer one of us." But Adjágbò felt pain at this. Ayakô would have nothing more to do with her, but Adjágbò felt sorry for her. Ayakô said that whenever he saw Paánza, it reminded him of the terrible thing the white man had done. But this didn't seem right to Adjágbò. He did not want to leave them behind, when they came to the forest.

Once in the forest, Adjágbò used to pick fights, take other men's wives, do every kind of mischief. Ayakô said to him, "You call me 'mother's brother.' What do you think you're doing, going around creating trouble that I'm left having to settle? You've been giving me trouble since I don't know when. . . . A little more, and they'll kill us because of you! Well, I don't want you to fight any more. You fight whites, you fight slaves, you fight Saramakas. It's no good." Adjágbò answered, "Well, if you don't want me to take other men's wives any more, you should go get that sister of mine, the one with the white father, at Kasitú, and bring her to me. Because [taunting] you're the great leader, you left Paánza to the whites. When we took to the forest, you refused to bring her. If you can

---

lie the adjoining plantations of d'Apas and Steenenberg, both owned during the late 1730s by a family known as Kastilho or Castilho.

Matjáus also preserve the name of Paánza's white father, who sold her to Kastilho—"Hendelíki." And indeed, I find that during the 1730s, Moses Nunes Henriquez owned a plantation only three kilometers downstream from Kastilho. Moreover, Paánza's brother Tjapánda—who marooned to Djuka and appears frequently in Djuka oral traditions as "Kofi Hendiliki Tjapanda"—is often called in archival materials "Coffij Champandro," and apparently lived for a time at plantation Charprendre, another five kilometers downstream.* The Saramaka traditions that insist that the slave crews of the Jewish plantations in this upper Suriname River region were routinely mixed in large harvesting gangs combine with these oral and documentary fragments to flesh out for us Paánza's plantation world, and to describe its boundaries. (See map p. 100.)

A letter that I found in the archives helps to complete the picture. On 28 October 1739, the governor of Suriname laconically described a recent incident to the Directors of the Societeit van Suriname in the Netherlands: a troop of maroons had just attacked the upper Suriname River plantation of Joseph Castilho, killing one white man and taking with them the few slaves that he had (SvS 266, 28 October 1739). It would seem that the lovers Paánza and Adjágbò were finally reunited. ✤

* Saramakas say that Tjapánda eventually took a Saramaka (Nasí) wife, and that they visited back and forth between Djuka and Saramaka. Documents report him to be visiting Saramaka for ritual purposes in 1772 (Hof 87, 26 February 1773 [21 January 1772]). And in 1776, he tried—but was denied permission by the Djuka tribal chief—to settle permanently in Saramaka, probably with his sister's people, the Kasitús (SvS 168, 21 June 1776 [12 June 1776]).

succeed in bringing her here, I'll quit." Ayakô asked, "She's at Kasitú? If we bring her, you'll stop causing trouble?" "Yes." "Well, then, no problem." (He wanted her for a wife, but it was his sister!)

Ayakô prepared [ritually] until he was satisfied. He prepared the *óbia,* Afíima. It was with Afíima that he took her. When he arrived, the person who was guarding Paánza while she was cutting rice . . . he fell asleep. (The *óbia* put Tjapánda, the watchman, to sleep.) Tjapánda was Ayakô's "sister's child," but he wouldn't have recognized Ayakô anymore. If Tjapánda had seen Ayakô! There he was, lying down, with his gun, his machete, everything. Well, Ayakô went and took these things and carried them off to hide them. Then he came and took Paánza. He said, "If you scream, I'll kill you. Because I've already 'killed' [worked *óbia* on] your brother. I am so-and-so and I've come to take you away. So, get ready,and let's get out of here." She "pulled out" her hair, took the rice seeds, and tied it in with the *angísa* [waist kerchief] from her skirt. That was all she needed. He took her to the edge of the forest and said, "You must stay here. I didn't really kill your brother. But if you try to escape, *nothing* can save you. I'll go wake him up so he can come away with his sister." So he went up to the man and knocked him hard with his hand. The man startled and awoke. Ayakô said, "Don't try to do anything. I already 'killed' you. [Taunting] Where's your gun and machete? I am so-and-so. I'm riper than you are! Get up right now and leave whitefolks' slavery! All this time since the white man sold you, and you're still here. Black man, come away to the forest. [Boasting] We already have everything we could want there. We fought. We escaped. And now we've come back here for you. We've taken your sister." Tjapánda's [*komantí*] *óbia* cried out. He jumped up and fled with his other sister in the direction of Djuka.

When Ayakô arrived [in Baákawáta] he said to Adjágbò, "Man, I've brought the woman for you. She's brought us rice." Then Adjágbò lived with her. He loved her so much that he ruined his relations with his own kinsmen. (Otjútju 3 August 1976) ❖

"Plantation 'the two good Friends,' or on the general Map [of Lavaux] called 'Steenbergen' belonging to R. de Castilho." Watercolor by J. H. Rotke, 1746. This lovely watercolor depicts Paánza's plantation as it appeared just seven years after her escape to join the Saramakas. (*CETECO, Diemen, Netherlands*)

THE EVENTS

TOWARD FREEDOM

1749–1759

The Battle of Bákakúun, 1749

147. They were living on the mountain top. And they dug a giant trench running from the very bottom up to the top. It was the only way to get in or out of the village. They cut big logs, just the width of the trench, and many men together rolled them to the top. When the whites came up the path, they did not know that things would come pouring down the trench to kill them. They came up and up until they were close. They could see the blacks. Then they [the Saramakas] released the logs. Well, there was no way to run fast enough to avoid them! They were mashed to a pulp. No way to escape alive. (Peléki 28 June 1976)

A series of vivid but disconnected fragments constitutes the Saramaka memories I have heard of the 1750s. They include traces of continued raids and battles, village movements, interclan rivalries, and the arrival of new groups, as well as a vision of the gradual but irrepressible process of building toward a peace treaty with the whites.

The Battle of Bákakúun, 1749 (147–51)

Saramakas remember the battle of Bákakúun as their finest wartime moment. Accounts from Lángu descendants of Kaási, from Matjáus, and from Nasís are pretty much of a piece: the defenders (in some versions, having first hidden their women and children in the forest) lured the whites up the great ditch and then, just as they approached the summit, rained down boulders and/or tree stumps upon them until they were crushed. The "House of the Wind," recalled in *151*, apparently refers to Bákakúun;* this fragment would seem to be preserving, frozen in time, the feelings of invincibility and pride that Saramakas during the 1740s felt about their greatest stronghold. Today, if a Saramaka knows only one fragment about ancient battles (and, of course, many know none at all) it would probably be that "Bákakúun is where they rained down those stones upon the whites."

I now believe that the battle of Bákakúun took place in November of 1749, during the massive expedition of Captain Lieutenant Carel Otto Creutz, which differed from previous military

---

* We have already met Folú and Wíi in other fragments; Boyón—sometimes called Gbôyèn—is said by Mètisên of Lángu to have been a "brother" of Alándo, the son of Kaási. Matjáus merge these identities, speaking of a single man, Kaási's son, whom they call "Alándo Gwéyan," or "Alándo Gbôyèn."

148. The village was not at the very top of the mountain but on a plateau. There was only one entrance, along a depression. But they had not dug it out. Water, rushing down the mountain had made it, not men. At the top, they poised [*séti*] boulders, all kinds of stones. When the whites approached, they released the stones and finished off the soldiers. (Peléki 30 June 1976)

149. Bákakúun! That's where they rained down those stones upon the whites. They couldn't get up the hill. (Faánsisónu 9 July 1978)

---

expeditions in its explicit goal of building toward a treaty.* By 1749, Governor Mauricius had become convinced that the only way to eliminate what he liked to call the maroon "Hydra" was

> to divide them [the various groups] and, insofar as possible, deal with each in turn. . . . [We should begin by mounting] one massive expedition and, even after conquering one or more villages and inflicting a crushing defeat, make peace, as the saying goes, with sword in hand. (Lichtveld and Voorhoeve 1980:166; SvS 285, 25 January 1750; Hartsinck 1770:768)

Accompanied by hundreds of men, and armed with detailed written instructions about the terms for negotiation with the Saramakas, Creutz set out in September, following the Saramacca River past Tuído (which he bypassed), and by early November arriving in the area of Agámadjá Creek. Sacking and burning villages and gardens throughout the area, the troops arrived at the "last village" on 5 November. As Creutz laconically described it in his journal (reproduced in full in R. Price 1983):

> We marched forward [up the mountain] and were awaited by the runaways on the hilltop, who with a terrifying shouting made it clear to us that they intended to prevent our getting to the top; but we made a charge up the mountain, in a little rush, sending a hail of bullets and hailshot before us, and finally arrived in the village, without their daring to do anything further.

The next day, having determined that "the runaways were now out in the wild forest, where they apparently had earlier hidden their wives and children" (before the battle, just as Saramakas report today), Creutz had the village put to the torch—"84 large houses and a considerable garden"—and sent an emissary out to them to begin the "peace" negotiations. By the time the expedition left for Paramaribo, after eight weeks in the forest, Governor Mauricius's fondest hopes had been realized: Creutz had found and destroyed as many as nine Saramaka villages containing some 415 large houses; he had negotiated a provisional cease-fire with "Adoe" (who said he was acting on behalf of aging Chief Dabí [-tatá Ayakô]);† and they had agreed to sign a final treaty, to be sealed with the transfer of a long list of goods to the Saramakas, the following September. Just as Mauricius had hoped, Creutz had made peace "with sword in hand."

---

* Too many of the potentially relevant archival volumes are sealed for me to feel absolutely certain of having successfully matched documentary accounts with memories of this battle; but Saramaka descriptions of the order (and nature) of events during this period make the scenario I sketch here seem highly probable, given my present information.

† The identity of "Adoe" is problematical, though he seems most likely to have been the man whom Saramakas today call Alúbutu. (By the late 1740s, as we have seen, Alúbutu had been made a kind of deputy to Tribal Chief Dabítatá Ayakô, as a result of having saved the latter's life.) However, Matjáus today insist that the "Adoe" mentioned in Creutz's report is their own ancestor Abíni—indeed, in 1975, they founded a short-lived political organization with the words "Adoe Abini" worked into their Paramaribo-printed logo. Nevertheless, no such connection was drawn by Louis Nepveu, who was the government negotiator both on Creutz's expedition and in 1762, nor by Abíni himself, when discussing the 1749 Peace with Nepveu (see R. Price 1983:document 10).

150. Bákakúun. The whites' guns were useless there. They killed those whites like no-thing. The big ditch. In order to get up the hill, you had to walk in it. They rolled the tree stumps down there, *zálálátjé,* all the way down to the bottom. So many were killed! (Aseedu 22 July 1978)

151. There was a village called Víntuósu ["House of the Wind"] on the Upper River. The whites said they'd come and destroy it. But the elders said, "No way. White men will never subdue Víntuósu. Because Boyón is there. Folú is there. Wíi is there. No way they can subdue Víntuósu!" (Bakáa 29 July 1978)   ✤

If the Saramaka and Dutch accounts of their respective "victories" seem overly discrepant, it is worth noting that each side's version was consciously developed—in one case written down, in the other passed down orally—*independently,* knowing that there would be no chance for the other side to respond.* Accounts of a 1755 battle (discussed in 170C–176C) provide a direct parallel, with each side claiming victory; however, in that case—unlike the present one—there exists independent evidence that demonstrates the relative vulnerability of the written word to manipulation by an interested party. Given the interpretive lessons from that 1755 case, Creutz's offhand description of his troops' assault on Bákakúun need not surprise. We know that he indeed returned to Paramaribo with a promise of peace; but given the strength of the Saramaka traditions about the battle, we cannot be at all sure that, first, Kaási and his people did not make a heroic defense of their hilltop redoubt and rain down those stones upon the whites. Indeed, weighing the bits of evidence currently available, I am strongly inclined to think that they did.†   ✤

* The documented exaggeration of "body counts" during the Vietnam War provides a modern example of this phenomenon; one journalist recounted that "a twenty-four-year-old Special Forces captain was telling me about it. 'I went out and killed one VC and liberated a prisoner. Next day the major called me in and told me I'd killed fourteen VC and liberated six prisoners. You want to see the medal?' " (Herr 1977:172).

† The Windward Maroons of Jamaica used an identical strategem during a battle against British forces in 1732. Their own oral traditions record throwing "sticks" (or logs) down upon the whites; the corresponding military journal describes "great Stones . . . roll'd down the Hill very thick." (This information, kindly supplied by Kenneth Bilby, is discussed in somewhat more detail in R. Price 1983.)

Saramaka wooden signal horn of the type used in the wars. (Hamburgisches Museum für Völkerkunde, photo Antonia Graeber.)

Down From the Mountain, 1750–1755

152. [After the battle of Bákakúun] some Kaapátus came down from the mountain and went to live at the head of Agámadjá Creek. On an arm of Upper Agámadjá Creek, called Kwamá Creek, there were [already] Folú and the Kwamás. The Kadósus also lived on Agámadjá Creek. There were villages all along the creek. (Mètisên 31 July 1978)

153. When we came down off the mountain, Papá Sentéa found the creek. Its head goes right to the mountain range called Wéényè. They called the village Sentéa, after him. (Agbagó 8 July 1978)

154. The Awanás and Dómbis lived together in the village of Sentéa. (Bayo 22 July 1978)

155. The Nasís and Biítus were living at Dosú Creek. With the [Túfínga] Indians. They lived there until after the Peace of Sentéa [1762]. (Góme 20 July 1978)

156. On the Gaánlío, we lived at Líomáu Creek. That's Abaísa territory. The creek above [current] Sitónuku is an Abaísa creek too. (Lántifáya 23 July 1978)

157. When those others settled in the Gaánlío area, the Matjáus still lived in Baákawáta. The Wátambíis and Paánza's people were with them. There were footpaths in those days. The main one began just above Sentéa Rapids and came over to Baákawáta. My father took me to see it. (Tebíni 24 July 1976) ✣

Down from the Mountain, 1750–1755 (152–57)

After the battle of Bákakúun, most of the people who had been living on the mountain moved down into the watershed of the Gaánlío, joining those who had built villages there during the previous decade. Saramaka evidence about village sites for this period is contained in songs, ritual, and oral fragments related to place names and contemporary events. By combining these with the extremely complex documentary sources from the 1760s, I have been able to reconstruct a general picture of village geography in the final decade before the Peace. (Detailed discussion of this evidence is presented in Price n.d.) ✣

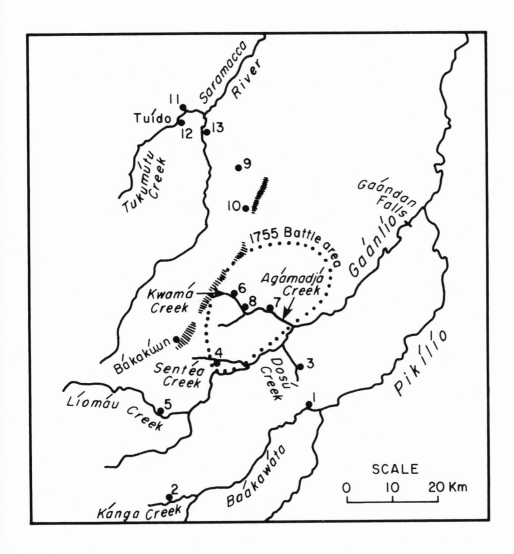

Main Village Locations, 1750s (Approximate) (Documentation is in Price n.d.)

1. Matjáus-Wátambíis
2. Kasitús (and later, Papútus)
3. Nasís-Biítus
4. Awanás-Dómbis-Agbós
5. Abaísas
6. Lángus (Kaapátus)
7. Lángus (Kadósus)
8. Kwamás
9. Lángus
10. Lángus
11. Matawáis
12. Matawáis
13. Matawáis

The Sinking at Gaándan Falls, 1750

158. Ayakô told Samsám, the Abaísa, that he was "going hunting" [that is, going to scout out the whites]. Ayakô left Samsám to take care of the village and went upstream. In the meantime, the whites arrived. Samsám told them to unload the presents while he went to fetch Ayakô. But he warned them that Ayakô was a very fierce man who might decide to kill them. "If you hear me hitting the tree roots [buttresses] with my machete on my return, run for your lives! It will mean Ayakô is coming to kill you." Samsám went off into the forest, but he didn't go far. After a while, he began hitting the tree roots with his machete and yelling, "Run for your lives! Dabítatá [Ayakô] is coming to kill you." The whites took to their heels. There were two blacks as well. They were all in one canoe. The man at the head of the boat was Kwasímukámba, a black in the employ of the whites. The canoe smashed over Gaándan Falls. Everyone was killed except for Kwasímukámba, who got away and returned to the city to tell what happened.

When Ayakô returned, he saw the presents, and he and Samsám divided them. The Matjáus and Abaísas shared the spoils. But Ayakô did not know that Samsám had killed the whites; he thought the presents had been properly received. Only later, at a great meeting, did Saramakas decide that no one—under severe [supernatural] penalty—could ever disclose to outsiders what really happened. (Otjútju August 1975)

The Sinking at Gaándan Falls, 1750 (158–61)

This most dangerous of all Saramaka First-Time stories describes the breaking of the 1749 Peace, provisionally established during Creutz's expedition. The central incident has been successfully protected by an elaborate cover-up for more than two centuries: in fact, no single event in Saramaka history posed a greater challenge in my fieldwork. "What really happened" in 1750 remained a crucial issue in the negotiations between whites and Saramakas for the next twenty years; it has remained a live issue among historically-minded Saramakas right into the present.

The bare background, as culled from the documents, can quickly be sketched. In March 1750, Governor Mauricius's political enemies persuaded the Council to renege on their part of Creutz's 1749 agreements regarding the treaty-signing ceremony and large gift distribution slated for the following September. Instead, they resolved to send a small delegation to Saramaka immediately—unannounced and five months before the date agreed upon with the Saramakas—to (once again) "sound out their sentiments" (GA 556, 20 March 1750). In April 1750, three whites including Sublieutenant François Picolet, a member of the Council, and Corporal Knelke—both of whom had been along on Creutz's expedition—accompanied by some twenty slaves set out for Saramaka bearing a small quantity of gifts. The expedition was never directly heard from again.

Instead, diverse indications began to reach the government as to its fate. (I list only the highlights here; see also R. Price 1983.) In January 1751, a leader of the raid on a Para River plantation was identified as a slave who had been on Picolet's expedition (SvS 287, 18 January 1751; SvS 201, 16 January 1751).* The following month, two Saramaka prisoners captured during

* Given the standard number of deserters from military expeditions to Saramaka—which often reached 50 percent of the slave force—it is highly likely that some of Picolet's men slipped off early on. Indeed, while modern Saramaka notions that Picolet finally arrived with two whites and a handful of blacks in a single canoe may be merely poetic compression, it is certainly not inconceivable that his twenty slaves and, perhaps, two canoes had in fact dwindled in this fashion by the time of his arrival on the Gaánlío.

159. Abíni met them [the whites, as they were coming upstream] at the mouth of the Sara Creek. He warned them not to go further, saying, "If you go now, you'll meet with evil. Let me go instead." But they insisted. They gave him the paper right there, at the mouth of the Sara Creek. But they didn't listen to his advice. Kwasímukámba was their guide. He consulted his *óbia*, and it said they would arrive safely. Well, they got to where Samsám was. (Tebíni 24 July 1976)

160. Samsám thought, "At last! It's in the bag now!" And he told the whites, "I'll go tell everyone else, at Sentéa, at Bákakúun, at Baákawáta." (This happened at Okóbúka, just below Béndiwáta and above Asigoón; just above Tomákôndè, at the straightaway in the river.) That's where Samsám met them. He told them to wait, he would go tell people. Because [he said] the others would kill the whites if they just showed up. And he told them to bring their cargo on shore, to unload everything. So they brought ashore all the goods intended for the peacemaking. Every single one! Then Samsám went off a bit. And he began hitting the tree trunks, *búnguung, búnguung, búngun, búngun,* over and over. When he came in sight, he yelled, "For God's sake, run for your lives. I went to those people, but they were so hostile that if you meet them, evil! Please run!" And they ran. Well that was the end of that! Then they descended Gaándan Falls, and of all those people, only one came out alive—Kwasímukámba. (Tebíni 28 July 1976)

161. After the sinking at Gaándan Falls, the whites decided they weren't going to come to the Gaánlío [to make peace with Saramakas] any more. (Tebíni 24 July 1976)   ✛

---

another plantation raid reported that Picolet and his men were prisoners of the Saramakas, were alive, and were being treated well (SvS 201, 18 February 1751, 3 March 1751). However, other captives from this same raid denied the story (SvS 201, 20 February 1751), causing the governor to comment ruefully that "the sources of our knowledge about all this are highly Confused and Romanesque," especially since all our information to date "rests solely on the word of blacks" (SvS 201, 18 February 1751). Meanwhile, Picolet's wife filed a complaint with the Court, citing the "Deplorable State to which she and her two children have been reduced . . . [having] no way of knowing whether her husband is alive or dead" (SvS 288, 2 October 1751). Later in the year, the widow of the owner of Plantation Mayacabo gave a gripping description of a November raid (R. Price 1983:document 5) in which her husband had lost his life, relating how the Saramaka raiders had made a special point of giving her a message for the governor: the three missing whites were alive, but if he wanted them he would have to come free them (SvS 288, November 1751). In March 1752, a Saramaka captured during a raid reported that Picolet was still alive, though his two white companions were now dead (SvS 202, 13 March 1752). And the following year Jan Pietje, a slave who had marooned but soon after turned himself in, declared before the Court that he had been told during his brief stay in Saramaka that "the three whites who had been sent . . . to make peace were still alive, and that the runaways were now holding them, just in case" (SvS 291, 29 January 1753).

A decade later, during the final peace negotiations of 1762, the whites remained keenly interested in the events of 1750. The fifteenth article of the treaty (R. Price 1983:document 11) is devoted solely to the issue of how to deal with the unnamed "murderers" of Picolet; and the government representatives lost no time, at their first opportunity, to interrogate both Abíni (twice) and Dabí intensely about the incident (SvS 154, 4 May 1762 [6 March 1762] [1 April 1762];

SvS 155, 20 April 1763 [4 November 1762]—all reproduced in R. Price 1983). Dabí's speech, though the least detailed of the three, is directly to the point:

> We are unjustly accused of having broken the Peace made with Mr. Creutz by murdering the whites who came bearing the agreed-upon presents. We are not guilty of their deaths. Indeed, we avenged their deaths by executing their own slaves, who had committed the murder. Have we not been misled by these blacks, just as the whites were? Instead of rejoicing, have we not come blowing the trumpet of war, saying that the presents came with a commando to destroy us? I say again, our people are innocent in this affair. (SvS 155, 20 April 1763 [4 November 1762])

It seems clear even from this scant summary of the documentary evidence that during the 1750s and 1760s Saramakas were taking great pains and using considerable imagination to manipulate the information that the whites were receiving about Picolet. From a Saramaka perspective, the cover-up was primarily designed to protect the Abaísas, for if it had been established that Samsám was the perpetrator, the government would never—Saramakas claim—have given the Abaísas a captain's staff or their share of the tribute. Yet the conspiracy was faithfully maintained by the Matjáus as well, since they were implicated as accessories, having—however unwittingly—split and enjoyed Samsám's spoils. Wedded by the events of 1750, these two rival groups uneasily maintained a cover-up that lasted for two and a quarter centuries.*

It was only in the early twentieth century that the cover-up was partially pierced, when the indefatigable missionary Father Morssink was given a fragment stating that Picolet and his men were killed at Gaándan Falls (Morssink n.d.:31, 33). During my 1960s field trips, I learned no more than that Picolet was indeed killed at Gaándan. In 1975, however, after a long, fruitless discussion with some older men at Djumú Mission, as I awaited the light plane that would begin my journey back to the States for the year, I was privately approached by Otjútju, who told me to meet him at the deserted airstrip where he would reveal what others dared not. Fragment *158* is a summary of what he told me, culled from notes handwritten while I was quite feverish with malaria; he told me that this version was told to him by his late Matjáu "great grandfather," Kositán, who himself had in turn learned it from his father, the Abaísa Adobóidi. It was this version, later retold by me as if it were well known to outsiders (as it logically could be, given Kwasímukámba's alleged return to the city with the news), that opened the doors to whole cycles of tales about treachery toward the whites. Fuller accounts of Samsám's act followed from this. Fragments *159–61*, from Tebíni, constitute my most coherent single account.†

Matjáu accounts of the sinking at Gaándan Falls stress the perfidy of Samsám and his betrayal of Ayakô, continuing the theme of their rivalry in their earlier accounts of settling the Upper River region (see *41*). In contrast, they depict their own ancestor Abíni as trying to uphold the ceasefire by warning the whites at the mouth of the Sara Creek, where they happened to meet, and receiving, in return, a "paper" or "letter." (Abíni's receipt of this paper—considered as a

---

* Hartsinck, whose monumental *Beschrijving*, written in the late 1760s, was based largely on official correspondence from Suriname to Holland, claimed in a passing reference that Samsám was the principal in the Picolet murder: "A certain Zamzam, chief of the Papa Village, who had not been present at the making of the Peace, intercepted the emissaries and murdered them all in a night" (Hartsinck 1770:777). I believe, however, that he simply inferred this information from misreading a 1767 report (SvS 331, 28 March 1767 [4 January 1767]); indeed, the fact that he surreptitiously deleted from his book the fifteenth article of the treaty, which shows that the whites did *not* connect Samsám to the murder of Picolet, suggests that he deliberately tried to remove any doubts his account might raise. (And all later published accounts that mention "Zamzam" simply copy Hartsinck.)

† There remain ambiguities in my oral materials concerning the clan affiliations of Samsám and Abámpapá—with some modern Abaísas claiming the latter but denying the former as their own, some Maipá (Kwamá) people claiming both Samsám and Abámpapá as theirs, and Matjáus and other clans viewing them as having been Abaísa and Kwamá, respectively. These apparent contradictions seem to stem, at least in part, from late-eighteenth-century shifts in clan composition and definition. For example, there is evidence that in the 1770s the Abaísas constituted only one major segment of the village that Samsám then headed (Hof 87, 26 February 1773 [12 February 1772]; SvS 167, 23 October 1775). (See, for detailed discussion, Price n.d.)

promise or token of future presents and staffs of office—is included in a number of Matjáu fragments relating to the preliminaries to the 1762 Peace; it seems to be connected to several actual events depicted in documents from the period, including those discussed in 197C–201C, below.)

The inclusion of the guide Kwasímukámba in these fragments is a poetic device. The documents make clear that during the wars there were many guides who were either born Saramakas, or who had joined the Saramakas and then deserted back (or were sent back) to the whites; but today, Saramakas consistently use the powerful image of Kwasímukámba—the prototypical secret agent (see *170–76*)—to stand for them all, in their stories. Saramakas often claim that one person escaped alive to "tell the whites the story," or in some versions that an African guide turned into a parrot and flew back to the city to tell the story, or even that a specially trained parrot itself flew back to tell the story—a convention that I interpret in part as grudging admiration on the part of Saramakas for the intelligence activities of their white adversaries. It must have sometimes seemed that the whites, with their magical powers of writing and technological skills, knew bits of information that would otherwise have been difficult to explain. Because of the nature of the event itself and the pact of eternal silence, it is not surprising that what is known (or admitted) today about the sinking at Gaándan Falls is fragmentary and contradictory. Abaísas, in my talks with them, vigorously denied the participation of their ancestors in the sinking, though they acknowledged having heard about the event itself. A Lángu man once proudly claimed that Bákisipámbo, not Samsám, was the perpetrator, while a descendant of Folú once made a similar claim about his man. In neither of these cases, however, was the speaker aware that complex political claims were at stake; rather, each was simply nominating his ancestor for what seemed at face value to be a heroic role.*

Saramakas commemorate the sinking at Gaándan Falls in two place names. The site of the sinking itself is called Potiléti ("straighten out") because as the canoe approached the falls, the last frantic commands of the whites were "potiléti, potiléti" to prevent overturning.† Yelling "potiléti," the crew rode into the falls, as one Saramaka said, with a "whoosh" and then a "bang."‡ A few miles downstream from Potiléti lies a sandbank still called Maátasándu ("Mulatto Sandbank"). It is said that it was there, several days after the sinking, that the bodies of Picolet's slaves were found, washed up by the great river.

Once, after hearing me mention Potiléti, an old Abaísa (who had claimed ignorance of who killed the whites) exclaimed excitedly to a friend: "That's where they finished off the *bakáa*s [outsiders]. Because one year, I remember that someone was going to make a garden there, down below Gaándan Falls, where they buried the *bakáa*s. At Maátasándu. So they realized that they couldn't make a garden there after all. Even though they had already cleared away the under- ~~on battlefields~~ growth!" This is, then, a fine example of how the naming and ritualization of geographic places keeps alive for Saramakas the meaning of the distant past.   ❖

---

* Published accounts based on oral fragments also mention the murder of white emissaries bearing gifts to Saramaka: Johannes King, the nineteenth-century Matawái evangelist, wrote a detailed description of how his ancestors tricked a group of whites coming to make peace and killed them all in a night (King 1983; for an English translation, see Price 1979b:300); and Junker took down a version from a Lángu man in 1920, which accused the Nasís of having killed two white emissaries (1922/23:463–64). I am unable to link any of these alternative traditions firmly to the documentary record.

† I suspect that Morssink's implication that Saramakas knew the name of the white leader of the expedition as "Pikoleti" stems from his misunderstanding their speaking about the place called Potiléti. In any case, I myself made this error at first.

‡ Gaándan Falls is indeed a formidable gauntlet to try to run. As the field geologist Ijzerman described it in the 1920s: "[The great river] has narrowed down here to a channel 10 meters wide, hollowed out in the granite, over which the water rushes with a tremendous force" (1931:115; see also his plate 14, facing page 212, for a photo). From above the falls, the water in fact appears quite smooth; it is only at the last instant that one sees the big drop.

The Coming of the Agbós

162. Sofía and her daughter Sialôtò, they were women from slavery days. Kekí Anáisa—a Maipá [Kwamá] man—and an Awaná caught them. The Awaná was probably Vumá because there weren't so many youngsters in those days, only great men. Well, they caught the women. I think they were [related to] Sara Creek Djukas, Mísidjáns. Sofía was a leper; she was Alábi's mother-in-law. Alábi's wife was Sialôtò. (Góme 21 July 1978)

163. The children of Alábi and Sialôtò are the Agbó clan. When Sofía died, they buried her at the mouth of the creek [now called Sofí Creek]. (Bakáa 29 July 1978)   ✚

The Coming of the Agbós (162–63)

These fragments concern the origin of one of the several Saramaka groups known as "Agbó," a word that Saramakas say means "wanderer" or "someone who has committed a crime."* Góme's reference to Vumá, and his interesting anachronistic comment that in those days there were only great men, suggests no firm tradition about the Awaná "finder" of the women. (One would, however, expect such traditions to be preserved, for related but different reasons, by the descendants of both the "finders" and those who were "found.") Other Awaná traditions suggest that Vumá died well before the Peace, and that this raid took place later, in the 1750s, when Sialôtò would have been a teenager.

Although literally hundreds of women must have been liberated on raids during the eighteenth century, all but a handful were assimilated conceptually (by genealogical fictions) into existing Saramaka groups and are not remembered as individuals today. The exceptions include Sofía/ Sialôtò, Paánza, and Piyái's Indian sister, each of whom is credited with founding a major matrilineal group. In the present case, these Agbós derive their special identity from Sialôtò's husband, their collective father, Alábi, tribal chief from the 1780s until 1820.

The German missionary diaries confirm that Alábi married Sialôtò during the early 1770s and that they had children together.† The special burial of Alábi's mother-in-law, at the mouth of the creek familiar to all Upper River Saramakas, is commemorated in the name Sofí Creek. To any Saramaka, its name implicitly preserves as well the memory of her illness: Saramakas do not bury lepers in cemeteries or with a coffin, instead simply interring the body in the bank of the river.
    ✚

* Potentially, there is an implicit genealogical tie between the two main Agbó groups—Asukúme's descendants in Soolán (who on genealogical grounds would be expected to be considered Dómbis) and Sialôtò's descendants (said in *162* to be Mísidján-related), who live among the Awanás. I have, however, never heard this connection mentioned by Saramakas. Jozefzoon derives the name of Sialôtò's group from the Kwamá *óbia* called Agbó; if true, this might provide a nominal link between the groups, if the Soolán Agbós had at some time been significantly helped by it.

† Jozefzoon, in a typically confused foray into oral history, depicts Alábi as marrying Sofía rather than Sialôtò (1959:12).

Adugwé's Indian

164. At that time, [the Dómbi] Adugwé had gone on a raid to the city. He had been hiding under the wharf at Paramaribo Creek. Then, when he got to Wefíngóto, he leaned up against a tree to rest. That's where the Indian spotted him. He took his bow and drew it back *háán, gbá*! The arrow went [made the sound] *heei, tjím*! It got him right in the collarbone. Stuck right in. He had to break it apart in pieces to get any of it out. He limped all the way to Púupángi Creek, and there he climbed a cashew tree. He took a liana and tied it around the remaining stub of the arrow until it was really tight. And then he yanked it out. His bone was broken! He opened his hunting sack. He took the Nawí *biòngò* and sprinkled a bit of it into the wound, *tê tê tê*. Until the day it was completely healed.

Well, the Peace finally came [1762]. They sat down to make the Peace at Sentéa. And that Indian came with the whites. They all sat down. Adugwé recognized the Indian. He kept pointing first to his collarbone, then to the Indian. Back and forth, slowly, sitting in that council meeting. The Indian began crying. The [white] officer asked him what was wrong. What happened next I don't know, but they killed the Indian there. (Bakáa 28 July 1978)

165. The person who told you this [*164*] did not know the full story. They had gone on a raid. They had caught [liberated] people. Then, as they were leaving, the Indian shot him. He hadn't seen the Indian. After the Indian shot him, he climbed the tree. But then he went after that Indian and caught him. . . . The Indians were really two. At the time he was shot, Adugwé was able to kill one of them. He cut off his head. Later, he caught the other one. He kept him for three days. Each day, he showed him the wound. The Indian would avert his eyes. This happened three times. Then, Adugwé killed him. (Tebíni 6 August 1978)   ✣

Adugwé's Indian (164–65)

This incident concerns Kúngoóka's famous brother-in-law, who played an important role (though he was not referred to by name) in "Kúngoóka's Story, Part 1" (*125* above). Like Kúngoóka's wife Dína, Adugwéungo—usually just called Adugwé—is remembered as the child of Sêsi, Momóimítji's "sister." This incident would seem to date from the early 1750s, while the Dómbis were living with the Awanás in their village at Sentéa Creek. My two fragments come from a non-Dáume Dómbi and from Tebíni, who has close Dáume connections. I first heard of this incident too late in my last stay in Saramaka to enrich or explore these fragments further. Nor have I yet been able to match the reported killing of the Indian at the Peace celebration with any documentary account.

From a Saramaka perspective, the story would seem to be preserved as part of the store of miracles attributed to the great *óbia* of Dáume, but it alludes to other matters of historical interest as well—the ambiguous role of Indians during the wars and the esoteric rituals of battlefield death. Saramaka memories of wartime Indians seem realistic and unromantic (and fit closely with what documents record): Indians harbored Lánu and his group at a crucial moment (*1, 4*); they aided Kaási throughout his early years in the forest (*50*); they made (often-reluctant) wives for several early Saramakas (*183–84*); and, as in this case, they often served the whites as scouts, guides, or bounty seekers, hunting down maroons for cash. (See also R. Price 1983.)

The matter-of-fact reference by Tebíni to Adugwé's cutting off the first Indian's head assumes knowledge by the listener of a whole complex of ritual and belief that involves both self-

"The Sculls of Lieu.ᵗ Leppar, & Six of his Men." Detail of an engraving by William Blake, after a 1773 drawing by John Gabriel Stedman (1796:Plate 25). Stedman depicted himself (right) mournfully contemplating his former companions' skulls, which had been ritually severed by his maroon adversaries.

---

protection from avenging spirits (see Price 1973) and central Saramaka ideas about manhood, derived in part from West African antecedents. As Peléki once told me: "In those days, until you killed someone and cut off his head, you were not a real man. . . . And if you didn't cut off the head, you hadn't really killed him. You hadn't mastered him. The head-cutting *is* the killing of a man. Because if you don't know how to do it, he'll come back to kill you." The proper handling of the severed head was undoubtedly complex. The related hunting rites performed after killing a large animal (for example, a deer, but especially a tapir), which I have witnessed, have the same explicit goal—to settle its spirit permanently so it will not return to take vengeance. Neither those whites who accused the maroons of wanton barbarity because of head cutting (for example, Stedman 1988:124, 398, 638) nor modern historians discussing the practice (for example, de Groot 1980) seem fully to have grasped its deeper significance as crucial self-protection and as a special source of power.* In the shrines of certain Saramaka *gaán óbias*, while preparing to go to battle, men drank from vessels made from the sawed-off skulls of their white enemies (see also Pakosie 1972). ✢

* Europeans, of course, have their own long tradition of dismembering corpses and displaying trophy heads—as in the many gruesome public executions of slaves in Suriname, as well as in war. Their intent, however—to incite terror as a means of control—was quite different from that of the Saramakas. In an unpublished paper, Saskia Keller suggests that the severing of heads as the crowning act in the "theatrical punishments" inflicted upon Suriname slaves may have also been motivated by the planters' conviction that the slaves themselves believed that head cutting disallowed the possibility of their being reborn in Africa as a whole person. Documentation for this notion in Suriname is, as yet, lacking—see Bastide 1965:11. Axtell and Sturtevant (1980) provide an excellent review of closely related practices, and their significance, among American Indians and their Euro-American adversaries.

THE EVENTS

Kúngoóka's Story, Part 2

166. Well, Kúngoóka and his brother-in-law were very close. ([To me:] His name was Adugwéungo, or simply Adugwé. Kabiténi Atjóko of Dáume just told me this the other day.) In the war years they were inseparable, going off on raids together, burning the whites' plantations, stealing everything, bringing it back home. They became like brothers. They killed whites together. Then when he became too old, he told Adugwé to go on a raid without him. Kúngoóka prepared him [ritually]. And he left. The time for his return came and went. There was no sign of him. Kúngoóka's wife's people "isolated" him [*butá bên a kapêè*, what is done as a first step to one responsible for a murder]. They said he had killed one of them, had sent him off to his death. In two weeks, they said, they would execute him. Well, he went to check his *óbia*, and it revealed that his brother-in-law was still alive.* But his wife's people would have nothing to do with him. He was left all alone. Days passed. He consulted the *óbia*. It said he was unharmed. The wife's people chose a day a week hence for the execution. "If he's not back by then, we shall kill you!" He consulted his *óbia*. It told him not to worry. The day before the execution, Adugwé appeared at the village gate. Did the old man celebrate! He said, "Who is this? You, brother-in-law?" They embraced and called their praise names. Then the old man emerged from the *óbia* house, *vóóm* [intensifier]. He flew! He flew above the house, circling it three times. Then he alit *tjêngèè* [intensifier]. And he called out to his wife's lineage, "You see the person you said I'd killed, right here with your own eyes? Well, take him. Whatever you've learned from me is yours. But that which I haven't yet taught you will stay [with me]." That's why Dáume people can't fly. He didn't give them that part of the *óbia*! (Peléki 27 July 1976)   ❖

---

* Some versions are more explicit about the "mechanics" of the *óbia*, which had been prepared in a clay pot: so long as the liquid was boiling, the missing person was safe; if it turned red, he was wounded; and if it boiled away, he was almost home (see also Jozefzoon 1959:11).

Kúngoóka's Story, Part 2 (166)

One of the keenest disappointments of my last field season was the illness of the favorite wife of one of the captains of Dáume, who was at last ready to work with me on a number of historical issues. Failing that, I am forced to rely on this second-hand version from Peléki, who had heard it shortly before from this captain himself.

The story, closely wrapped up with the history of the great *óbia* of Dáume (see *125*), balances Kúngoóka's warm relationship with his brother-in-law against his permanent and precarious status in the village as an outsider and affine. Its reference to "flying" is meant to be taken quite literally: this was a gift said to have been possessed by various African-born Surinamers, as diverse as the Awaná Vumá (see *96*) and the enemy secret agent Kwasímukámba (see *176*).

Adugwé's famous raid most likely occurred while the Dómbis were at Sentéa, during the waning years of the war. Those scattered fragments that I have heard from Saramakas describing Kúngoóka's residence are limited to later periods. They tell how the aged Kúngoóka lived near Kudébaku Creek on the Gaánlío (where the Dómbis had a village during the mid-1770s) and how he finally moved to Kofí Creek, near where Dáume is located today. The German Moravian diaries provide a touching vision of a man who may very well have been Kúngoóka, at the very end of his life. On a visit to a village he called "Coppi," in 1781, one of the missionaries wrote of meeting "an

The Great Papá Contest

167.

Dokubónsu wíni Doísa
Gamánti dè gbèdé, gamantí bái moyôn
Ma dí Doísa kó wíni Dokubónsu
Hên gamantí dè gbèdé, awó kabái wiyê.
—(Tebíni 24 July 1976)

---

old captain who is the most respected servant of the idols and with his magic produces the greatest deceptions. One can actually see the evil spirits in his eyes" (Staehelin 1913–1919, 3:ii:48). And by 1788, the missionaries were referring to the village at that place as "Dagome." Kúngoóka—who must have been born soon after 1700 and come to Suriname and fled to the forest in the 1740s—seems to have died in the 1780s, in the village that (in spite of minor moves within a small area) is still called after his African birthplace (Dahomey), Dáume. In lighter moments, when a nickname is called for, Saramakas celebrate Kúngoóka's legacy by using an alternative name: "Kôndèbúnu," the "Village of Good." ❖

The Great Papá Contest (167–68)

Saramakas express the rivalry between Matjáus and Abaísas in various ways. One of its neatest formulations—in the ritual language known as Papá—recalls a famous singing contest. *Papá* performances take place as the climactic event of funerals. They last throughout the night, and a good deal of liquor is customarily consumed. Each song has a leader and a chorus. This famous contest involved two leaders—one Matjáu and one Abaísa—who agreed to sing, as it were, "to the death."*

This story is not normally told in narrative form. Fragment *168* is part of an explanation for me of a veiled reference I had overheard in speech to "the thing of Dokubónsu and Doísa." Today, the story is elliptically invoked by knowledgeable Matjáus whenever confronted by an Abaísa in a particularly tight situation. In such a context, it would mean, "You have beaten me today, but tomorrow I will beat you doubly."

As an extended example of the uses of First-Time by Saramakas, I quote part of a conversation between Peléki and Tebíni that I was able unobtrusively to record in 1976. (Since this is a fragment of normal Saramaccan speech, it contains a good bit of redundancy as well as veiled allusions.) Peléki was reminiscing:

> I was having some trouble with Abaísas in Sántigoón. And I spoke the thing [the Papá formula]. I said, "It already happened in early times." There was the [Abaísa] fellow called Asantíkáki, with the Abaísa man called Adantífi who is in charge of Bòòfángu there.† Well, I said to them, "The thing these youngsters are talking about, when I adultered with the wife of that [Abaísa] fellow. Well, they beat me up. [So], I don't owe anything further to them. Once they beat me up, I should be able to assume

---

* I tentatively date this contest to the 1750s, after the sinking at Gaándan Falls, but I do not have genealogical connections for the protagonists.

† Bòòfángu is a *gaán óbia* of the Abaísas, traditionally located at a shrine at Tjíbihédi but during the past decades moved to Sántigoón, near the coast. Its specialty is difficult *yoóka* ("ghosts"). Whenever, for example, a pregnant woman dies anywhere in Saramaka, Bòòfángu priests will be summoned to supervise the funeral.

168. The Abaísas and Matjáus met at a *papá* performance. They were enemies; it was to be a grudge match. They agreed on the rules for the contest: the first one to doze off would be killed. Well, the Matjáu, he was the first to doze off. That was Doísa. So Dokubónsu, the Abaísa, had bested him. He "killed" him; he knocked him with a club. But Doísa wasn't dead! They gave him water and he regained consciousness [*a wéki báka*]. So they returned to the contest and continued playing. And then Dokubónsu was the one to doze off. Well, Doísa knocked him *bôbô bólo* dead! He killed him. (Tebíni 28 July 1976).

❖

---

that the thing is finished. But it seems not to be finished for them! They continue to hound me. Well, I'm telling Adantífi publicly now; get those [Abaísa] 'children' of yours off my back. Lánganéki, Kombésónu [other older Abaísa men of the village], call them off! Tell them they mustn't become victims of I-told-you-so. But if they want I-told-you-so, they'll get it, a broken bottle in the face! . . . [more of the same boasting threats] Because that's the way it happened in early times. *Dokubónsu bi wíni. . . .*" [He speaks the whole Papá fragment.] Then Adantífi called out, "You, those Abaísa boys! I'm warning you. Those people called Matjáus, when you go out looking to catch them, you never succeed in bringing them home."

Tebíni greeted the climax of Peléki's story with excited shouts of "Perfect! Perfect!" In this way, then, an obscure event of more than two hundred years ago continues to serve Matjáus in their ongoing interactions with their traditional rivals, the Abaísas.

The choice of *papá*-playing as the idiom for expressing Matjáu-Abaísa rivalry is not gratuitous. Abaísas, since the time of their collective escape nearly three hundred years ago, have referred to themselves by variants of this name (Alabaisa, Labadissa), derived from the Labadist owners of their plantation (see 34C–41C above). Outsiders (non-Saramakas) during the eighteenth century, however, generally called them instead "Papa negers," and their village "Papa Dorp."*

Today, Abaísas and Matjáus are considered the best Saramaka *papá* players, with everyone (including Matjáus) agreeing that the Abaísas are the true masters. However, Matjáus consider themselves superior in the other two "plays" associated with funerals—*adugbá*, the drums played just after the *papá*, beginning at cock's crow on the climactic morning of Saramaka funerals, and *adjú*, the drums that follow them at full dawn to accompany the final chasing of the ghost from the village. Basiá Tandó, a Matjáu who is a pretty fair *papá* player himself, tells a neat tale to explain this division of labor and knowledge.

Once, an Abaísa man married a Matjáu woman. A Matjáu man married an Abaísa woman. They went off, all four of them, to make a garden together. (It was on the site of an old cemetery but they didn't know that.) In the evening, the two Matjáus fell asleep but the Abaísas didn't. And the dead people began to play *papá*, all night long until cock's crow. Then the Abaísas fell asleep and the Matjáus awoke. The dead people began to play *adugbá*. Until full dawn. Then they began the *adjú*. The Abaisas slept right through the *adjú*. Which is why each clan knows what it does.

When Matjáu *papá* players like Tandó are invited as specialists to play at a funeral and are presented with the traditional baskets full of cloths, bottles of rum, and so on, they always transfer the baskets' contents as well as the rum to their own containers, brought for the purpose. But when the Abaísa *papá/aladá* masters perform at a funeral, it is always their prerogative, and their practice, to go home with baskets, rum bottles, and all. ❖

* It is quite possible that the original Labadist maroons included a disproportionate number of Papá (Popo, "Slave Coast") people. Before 1700, the Slave Coast contributed nearly two-thirds of all Suriname slaves (Price 1976:13). Matjáus, whose initial maroon ancestors escaped even earlier than the first Abaísas, would also have included a significant Slave Coast contingent, but their own traditions signal considerable regional diversity in Africa—stretching from the Gold Coast to Yorubaland to Loango. Its speakers/players refer to *papá* as *aladá*, confirming its specific African roots (see 44C–47C above).

The Asáubásu Mystery

169. [R.P.:] Let's discuss the people of Asáubásu [a small village on the Pikílío, near Djumú Mission].

[Peléki:] Who their great ancestors were. Where they escaped from. Where they "walked" [in the forest].

[Tebíni:] [long silence] Well . . . they came very late. Avó Adjágbò brought them. Paánza's husband, he found them someplace way downstream. (I've forgotten which of these places down there it was.) From where he found them, he brought them to Paánza, in Baáka-wáta. Because . . . they and Paánza were close [matrilineal] relatives. But Anóya of Lángu, he once told us that these people are Béndiwáta! [the Kaapátu—Lángu—village on the Gaánlío]

[Peléki:] So! Afiiká [of Lángu] told me the same thing. But it's more complicated. He said, "The people of Asáubásu, they're Kaapátus." I said, "Well, these 'Kaapátus,' who was their first ancestor?"

[Tebíni:] Exactly [the right thing to ask]!

[Peléki:] "Where did thèy walk [to Saramaka]?" And he said, *"Máti* [friend]." I answered. He said, "It's not a long story. The person I can name. Their first ancestor, the one who ran away. When I get out of the hospital [in Paramaribo, where Peléki and Afiiká were both confined at the time], I'll come and visit you from Lángu. I'll have found out who all their great ancestors were. I must come down from Lángu anyway, because I have to discuss a matter with the tribal chief. So, we'll meet and I'll tell you. It's not difficult. But I want to check it through fully. Logofóu knows it." Afiiká was saying all this. We talked about it every single day! "Linzékióo [the present Asáubásu captain] is really one of us [Béndiwáta, that is, Kaapátu]! That god that they have there, it's not one they came and got from us. It's their own lineage's god!" Afiiká said all this.

[Tebíni:] Only recently, I heard the same thing.

[Peléki:] That's what I'm talking about. At last New Year's, I was in the hospital. I was released before Afiiká. Finally he returned [from the city] to Saramaka. He shook my hand when he got off the plane. *"Mati,* you've come?" I asked. He answered yes. He said, "Let me go to Lángu, then I'll come back down. The things we discussed . . . I have not forgotten them" [Tebíni chimed in on the second half of this "formula"]. Well, Afiiká left and became deathly ill. He was hardly alive. Now I go to see him in the hospital [at Djumú Mission, where Peléki lives]. But he can hardly speak any more.

[Tebíni:] [With real sympathy] *Ké!* It is lost.

[Peléki:] I've prayed on his behalf until I don't know what else to do. . . . [more discussion about Afiiká]. . . . Batelêi said to me with surprise once, when I asked him, "You don't know that, here [in the Pikílío]?" And he chuckled a bit. "Well, you should just ask Lángu!" I said, "Well, then, who *are* these people?" He said, "I'd better ask to be sure." ([To Tebíni:] This thing is difficult, brother-in-law!) Then I sent a message to Captain Faánsisónu [the Matjáu headcaptain who was brought up and spends much time with his father's people in Lángu]. Well, [he is like a] Lángu! . . . Once, Kositán [an important Matjáu, now dead, of the generation born ca. 1880], Tribal Chief Agbagó—he wasn't tribal chief yet—and I were working at the Commewijne River. When they [the two older men] discussed things, I used to listen. Kositán said, "Ómi Boní [a previous nickname for Agbagó], those people of Asáubásu. What do you know about them?" And Agbagó replied, "Kositán, that's not the way to talk to me. You [the older one] are the one who must know." "Well, Wómi Bóikóni [another nickname], as I am here before you, I haven't got a clue about them! I know they're called '*paáti nêngè*' ['island people'], but I haven't a clue as to who they really are!" ([To Tebíni, excitedly:] Kositán didn't have a clue!)

[Tebíni:] Absolutely not!

[Peléki:] And I never learned anything else about them from those men. The number of times I overheard them sitting down to discuss First-Time—not for my ears, just between themselves! Well, so I sent a message to Faánsisónu. (This knowledge is not in the Pikílío!) Since Afiiká said that it is known in Lángu . . . well, Faánsisónu, he's [almost] a Lángu person. Let him search it out up there [in Lángu] and bring it back down to us. And so it stayed until now. We met recently and he said, "Peléki, I got your message. What Afiiká told you about these people is true!" ([To Tebíni and me:] Well, is that what you call answering a request?)

[Tebíni:] [derisively] They really don't know!

[Peléki:] The thing doesn't make sense yet.

[Tebíni:] Because Tribal Chief Binótu [Atúdéndu, who held the office from 1934 to 1949] once asked me, "How is it they live in the Pikílío [Matjáu territory], but we don't know a thing about their origins?" I said, "Well, *I* know. Avó Adjágbò brought them to Baáka-wáta. That's all there is to it!"

[Peléki:] [musing:] I've heard it said that Matjáus brought them here, too. That's a part of what I've heard. But when I went to hear this other story from Afiiká. . . .

[Tebíni:] [interrupting] But the story as I've heard it. After I'd discussed it with Tribal Chief Binótu, I went to Bakáapáu [a Kasitú, a descendant of Paánza and Adjágbò] to ask him. Then he said, "Mamá Paánza. It was her sister. But she [the other one] was the younger. They were following Paánza. And Avó Adjágbò brought them here." Well, this whole business continues to trouble [confuse] me!

[Peléki:] That's why, last New Year's—not the one that just passed but the one before that—I brought some rum as a gift to Linzékióo [the elderly Asáubásu captain]. I said, "*Máti,* I've brought a little rum for you, since we're both enjoying [living to see] another year. [apologetically:] I'm all messed up [physically], but I've brought you a little rum anyway, so you can drink." And he said, "Yes." ([To Tebíni and me:] Well, older men, when you want to find out something from them, you must know exactly how to proceed.)

[Tebíni:] You bet!

[Peléki:] And he took the rum, held out the bottle. (It was a *pêngi* [about 33 cc.].) He said, "Well, *Máti,* the rum you've brought me, I cannot drink it by myself." So he took the glass, leaned it so the rum dribbled out.

[Tebíni:] *Tjôôôô* [the sound of rum pouring out].

[Peléki:] And he prayed, "Well, ancestors, don't you see? The fellow here has brought me rum. New Year's! That's why he's brought me this rum. Look how sick he is! Consider what he's done, the thoughtfulness. He hasn't become impolite! Well, as long as it's still beating, your feelings are still alive! I give you rum, then. The rum he carried to give me. I can't enjoy it by myself. Tatá Adúngu, I pour a libation for you." Then—in the middle of the prayer—he turned suddenly to me and said, "Peléki, who is Adúngu?" So I said, "*Máti,* I'm not the one to ask that to!" Then he said, "Really? Why not?" And I said, "You're the one who must tell *me.*" So he said, "Peléki, you don't *want* to tell me." I protested, "It's not that I don't want to." "Peléki," he finally said, "Well, Adúngu was a Dángogó [Matjáu] person!"

[Tebíni:] What did you hear there?

[Peléki:] Linzékióo. He who is right over there [in Asáubásu] today. He said, "Adúngu was a Dángogó person." So I said yes. And he went back to his prayer. "Ancestors, we give you rum. Drink it with pleasure. Tatá Adúngu, I give you rum." [the prayer continues]

. . . Later, I went to the tribal chief. I asked, "Was Adúngu really a Dángogó person?" And he said, "Man, where did you hear *that* one?" And I said, "Linzékióo told me so." So he said, "Well, listen. It makes sense. In those days people did used to 'catch' other people" [find them in the forest].

[Tebíni:] Well, Peléki, what he said there, isn't that what I just finished telling you? What Maáku [the famous early twentieth-century female captain of Kámpu] told us? She said, "Those [Asáubásu] people . . . Avó Adjágbò brought them to Paánza at Baákawáta." Well, was I wrong?

[Peléki:] No, it's exactly what you said. But then I got this [infected] thorn in my foot. Otherwise, I would already have gone back to Linzékióo about this. After all, every older man has a very particular way you must approach him [on such matters]. I know the

---

The Asáubásu Mystery (169)

This conversation is the fullest single transcription/translation in this book. I present it in this form because it so effectively captures—in spite of its inconclusive substantive results—the rhetorical tone and the research strategies of my best Saramaka collaborators.

I know little more than is contained in this conversation about the origins of the people of the small village of Asáubásu, which is sandwiched between the Kasitú village of Bêndêkôndè and Djumú Mission, on the Pikílío. After the post-Peace Treaty migration of the 1770s, from Baákawáta to the presently-inhabited region of the Pikílío, I know that these people established themselves on an island across from their present village—hence their nickname, "Island People." And today, they serve as priests for the river god, *tonê*, and are said to possess special powers over the rain and the sun. Their arrival in Saramaka would seem to date from between the 1740s (after Paánza's coming) and the 1770s (when Baákawáta was abandoned). My placement of this fragment at this point in the text, suggesting a 1750s arrival date, is tentative.

There are two substantive messages contained in this conversation. The first concerns relations between Asáubásu and the Kasitú clan (who are their immediate neighbors), and Asáubásu and the Matjáus (on whose land both they and the Kasitús live). In this context, to say that the (unnamed) Asáubásu ancestress was Paánza's younger sister, and/or that Adjágbò (or Adúngu) "found" these people and brought them to Paánza, is to stress that there are special ties binding each of the two "client" clans to each other, and binding each to their "finders" and "hosts," the Matjáus.* The significance of the second message, relating the people of Asáubásu to the Kaapátus, remains obscure to me. My Kaapátu friend, Mètisên, once told me that his Kaapátu ancestors had special connections with the plantation called Rama, which is next door to Paánza's "Kasitú" plantation. This particular web of Lángu-Asáubásu-Kasitú threads should prove amenable to unraveling through further fieldwork. ✥

---

* I have found an interesting archival fragment suggesting that Adúngu may indeed have been a Matjáu, and a habitual "finder" of new recruits. A postholder's letter from 1772 notes that a Saramaka named "Adongroe" was arrested on the coast for slave stealing, and it requests that he be released into the custody of his captain, apparently a Matjáu (SvS 165, 31 December 1772 [13 December 1772]).

proper way with my brother-in-law Tebíni. I know the way with [Headcaptain] Faánsisónu. I know the way with Atjóku [the captain of Dáume]. I know exactly where to walk so they will speak; I know exactly where not to walk lest they won't say a word. Well, I shall go to Linzékióo and seek him out on this. He said, "Adúngu was a Dángogó person." I had never heard that! (Conversation, Peléki/Tebíni 28 July 1976)   ❖

Kwasímukámba's Gambit, 1755

170. One day, Kwasímukámba told the whites he could find the way to Baákawáta. "Let me go all by myself," he said. "I'll deceive them . . . prepare them until they're ripe [for plucking]." And that is what he tried to do. (Tebíni 28 July 1976)

171. Kwasímukámba came all alone. He went and made peace with them at Baákawáta. He said he didn't come to do mischief (exactly like what this man here [R.P.] claims!) He arrived and became their *máti* [close friend], and they lived together for a long while. (Tebíni 24 July 1976)

172. When Kwasímukámba came to Baákawáta, Ayakô received him like a *máti*. Over and over again, Kwasímukámba used to ask Ayakô to reveal the secret of his *óbia* [which made him invulnerable]. Ayakô trusted him until one day Wámba [the *apúku*, once in Lánu's

---

Kwasímukámba's Gambit, 1755 (170–76)

Of all the stories in this book, Kwasímukámba's Gambit is my personal favorite: it expresses more sharply than any other the central dilemma of studying Saramaka historiography, and it permits a comparison of unmatched richness with contemporary written accounts.

One day in 1976, just after telling me some details about this highly secret and dangerous story, Peléki explained:

And that's why, Friend, Bush Negroes [Maroons] do not trust Creoles [non-Maroon Afro-Surinamers]. Which is why it is so hard for us to get ahead [in the modern world]. We don't believe them. Because of what happened to our ancestors. If you take one of them as a *máti*, that's what they'll do with you. You must not trust them with a single thing about the forest [our life]. City people! They fought against us along with whites. Like you. I must not [am not supposed to] tell you anything! It isn't good. Because whites used to come fight them. Well, Kwasímukámba was a Creole [*nêngè*], and he joined up with the whites to bring them here. . . . But if you teach an outsider something, well, little by little he'll use it to come kill you. That's why, Brother, Maroons don't teach whites things. . . . All these Maroons still believe that outsiders are always trying to learn our secrets so they can someday come kill us. Because if they'd really known Ayakô's secret, they wouldn't have shot [wasted their ammunition on] the sugar cane. . . . Well, they didn't trust him fully. They didn't teach him *all* of their knowledge. And that's why he didn't triumph in the end. That's why we say, if you teach a Creole or a white person, that's what they'll do with you. This is the one thing Maroons really believe. It's stronger than anything else. . . . This is the greatest fear of all Maroons: that those times shall come again.

For historically-knowledgeable Saramakas, Kwasímukámba represents the prototypical symbol of betrayal, a constant reminder of the necessity to be guarded in all relations with outsiders. As we have seen in the first section of this book, everyday Saramaka proverbs and folktales are filled with morals about not trusting other people, and the story of *nóuna,* outlined there, was considered emblematic of such concerns. But the idea— expressed so often in daily life—that knowledge is power, and that one should not reveal all of what one knows, becomes magnified enormously for Saramakas whenever dealing with First-Time, with ritual, or with

head, now in that of Yáya] warned him, "Evil is on the way, beware." So Ayakô decided to trick Kwasímukámba! He told him that his power resided in the small stand of sugar cane growing at the rear of his house. Ayakô said that if the sugar cane were shot at until it withered and dried, he would die. (Otjútju August 1975)

173. Before the year was up, Kwasímukámba went downstream [to the city]. One day they simply didn't see him any more. Then he went and loaded those soldiers into boats *sílílí* [intensifier indicating how very many there were]. He led them all the way up the river until they were very close. (Tebíni 24 July 1976)

174. Then one day, at cock's crow, Wámba appeared in Yáya's head and sang out:

Lu-kéin o,   ba-ná- ngo-ma hé-si é.   Lu-kéin o,   ba-ná – ngo-ma hé-si.

Kwa-sí – mu-kám-ba   tjái ki-bám-ba.   Ba- ná-ngo-ma hé – si   o.

This song is in the esoteric *apúku* (forest spirit) language. "Lukéin" is the special term of address for Ayakô used by his sister's daughter's god; "banángoma" is the *apúku* word for "[black] person" (*nêngè* in standard Saramaccan); "kibámba" is the *apúku* word for "white person" or "outsider" (*bakáa* in standard Saramaccan). The song, then, roughly translates, "Ayakô, hurry, man! [repeat]/Kwasímukámba is bringing the whites./ Hurry, man."

---

outsiders. And the highly secret story of Kwasímukámba combines all three of these contexts of heightened danger. This is why it has come to epitomize for Saramakas all of the fearsome risks of sharing confidences with outsiders.

I first heard mention of Kwasímukámba on the final day of the 1975 field season (during that same feverish session at which I first learned about the Sinking at Gaándan Falls; see 158C–161C), more than nine years after I had begun working with Saramakas. (A careful examination of those oral traditions recorded by others from Saramakas [see Price 1976], as well as discussions with other anthropologists, indicates that until that moment, Kwasímukámba had never been discussed with an "outsider.") During the summer of 1976, and again in 1978, I was able to collect a number of additional fragments about the man, mainly from Matjáus. (Men from other clans, even those quite thoughtful about the distant past, seemed to have little detail to offer about the story.) Occasionally, I heard variants: that Kwasímukámba eventually died from his infected ear; that the Saramakas devised various punishments or tortures for him; that it was his nose, not his ear, that was excised; and so on. It was, however, the Matjáus, who are most familiar with the incident, who were able to enrich it with considerable detail. For them, it is the song of the Matjáu forest spirit Wámba that stands firmly at its center, as the mnemonic kernel for the various discontinuous fragments that swirl around it.

The Matjáu accounts that I have transcribed in *170–76* place the site of Kwasímukámba's encounter with the Saramakas at Baákawáta, the homeland of the Matjáus during the 1750s. However, other Matjáu fragments make clear that Chief Ayakô, who harbored Kwasímukámba, was in fact living during this period with his sister's child Yáya, apart from their Matjáu kinsmen, near the Awanás at Sentéa. And this location is confirmed by the documentary record of relevant events (see below).

It was saying, "They've come. That Kwasímukámba who disappeared. Well, he didn't just disappear. He's returning!" They went and consulted the great *óbia* pot. It was boiling! [indicating danger] And that very day, the whites arrived. (Tebíni 21 July 1976)

175. They abandoned the village as the whites approached, and hid at the edge of the forest. When the whites arrived, Kwasímukámba showed them the small stand of sugar cane. They stood shooting at it for so many hours! But it did not dry up. Their ammunition was finished. Then Ayakô appeared with his cutlass. He had been hiding. He came out and fought with them. He cut off every single head except that of Kwasímukámba. Then Ayakô said to him, " Kwasímukámba, when I gave you food, you ate till your belly was full. Now look what's become of you. Well, I am not going to kill you. But I will fix you so that everyone will laugh at you." Then he grabbed him and stretched his ear out hard like this [demonstrates the stretching of his right ear]. And then he sliced it cleanly off! He said, "Take this and show it to the whitefolks." (Tebíni 11 July 1978)

176. Kwasímukámba said, "This is one hell of a thing for Kwasímukámba of Tjedú!* When a person's ear is cut off, his face is spoiled!" And he left for the city. [Some people say he actually "flew" off.] (Otjútju August 1975)   ✥

* Tjedú, or "Kwedú," is now thought to be Kwasímukámba's father's name (or the name of his father's clan or tribe), which he—as a Saramaka still would—called out when "recounting his [praise] name" (*kondá nên*); see Price and Price 1972:343.

The rich eighteenth-century written accounts of the man whom Saramakas call Kwasímukámba provide a special perspective from which to consider the nature of Saramaka selectivity about the distant past. (Comparison of these with the oral fragments will also help remind us of some of the ways in which the *written* word is especially vulnerable to distortion by interested parties.) These documents depict Kwasímukámba playing several major roles in eighteenth-century Suriname; as I have presented this information in some detail elsewhere (Price 1979a), I here provide only the barest summary.*

The man whom eighteenth-century writers referred to as "The Celebrated Graman Quacy . . . one of the most Extraordinary Black men in Surinam, or Perhaps in the World" was born "on the coast of Guinea" about 1690 and transported to Suriname as a child (Stedman 1988: chapter 29; Price 1979a:151–52). By 1730, he had discovered the medicinal properties of the tree that Linnaeus named in his honor *Quassia amara* (called in Suriname "Quassiehout" or "Kwasi-bita"); and during the next six decades, amidst his many other activities, Kwasi served as the colony's leading *dresiman* (curer) and *lukuman* (diviner), with vast influence "not only among blacks and Indians but also among the European colonists" (Lichtveld and Voorhoeve 1980:181). Kwasi's fame among the Europeans was not, however, based solely on his medical and spiritual talents; for more than forty years he was the colony's principal intermediary in dealings with maroons, serving first as a scout, then as a negotiator, and finally as spiritual and tactical

* Major sources include Hartsinck 1770; Nassy 1778; Stedman 1796, 1988; van Sijpesteijn 1858; Wolbers 1861; the satirical "rouwklagt" written upon the occasion of Kwasi's death in 1787 and published in Lichtveld and Voorhoeve 1980; and various documents from the archives of the Societeit van Suriname, in the Algemeen Rijksarchief (see also Price and de Beet 1982). One additional source, Sack 1911, was recently pointed out to me by Drs. G. W. van der Meiden; it gathers together a number of obscure archival references relating to Kwasi's life and presents a numerical table of "Quassiehout" exports showing, for example, that in 1869 Suriname exported 245,622 kilos of this wood that Kwasi "discovered"—partly for pharmaceutical use but also, apparently, as an additive in various English beers (Sack 1911:1184–85).

"**The celebrated Graman Quacy.**" Engraving by William Blake, after a drawing by John Gabriel Stedman (1796:Plate 76).

advisor of the specially selected black troops who in the 1770s and 1780s fought alongside the Europeans in the great battles against recent (non-Saramaka) maroons. Always the opportunist, Kwasi—who as early as 1730 had received from a member of the Council "a golden breastplate on which was inscribed 'Quassie, faithful to the whites' " (van Sijpesteijn 1858:92)—became in 1744 the slave of Governor Mauricius himself. His varied antimaroon activities during the next decade won him a letter of manumission, but personal freedom did not significantly alter his customary activities: he continued to conduct expeditions against maroons and to hunt them for a bounty, and he continued his diverse medical activities. In due course, Kwasi also became a planter in his

THE EVENTS

own right and, in 1776, in recognition of his many services to the colony, the governor sent him all the way to The Hague, to be received by Willem V, Prince of Orange, who feted him with gifts. It was after his triumphant return to Suriname, wearing the elegant outfit given him by the prince, that Kwasi posed for the famous portrait drawn by Stedman and later engraved by William Blake. Kwasi remained active on behalf of the colonists into his nineties, while he lived "in a good house in Paramaribo, which was given him for his use, free of charge by the Government," along with the services of three slaves, two male and one female (Wolbers 1861:436; Sack 1911:1178). And it was during these final years that he became accustomed to receiving letters from abroad addressed to "The Most Honorable and Most Learned Gentleman, Master Phillipus of Quassie, Professor of Herbology in Suriname" (Lichtveld and Voorhoeve 1980:179).

This summary biography may serve as background for the events of the 1750s, when Kwasi's life suddenly intersects with Saramaka memories.* The relevant documents provide a fascinating counterpoint to the Saramaka story of Kwasímukámba's Gambit. (Again, I merely touch on the highlights, having presented a more detailed account elsewhere [Price 1979a].)

In 1753—four years after Creutz's cease-fire with the Saramakas, and three years after the mysterious disappearance of Picolet—the news reached Paramaribo that a group of Saramaka raiders had sacked a plantation on the Cassewinica Creek, carrying off with them about seven slaves (SvS 145, 2 November 1753). Eleven months later, Kwasi suddenly emerged from the forest and announced to the surprised whites that he had just spent the past year living among these Saramaka rebels:

> He says that he had gone to the Cassewinica for medical reasons . . . and was taken away along with some nine or ten other slaves, small and large, when the runaways raided there. He believes this must have occurred some twelve to fifteen months ago. [After a journey, part on foot, part by canoe, described in some detail] they finally came to the landing place of the runaways. . . . He says further: that the villages are very strong and that there are a great many Negroes; that they are the same villages with which Captain Creutz had made the peace [in 1749]. (SvS 294 "okt. 1754")†

Kwasi then described his "escape" back to slavery, while he was on a raid of the Castilho plantation with a group of Saramakas, and he assured the members of the Council that he was now both eager and fully equipped to lead a major expedition against the Saramakas.

> He said that if they [the whites] would bring him to the Sara Creek, he would be able to point out the route . . . that they would then have to go in boats upriver until they reached the landing place of the runaways. That he could also find the [previous] night campsites and guide them from one to the next. But [he warned] that the trip is very long and he thinks it will take a good three months to get there . . . He has heard that the runaways have patrols out and sentries posted, with instructions to poison the rivers and streams if the whites are seen to be coming. (Ibid.)

Within the year, Kwasi's plan was realized and a massive expedition consisting of some five hundred men was organized. Its purpose was "either to make one last attempt at a permanent Peace or else to set up positions in the [rebels'] villages, and insofar as possible search them out and completely destroy them" (SvS 202, 9 December 1754). Captain E. G. Hentschel was chosen as commanding officer, and his report of the expedition represents the most detailed of all such military reports I have seen regarding Saramakas.

---

* It is worth noting that until 1977–78 I was unaware of the equivalence of the two "Kwasis," so that my Saramaka traditions are insulated from the colonial accounts. Saramakas themselves, though they knew something of the famous slave healer Kwasi, did not relate him to Kwasímukámba.

† The two main documents regarding Kwasi's Saramaka adventure have been hitherto ignored in the standard histories of Suriname. They are "Informatie over de Neger Quassie" (SvS 294, "okt. 1754") and "Journaal Gehouden op de Tocht teegens de wegloopers in Suriname, onder aanvoering van den Capitein Ernst Godfried Hentschel" (SvS 297, 16 September 1755–25 December 1755). Both are reproduced in full in Price and de Beet 1982 (in Dutch) and in R. Price 1983 (in English).

On 17 November, after two months of extraordinary difficulties, hacking their way through thick forest and dragging themselves over innumerable rapids, the expedition finally arrived at the foot of a rapids where Kwasi declared "that this is surely the true landing place of the runaways, from which he escaped a year ago." During the next two days contact was made with the rebels, and firefights occurred. They had arrived in the heavily populated area around Agámadjá Creek (see map on p. 100). On 20 November, after a day of intermittent battles, Hentschel wrote in his journal that

> the runaways constantly swarmed around us, yelling out to us that we shall never get to the top of the mountain at the fourth village [they had thus far found and destroyed three]. They cursed Kwasi hideously, saying that the whites were right [justified] in coming, but that the fault was his.

The following days were spent in search-and-destroy missions, resulting in the destruction of several villages, including that in which the "gouverneur" of the Saramakas lived. There were heavy casualties on both sides. On 27 November, Hentschel finally sent out a slave emissary with an offer of peace. The Saramaka response was simple:

> They would provide us with whatever provisions we required [from their gardens] as long as I would turn over to them two kegs of gunpowder and the guide Kwasi.

Two days later, the Saramakas requested that a slave again be sent to them, to receive a message, and the same old man was dispatched. He reported back that the rebels were still insisting on the "two kegs of powder and Kwasi." An hour later, a second messenger was sent, and he in turn told Hentschel:

> The runaways have only two demands—the two kegs of powder and Kwasi. If these were met, they would within a day bring all needed provisions to our boats.

By this time, the expedition was sorely in need of provisions and was subsisting largely on manioc cakes; Hentschel noted that 19 whites and 14 slaves were sick or wounded, and that he himself was suffering a high fever. The following day, the Saramakas once more requested that an emissary be sent.

> I sent the old slave once again but with the message that they will receive neither powder nor the guide [Kwasi], and that we can never make peace with them on those conditions.

The old man never returned, and the next day Hentschel decided it was time to leave for the city, where the expedition finally arrived on Christmas Day, 1755, after more than three grueling months in the forest. This seems to have been the last significant wartime expedition to Saramaka.*

In what ways do these documentary testimonies throw light on Saramaka accounts about Kwasímukámba? First, they show that Saramakas have collectively preserved an uncannily accurate memory of these diverse events of more than two centuries ago. Let me briefly recapitulate: Saramakas today say that Kwasi (1) led several expeditions against them in the area of the plantations, (2) later led a peace-making expedition far upriver, (3) still later came to Saramaka on his own, where he lived for some time as a spy who feigned amity, (4) escaped back to the coast, where he (5) gathered an expedition against them, and (6) ultimately had his ear cut off in punishment by the Saramakas, in the wake of a great battle at the village of their chief, after which he (7) fled to the city. The documentary sources regarding Kwasi's activities viz-a-viz Saramakas report that he (1) led expeditions against them in the area of the plantations (see Price 1979a), (2) led a peace-making expedition far upriver (in 1747, he served as a guide on Brouwer's expedition), (3) was taken to Saramaka, where he lived for about a year, feigning amity, (4) escaped back

---

* There was one other expedition, of similarly massive size (161 whites and 345 slaves), sent out in the early months of the following year; but as far as I can tell from the documents at my disposal, the troops returned by May, "utterly defeated by the torrential rains," and with fully half of the slaves having died or deserted (SvS 148, 1 May 1756–31 May 1756). Kwasi seems to have been along as guide (SvS 297, 27 March 1756), but I have seen no record of their having made contact with the Saramakas.

to the coast, where he (5) brought a giant expedition against them, and (6) himself became a central issue in the negotiations between the whites and Saramakas that came in the wake of a battle at the village of the Saramaka "gouverneur" (chief), after which he (7) returned to the city.

Second, this comparison nicely highlights those moments in the story that Saramakas have interpreted from a special perspective. While Kwasi, for example, depicted himself to the whites as having been abducted from the plantation, Saramakas view him as having come of his own (evil) volition. We shall never know what Kwasi's motivation really was at the time he joined the Saramakas as their temporary "friend" (and in fact the distinction might, at the time, have been an extremely fine one). Nonetheless, the modern Saramaka view does fit Kwasi's opportunistic character, as we know it from documentary sources; it raises some especially rich psychological possibilities; and it is fully consistent with the activities of other secret agents who appear in the eighteenth-century documents. (It is, however, so dramatically satisfying that one cannot rule out its simply being a rhetorical device.)*

Another obvious contrast between the sources involves the outcome of the battle, in which each side claims victory. Commander Hentschel reported that the Saramakas wanted Kwasi badly, but he did not indicate that their wishes were realized. In contrast, the Saramakas depict a great victory, capped by their revenge on Kwasi. This sort of difference of perspective is every bit as expectable as it ought, in retrospect, to be impossible to resolve. After all, Hentschel—like commanders of similar expeditions (see 147C–151C above)—knew that the Saramaka enemy was in no position to challenge his official report; and similarly, Saramakas two centuries later could certainly be excused if they exaggerated the battlefield success of their ancestors. Nevertheless, there does exist one extraordinary piece of evidence about "what really happened," which I noticed only while writing an early draft of these pages (though I had had it before my eyes many times before). It suggests that there may be more to the Saramaka version of the battle than one might otherwise suspect. A close look at the famous Stedman-Blake engraving of "The Celebrated Graman Quacy" clearly reveals that, under his curly "grey head of hair" (Stedman 1796, 2:348), this extraordinary nonagenarian is missing his right ear.† ✤

* The whole rhetorical structure of the Matjáu story is noteworthy. Indeed, it parallels almost exactly the structure of the *nóuna* folktale. Both the folktale and Kwasímukámba's story include the sending in of a secret agent (in one, a Bush Cow in disguise; in the other, a faithful slave feigning friendship) who comes within an inch of succeeding in extracting the ultimate secret; the timely warning by a god, speaking through an old woman; the final victory in which the enemy is decimated and the sole survivor is maimed or "marked"; and the general moral about knowledge, power, and distrust. Both stories, through their structure and content, seem somehow to encapsulate principles that stand at the very heart of Saramaka life.

† Although Kwasi had leprosy many years before, its progress had long since been arrested. The published sources that comment directly on his disease and his famous self-cure make it clear that his face was not in any way affected (Stedman 1796, 2:347–48, Nassy 1788, 2:72–73, Lichtveld and Voorhoeve 1980:179–86). Nonetheless, there is evidence that Kwasi characteristically showed only the "good side" of his face during his later years. In a satirical poem written on the occasion of his death, he is likened to the King of Diamonds (Lichtveld and Voorhoeve 1980:185). In a clever footnote Lichtveld and Voorhoeve—who knew nothing of the ear-cutting tradition—nevertheless speculate on the meaning of this metaphor, pointing out that the King of Diamonds is the only king in the deck who shows only half of his face.

Yáya's Prophecy

177. When the whites came [to explore peace possibilities], the Saramakas were hostile; they didn't want peace. It was at Baákawáta. [It's as if] I wanted us to make peace; you didn't want us to make peace; that man over there didn't want us to make peace; that other one wants us to make peace. That's how we disputed the thing!

. . . Avo Ayakô had said that he couldn't [stand to] see outsiders [*bakáas*]. Whitefolks [*wéti sèmbè*], he simply couldn't stand them. Then they asked [themselves], "If the whites want peace, how will we respond?" It was as part of this discussion that Yáya said "that thing" [her famous pronouncement]. It was she who had the god [Wámba, in her head]. She said that they should not be hostile [to the whites] any more. She said, "the person to whom this is unacceptable [Ayakô] is the oldest of us all. When he is no longer here, well, peace will come." (Tebíni 10 August 1976)

178. She said, "Tei u tei huena, vunvu sa fúu tjéni pôtò." [The first phrase, not in normal Saramaccan, means "little by little" or "over a long period of time"; the second means "hummingbird will fill up the sugar cane cauldron."] Then the old man, it wasn't too long before . . . he died. And when he had died, peace finally came. (Peléki 22 July 1976)

❖

Yáya's Prophecy (177–78)

This final set of fragments relating to the peace preliminaries refers to the late 1750s. For Saramakas, the famous phrase spoken by Yáya remains the mnemonic heart of the story. (Discussions with Matjáus make it clear that it was actually Yáya's god Wámba who made the prophecy, using Yáya as medium.) For Matjáus, Ayakô's death, sometime between 1756 and 1758, symbolizes the end of an era and the transfer of leadership to a new, "creole" generation.* Yáya plays a pivotal role conceptually, as she was Ayakô's sister's daughter (and the medium for Wámba), but also the mother of the first post-Peace Treaty tribal chief, Abíni. This "bridging" role appears in traditions regarding Yáya just after the Peace as well, when she is once again credited with decisively swaying public opinion in favor of the whites, at the time the first Moravian missionaries arrived (in 1765). According to Christian Saramakas, it was Yáya who persuaded the others to permit the missionaries to give their "book" (Bible) to her Awaná grandson, Alábi, and it is to commemorate this act that the hospital at Djumú Mission is officially called "Jaja Dande Hospital."†

❖

* By the time of the Peace, leadership throughout Saramaka was clearly passing from the first generation of runaways—African-born men like Ayakô, Vumá, Kaási, and Abámpapá—to those born in the forest (or, in a few cases, brought to the forest as children). Of the "40–42" Saramakas who journeyed to Djuka to arrange the 1762 Peace, only "3–4" were African-born (SvS 154, 16 February 1762 [5 February 1762]). During the first decades after the Peace, Saramaka society was led by men and women whose early life had been shaped by the dual experiences of freedom and constant war.

† Tribal Chief Abóikóni, upon whose advice this name was bestowed, gives the praise name of the person usually referred to as Yáya Wedéwe as follows: Yáya a Dánde, Tjínaweebí, Anákiéndukúme kóóaden. Hên da Amámè.

The Papútus Arrive, 1759

179. They lived in Para. That is where the war "met" them. One of the final battles. When they came [to Saramaka], it was like Creoles [coastal people]. . . . The whites had followed them and fought with them there. (Otjútju 3 August 1976)

180. They lived at the plantation called Kutí, what whites now call Vier Kinderen. Atjó was *basiá* ["driver"] there. (Anikéi August 1979)

181. The Matjáus were in Baákawáta. The Wátambíis had come to live with them there. . . . Then much, much, much later, the Papútus came to Kánga Creek [in Baákawáta]. They came [to Saramaka] as a group of seventy people. (Otjútju 3 August 1976)

182. When they first came, they lived with the Nasís at Dosú Creek, then at Awásitónu above Gaándan Falls. . . . Ayakô's wife [Asukúme] had a brother called Ngweté [like her, a Dómbi]. He married one of the Papútu newcomers to Saramaka, and he brought all of her people to live with his own in-laws [the Matjáus]. Tata Kánga and Tata Atjó were the main Papútu men. Matjáus gave them the creek and they made their village, Kánga Creek. (Tebíni 10 August 1976) ✜

The Papútus Arrive, 1759 (179–82)

The Papútus trace their origins to Plantation Vier Kinderen on the Para River. Today, this clan still possesses many of the same *óbia*s (for example, the medicine for snakebite) as do their former fellows who remained on that plantation as slaves; and Saramaka Papútus continue to visit the plantation site to express kinship with these distant relatives. I have been able to trace the Papútu rebellion to 1729, when this largest of all Para River plantations—at the time owned by the Widow Papot—was raided, and "almost every single slave deserted" (GA 1, 12 November 1729).* A few of the new maroons seem to have headed south and joined the Nasí group (see 107C–120C above), but the bulk remained in the Para region, living on the outskirts of the plantations. In 1758, Sergeant Dörig led a military expedition against a maroon village in Para, destroying ten houses, one shrine, and a large garden, and taking two captives; a commando sent out soon after encountered some fifty maroons still in the area (SvS 305, 9 September 1758; SvS 204, 15 September 1758, 23 September 1758). I now believe that the main group of Papútus to come to Saramaka was composed of these 1729 maroons, who managed to live for nearly thirty years in a hidden village in Para until Dörig discovered them in 1758. Fragment *179*, which was related to the Matjáu who told it to me many years before by the late Papútu Alínzofíti, provides strong Saramaka support for this scenario.

The incorporation of a large new group must have posed all sorts of problems for Saramakas in the late 1750s. Unfortunately, I have only limited fragments about the Papútus' abortive stays with the Nasís and at Awásitónu. The most interesting set of fragments—which I heard very late in my research and cannot quite piece together yet—involves a Papútu woman (or possibly a Dómbi woman, married and living with a Papútu man) called Aéfadámba and an *apúku* called Malúndu, which she "found" while she herself was lost in the forest at the time the Papútus lived on the

---

* I do not know at what date this plantation was owned or managed by "Kutí" (see *180*), or whether this was the Coutier-owned plantation unsuccessfully raided by Adjágbò and other Saramakas in 1747 (see 61C–65C).

Twofingers

183. When they lived at Dosú Creek, Akwádjaní and his brother [Kwakú Étja] had a garden near Kánga Creek. Something kept stealing from their garden, but they couldn't figure out what it was. Each morning things would be missing, but there was no sign left behind. It was Indians. They had been coming there every night and then, during the day, staying in a large cave. They [the Saramakas] decided to post a watch near the cave to see what lived inside. Now, when the sun got hot, these people [the Indians] used to come out to warm themselves in the sun. But they'd come only one or two at a time. Then they'd go back in, and another would come out. Well, two girls came out to warm themselves, and they caught them. They took them away.

The girls' hair was very long. The men divided them; Kwakú [Étja] had one, Kwádjaní had the other. They discussed how to make them look more acceptable to bring to the village. Kwakú cut the hair of his girl, but Kwádjaní said he wouldn't, that it was a *tjína* [taboo] to cut an Indian's hair. The girl just stood there. Well, a week later, Kwakú's girl

---

Gaánlío. This forest spirit is credited with having "made" (created) the powerful Dómbi *gaán óbia* Mafúngu, which is what Saramakas still use to find someone lost in the forest.*

By the time the whites arrived to make peace in 1762, we know from contemporary documents that the Papútus were firmly settled, just as Saramaka traditions indicate, on the arm of Baákawáta named after their main man, "Kánga Creek." ❖

Twofingers (183–84)

During their stay at Dosú Creek, ca. 1759, the Nasís captured some fleeing "Indians" and brought them to live with them. The story of the armadillo father would seem to be the Saramaka explanation, undoubtedly discovered by them through divination, of the strange shape of the "Twofinger" child who was born to Kwádjaní's Indian wife. Nasís preserve this story mainly because one of their current descent groups traces its ancestry to these Indians. Yet the story attests as well to the important (if occasional) cooperation between often-unwilling forest Indians and early maroons, from which the maroons must have derived a great deal of useful environmental knowledge. The two fragments transcribed here are from a Dómbi and a Matjáu, respectively. In my very tense meeting with Nasí elders in 1978, one of the questions I asked was about the "Twofingers," but it was met with stony silence. Finally, one old man said, "Friend, we Saramakas have a way. . . . We know something, but if it's not absolutely necessary to say it, we simple say we don't know it. With this question, it's best just to leave it alone." Another added, "All we've heard is 'Bafílángu.' That's those Indians. They had only two fingers."

Contemporary written sources provide a curious counterpoint to these Saramaka memories, a fine example of the contrastive play of the European and Saramaka imaginations. Today we can be sure only that eight or ten Twofingers—people of non-Saramaka origin who had varying degrees of genetic deformity— in fact lived among the Nasí at Dosú Creek during the early 1760s. Little

---

* Government official L. Junker provides an interesting confirmation of this skeleton story. In 1920, he was present at a celebration in honor of Mafúngu, and he asked the Dómbis whether the god had come with their ancestors from Africa. "They denied this and told me that their ancestors had found this god . . . in the forest on the Upper River" (Junker 1922/23:461). Secrecy about Papútu-Dómbi rivalry, vengeance, and unfulfilled "payments" regarding this case—combined with the lateness of my hearing about it—make it one of those events still unclear to me.

was dead. But Kwádjaní's girl, the one whose hair hadn't been cut, she made the Túfínga-luángos. Her descendants are still at Kambalóa [a present-day Nasí village].

Later, the Indian woman became pregnant. But no one knew who the father was. She refused to tell. So, at night, they set watch. One night, after dark, they heard, "knock, knock, knock!" Whoever it was stayed till cock's crow and then managed to slip off. The third time he came, they caught him and were about to kill him. He said, "Don't kill me." The animal! It was an animal that had made her pregnant. An armadillo. That's why Nasís don't eat armadillos. The animal had been betrothed to the young woman while she lived in the forest. Now that she was old enough, he had returned to make love to her. The girl child she bore was called Lusí. This was the Túfínga child. (Bakáa 28 July 1978)

184. Túfíngaluángos were one kind of Indian. They had only two fingers. . . . Luángo Indians can survive for a really long time in the forest. They're very fierce and wild. They're still here in the forest. The Nasís went out and caught them, and brought them back to live with them. They became like family. One of them was Ma Kôndè. (Tebíni 11 July 1978) ❖

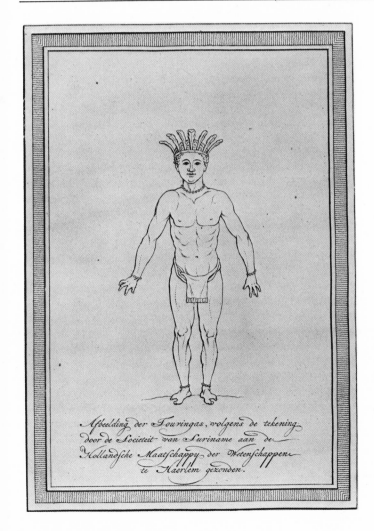

"Depiction of Two-fingers, after a drawing sent by the Societeit van Suriname to the Holland Learned Society at Haarlem" (Hartsinck 1770: 812–13). The original drawing is no longer in the possession of the Society and is presumed lost.

else about them seems certain. Most likely, they had split off from a much larger group of Indians who had intermarried with (non-Saramaka) maroons and who had lived in the savannahs to the west of the Saramacca River; future research may well permit more precise identification. The contemporary sources make it clear that during the period immediately preceding the 1762 treaty, Abíni and the other Saramaka chiefs went to some pains to exaggerate the size and importance of the Twofinger group to the whites, in order to represent them as a potential additional "unit" (village, clan) to receive tribute gifts. This strategy met with limited success, in that an emissary of Ma Kôndè, the Twofinger female "chief," was among the final signatories of the 1762 treaty. After the white postholder had made his first tour of inspection through the Saramaka villages in early 1763, however, the Twofingers were simply lumped, for purposes of tribute, with their Nasí hosts.*

The whites, whose hunger for the exotic was fueled by Saramaka stories about the Twofingers, were fascinated with what they heard. The first postholder to the Djukas produced the earliest report:

> I find myself intrigued by an account told me by the Saramakas about a village [people] that they call "Twofinger," who have on hands and feet but two "fingers," long like a crab's claws. They build large houses like the whites and cover them with planks. They have nails and gunpowder. It has been less than two years since they were discovered by the Saramakas. (SvS 16 February 1762 [5 February 1762])

Shortly afterwards, another white official in Djuka territory interviewed visiting Saramakas and wrote more detailed descriptions. He reported that the Twofingers could find their way in the forest by night as easily as by day; that the Akurio Indians who lived in the Saramaka village at Tukumútu considered them "Black People" rather than Indians (as some appeared to resemble Indian-African mixtures); that the "Spaniards" had attacked the Twofingers six to seven years previously (and the Twofingers had several battle "souvenirs" to prove it); that the Twofingers had been "found" by Saramakas who were on a hunting expedition on the Upper Pikílío; that they held everything communally, including their women, "the children not knowing who their fathers are"; and that

> the houses or huts of the women are built apart and divided into rooms. When a man wishes to have a woman he goes to her room and, if he is admitted, he leaves his bow, lance or club in front of the door, so that another who comes by sees it and knocks on another door. . . . They are every day happy, dancing and playing. (SvS 154, 4 May 1762)

After the treaty of 1762, the new Saramaka postholder visited the village at Dosú Creek where the Twofingers lived, determined that there were only eight or ten of them, and finally brought one of them back with him to Paramaribo, "in order to show this remarkable spectacle to your High Mightinesses of the Court [of Policy]" (SvS 155, 15 November 1763). The whites treated this Twofinger with considerable scientific curiosity and even sent a drawing of him back to the Holland Learned Society in Haarlem. Documents relevant to the Twofingers span the period from 1762 until 1780, when the last of the Twofingers related his woeful tale to a missionary.† ✛

---

* During this same period, Abíni was making similar efforts regarding a small group of Akurio Indians who had come to live among the Matawái; they, too, had representatives at the treaty signing but, in the end, once the postholder had visited in person, they—like the Twofingers—faded into the background (R. Price 1983).
† Relevant references include Hartsinck 1770:811–12; Staehelin 1913–19, 3:i:88; 3:ii:225; SvS 154, 4 May 1762 (1 April 1762); SvS 155, 20 April 1763 (20 February 1763); Hof 87, 26 February 1773 (29 January 1772); Stedman 1988:514–15, 658; and Benjamins and Snelleman 1917:682. Several of the better contemporary descriptions are included in R. Price 1983.

"**Depiction of Twofingers**" (Hartsinck 1770:810–11).

FREE AT LAST

1760–1762

How Wíi Brought the Peace

185. Sángonomitólola   Sángono, Me-of-the-magical-leaf [Wíi's praise name]
Sángonomitólola   Sángono, Me-of-the-magical-leaf
Lángu nêngè tjá fíi kó   The Lángu clan has brought the Peace
Baawíi nêngè tjá fíi kó   Baawíi's [an *apúku*'s] people have brought the Peace

Sángonomitólola   Sángono, Me-of-the-magical-leaf*
                        —(Tebíni 6 August 1976)

---

* Wíi's praise name for himself includes an eighteenth-century word no longer in Saramaccan: "*tol-ollà . . .* ein gewisses Kraut" (Schumann 1778; cf. Spalburg 1913:85); see also footnote to 185C for a discussion of Wíi's names. A variant for line 4 says, "A *Mapána nêngè* [Mapana person] has brought the Peace," which probably simply refers to Wíi's stay in Djuka territory (since *Mapána nêngè* was a standard Saramaka term for the Djukas—see Price and de Beet 1982); but it is just possible that it links him to a 1717 maroon village reported to have been under the leadership of a certain "Will" in that area (Schiltkamp and de Smidt 1973:272), though no supporting oral evidence is known to me. The *apúku* named Baawíi is said still to live in Bundjitapá, the village of Wíi's descendants on the Gaánlío.

How Wíi Brought the Peace (185–96)

Saramakas' pride in their ancestors' antiwhite fierceness does not prevent strong pride in their role in the forging of the Peace. Two groups—Lángus and Matjáus—actively dispute their respective roles in these events. The main protagonist is Wíi, the Lángu ancestor whose escape from slavery was discussed in *52–54.**

Knowledge of how, after nearly a century of warfare, the Peace of 1762 came to Saramaka is encapsulated in two adversarial song/speech fragments. The first (*185*), said to have been sung by Wíi himself on his return to Saramaka in 1762, is in the esoteric Luángu language. Today it is sung by his Lángu descendants at ceremonies for *apúkus* (with whom Lángu people are said to have a special affinity). The second (*186*) is in the esoteric Papá language and is sung by Matjáus as the standard response to the Lángu claim. Both are considered extremely powerful, and Tebíni

---

* Saramakas insist that this man's "real name" was Tjukúnda, the word for a long pod used as a rattle in *apúku* rituals. Matjáus gave him the *sêkêti* name ("romantic play name"—see Price and Price 1972) Uwíi, or Wíi ["leaf"], since he had been named after a tree part. The usual Matjáu reference for him today is Pái Uwíi ["son-in-law" Uwíi], which was the name used for him by his "father-in-law," Ayakô. Lángus today call him Tatá ["Father"] Wíi.

186.   Adjoto kaako, kaako siló   Stole it, you just stole it
                 Kwême djidjiló   Like the thief
                 Avúvu míndo djádja   From the land of the dead*
                                             —(Tebíni 6 August 1976)

187. The Matjáus gave him [Wíi] a wife. Then he came there [to their village], did witch-craft, tried to take over the whole place. When they shot him, he went into the forest. He went and took the Peace. That is what is said. (Agbagó 8 July 1978)

188. [After Yáya's "hummingbird" speech, see *177–78*] it wasn't long before the old man [Ayakô] died. Then they accepted the Peace. It was during his funeral rites that Wíi went into the forest. He went all the way to Djuka. And he saw the whites. He said, "What are you doing here?" They said, "We came to you [Saramakas], but you killed us, so we went back [to the coast] and never came again." Then they gave him the Peace. "Take it," they said. The old woman [Yáya, back in Saramaka] said, "Hasn't it happened exactly as I told you it would?" They all said, "Yes." (Tebíni 24 July 1976)

189. Wíi had a wife at the Pikílío. He was married to one of the daughters of Ayakô and Asukúme. After a time Ayakô became gravely ill, and divination accused his son-in-law, who had come to pay a visit to the sick man. . . . Ayakô took aside his son, Dabí, and told him, "I am going to prepare [ritually] something to give you. If Wíi is really a witch we will know it. It will be something for you to shoot him with. If he really is not a witch, it will not harm him. (Mètisên 2 July 1976)

* This is a very loose translation. The second and third lines apparently allude to the way Death steals its victims unawares. I have also been told that this Papá fragment means, "You're a liar. It wasn't you who brought the Peace. You stole it. By theft you brought the Peace." As with other fragments in esoteric languages, this Papá fragment is spoken differently by different people. I have also heard, "Nóno. Yú! [No way. You!] Adjoto kaako kaako/ We maasi djilo [also: Akwé maasi siló]/Awemé djadja."

---

would not utter them for the tape recorder (though he dictated them for me to write down); however, the tribal chief once chanted them with abandon into my machine, in the midst of an excited exposition of how it was really the Matjáus who had caused the Peace to come. The story of Wíi's exploits is not usually told from beginning to end, in narrative form. Fragment *187* is a full transcription/translation of the tribal chief's "explanation" of the story, after chanting the two songs—another nice example of typical narrative condensation. An interested Saramaka would very gradually piece the story together for himself from such overheard explications of these two esoteric songs, over the course of many different sittings with older men.*

The central events are not disputed among Saramakas—Wíi "found" the Peace in Djuka and arranged for it to come to Saramaka; but how and why he was in Djuka in the first place is a matter of considerable contention, and it bears on whether Lángus or Matjáus deserve ultimate credit for "having brought the Peace." Both Matjáus and Lángus agree on the outline of events: (1) Wíi took a Matjáu wife, becoming Ayakô's "son-in-law." (2) On a visit to the Matjáus, during Ayakô's funeral,

* There exist several published accounts of these events, based ultimately on oral testimony from Saramakas (Hartsinck 1770:800–801; Morssink n.d.; Junker 1922/23:463–64). Because an analysis of these texts would require considerable familiarity with contemporary politics (since most of the accounts represent clear attempts to manipulate information being given to the whites for then-current political ends), I do not consider them here.

190. Ayakô told Dabí that when he was dead, Dabí should put a musket ball in his mouth. Then, before they buried him, he should remove it and use it in a gun to shoot Wíi. If he had really killed Ayakô [by witchcraft], the shot would kill him; if he was indeed a witch but had not killed Ayakô, one of his fingers would fall off from the shot. (Peléki August 1975)

191. When Dabí shot at Wíi Tjukúnda, one of his fingers fell off. They knew he was a witch! Wíi ran off into the forest. It was at Baákawáta. (Peléki August 1975)

192. When dawn came, Wíi came back to the edge of the village and called out to his friend Kofíkióo. (Kofíkióo was a Nasí. He and Wíi had given each other wives [that is, were affines, doubly].) Wíi said, "Friend, I am not dead, but I can't go off [like this]. Call my sister's daughter and bring her for me." (Well, this sister's daughter was Tjámba-luángo.) He said, "I can't go without her. Let her bring one bunch of bananas with her when she comes." Those bananas! They kept peeling them and eating them all the way to Djuka [many days' travel]. They would go to sleep at night and when they awoke, the banana skins would be full again!* (Peléki 9 August 1976)

193. Wíi never came back [to live in Saramaka]. He lived on the Tapanahoni [really, the Djuka Creek] with his sister's child, the girl. The descendants of Tjámbaluángo are still there, in Djuka. But they call her by another name, Betú Kadósu. (Mètisên 31 July 1978)

194. They [the whites] gave Wíi the things necessary to make peace. He walked down Mándjuka [Creek] to Lokotí Creek. . . . He had been gone for so long that [Saramaka]

---

* Once, when discussing Maáku, the famous female captain of Kámpu whom Tebíni knew in his youth, he reminisced, "She was the last one to know the 'banana' *óbia.* The one where you peel the bananas but leave the peels attached to the stem. When she died, it was lost." I believe (but am not certain) that this was the *óbia* used by Tata Wíi.

Wíi was shot at with a gun by Ayakô's son Dabí.* (3) Wíi fled into the forest and was presumed dead. (4) He arrived at Djuka during the final peace negotiations there. (5) He returned to Saramaka, turning back a raiding party he met on its way to devastate plantations, and he brought Saramakas the opportunity to negotiate in similar fashion with the whites.

In conversation with me, Lángu people maintained simply that Dabí unjustly and without provocation shot a musket ball at Wíi (there is no mention of an "ordeal"), but that Wíi was so "ripe" (ritually powerful) that he was not hurt and was able, singlehandedly, to bring the Peace to all of Saramaka. In contrast, Matjáus stress that if it were not for their having rightfully chased Wíi from Saramaka, he would never have "happened upon" the Peace.† Peléki, for example, once

---

* Matjáus now say that, as was the custom, there had been a massive "play" (dance/drum/song performance) throughout the night preceding the burial, and at cock's crow there had been a *sangáa*—a wild melee in which men armed with machetes and guns (and many possessed by *komantí* spirits) dash all around the village chasing away evil. (Nowadays, this *sangáa* is done only during the "second funeral," long after the corpse has been buried, but Saramakas tell me that in the old days it was done on the early morning of the burial day itself.) It was during this *sangáa* that Dabí is supposed to have shot at Wíi.

† "Perspectival" disputes about First-Time history commonly include such agreement on the basic facts combined with disagreement about motivation or signficance. Matjáus, for example, like to denigrate the "jacket" that the Nasí Kwakú allegedly received from the whites after the battle of Kumakô (*107–20* above) by insisting that the whites did not *give* it to him, but that he simply "found" it—"an old shirt or something like that"—lying around when he went to the coast.

people had stopped even talking about him. . . . At its mouth, on the Suriname River, he saw Alúbutu, who was on his way to a raid. Wíi called out, "Mi Akwábosu!" "Well [Alúbutu said in surprise] the person with whom I used to call that special name* has been dead for a long time." [But he again distinctly heard] "Mi Akwábosu!" So he answered, "Mi Aliábosu!" And he cut across the river and he saw Wíi. Pái Wíi! "You're alive?" "Yes, I'm alive." (Tembái 23 July 1978)

* Special friendship between two Saramakas may include the creation of special (reciprocal) address terms, referred to as "calling name" (see Price and Price 1972).

---

exclaimed to me with considerable passion: "Wíi didn't go to Djuka because he wanted to! He went there because he had gotten in trouble [with the Matjáus]." Any credit or positive motivation is relentlessly denied him by Matjáus. Tebíni put it this way: "The whites went to Djuka. They got there before Wíi happened upon the Peace there. He brought it back. . . . [But] the time had come, anyway. At that time, the old man [Ayakô] was already dead."* These Matjáu counterclaims and deprecations are sometimes backed up with further elaborations upon the story itself. Otjútju, for example, explained:

> When Dabí had prepared the musket ball ritually, he told his sister [Wíi's wife] what he had done. He said he was going to shoot Wíi. But she [surreptitiously] removed the ball from the gun, leaving only the [other] óbia ingredients with which he had loaded it. Dabí did not know the ball had been removed, and when he shot at Wíi, that is why only his finger fell off. Otherwise it would have killed him [for his witchcraft].

Leaving aside the questions of Wíi's motivation and of Matjáu-Lángu contention for the ultimate glory of "having brought the Peace," we find firm confirmation in contemporary documents of the basic Saramaka story. (I summarize only those documentary materials that bear directly on the Saramaka accounts, drawing on a large number of available pages; see, for details, R. Price 1983.)

Within a year of having successfully negotiated a treaty of peace with the Djukas in 1760, the whites received a message from Djuka—originating from Wíi, who had been living there for some time—that the Saramakas also wanted peace. Toward this end, the Council in Paramaribo decided to send Quakoe (a Djuka headman then serving as official emissary to the whites) to Saramaka. With a solemn handshake, he promised that he would undertake the mission, and he accepted in advance a reward for this service. Instead of going to Saramaka, however, he simply returned from the city to Djuka, making clear to his compatriots that he had no intention of actually making the trip. The Djuka headmen claim to have tried to force him to go, but to no avail; and they finally "summoned Wíi, who some years ago had fled from Saramaka . . . and they persuaded him to go [instead of Quakoe], and they gave him four men [said in another document to have been eighteen men] to accompany him. Wíi accepted" (SvS 154, 4 May 1762 [8 March 1762]). Wíi's expedition to Saramaka left in late 1761 (after considerable discussion among the

* The death of "the old man" is the event that allows Matjáus to resolve the dilemma of wishing to depict themselves as having been both warlike and conciliatory toward the whites. Yáya's "hummingbird" speech (177–78), marking the official shift in attitude, likewise alludes to this death as signaling, in a sense, the passing of the Age of Heroes. In the same breath as deprecating Lángu claims to bringing the Peace, and stressing their own positive role, Matjáus sometimes flaunt their warlike postures and inclinations. Here is an old Matjáu headman talking, with pride, on tape to his grandson (not in my presence): "This is why Matjáus were not for peace. It's not that they were inherently fierce [or evil]. But Matjáus are stubborn! Once you cross them in some way, they'll never let you forget it. Well, they were not about to 'forget about' what bakáas had done. And this not-willing-to-let-bygones-be-bygones is why peace wasn't made earlier."

THE EVENTS

195. Wíi sang out, *"Mi kwanda bilúngu ge malúngu. Mi bi gó fu ógi, mi kó fu búnu."** (Otjútju 13 August 1976)

196. He said, "When they shot me, I didn't die. I went all the way to Djuka. I saw the Peace they made, and I'm bringing it back here." Alúbutu told him to wait. (The other canoes of raiders had gone on ahead.) And he went to Dabí and asked him, "If you should see your brother-in-law [alive], what would happen?" Dabí mused, "But Wíi has been dead such a long time!" Then Alúbutu told him how he had seen Wíi. Dabí said, "If Wíi isn't dead, then we have no more grudge with him any more. I am finished with that." Then Alúbutu gave Dabí some salt and a knife that Wíi had given him to prove that peace had come [to Djuka]. (Peléki July 1974) ✤

* The first phrase is not normal Saramaccan but a praise name; *malúngu* is an *apúku* word whose meaning is not known to me, and *bilúngu (biòngò)* refers to certain crucial, helpful ingredients of ritual recipes. The second phrase, in rhymed Saramaccan, means, "I went [there] because of evil [or, to do evil] [but] I've returned for good [having done good]."

Djukas about whether or not Wíi was in fact a witch); its successful return to Djuka took place in February 1762. Some forty Saramakas, including six headmen, accompanied Wíi back to Djuka; all were seeking peace.

A fascinating postscript to one of the letters written from Djuka to the governor to describe the expedition reported that on their way to Saramaka, Wíi's group had intercepted a group of Samsám's men on their way to raid the governor's own plantation (which, the letter adds, had already recently been raided by the Nasís), and were successful in convincing the would-be raiders to return to their villages in Saramaka (SvS 154, 16 February 1762 [5 February 1762]). This postscript, then, points directly to the event described by Saramakas today in *194:* Wíi's journey from Djuka down the Lokotí Creek (see map p. 100), at the mouth of which he met a group of Saramakas heading downriver on a raiding party, showed them evidence that peace had come to Djuka, turned them back, and thereby set the final peace negotiations in motion.*

Taken as a whole, the documents from 1761–62 (which are too complex to examine in further detail here) reveal that Wíi was in fact a refugee from Saramaka harbored by the Djukas; that he was involved in troublesome relationships with both Saramakas and Djukas that included frequent accusations of witchcraft; that he successfully communicated the Saramakas' wishes for peace to the whites;† that he led a peace-making expedition from Djuka to Saramaka (that met on the way a party of raiders whom he turned back); and that, as a result of the subsequent negotiations, peace finally came to Saramaka. Born in Africa, an early maroon leader of the Lángu clan, a refugee among the Djuka for alleged misdeeds in Saramaka, Wíi in his own complicated way indeed "brought the Peace." *Sángonomitólola!* ✤

* Another document describes how a few months later, a group of Matjáus came separately to the whites to chide them about trusting Wíi, who they explicitly said was a fugitive from Saramaka who had killed their own senior man (Ayakô) by witchcraft. The Matjáu version of these events, then, has been consistent for over two hundred years (SvS 154, 2 October 1762).

† There is further complex evidence in the documents that Wíi's motives included revenge on his "enemies" Samsám and the Matjáus, both of whom had apparently been among the Saramakas most strongly against the Peace (see Price n.d.).

The Separate Peace of Afadjé

197. When Afadjé heard that peace had come to Suriname, he went to the city. . . . They gave him *two* staffs of office! He grasped them like this, one with each hand. He sat down and broke two chairs, that's how big he was. They gave him a wooden chair; it bent *gándán* [intensifier]. Finally, they took a big pot and laid a [iron] manioc griddle across its mouth, and he sat down. No chair could hold him!* (Tebíni 6 August 1976)

198. As they were coming south, Afadjé died. At Béiki-lánga-úku [near Berg en Dal]. He was sick in his belly. That's the thing they sing in Papá. (Otjútju 3 August 1976)

199. As Afadjé lay dying, he sang:

> Mása fu alúnya [the name used for the *kúnu,* repeated several times]
> Ahunudé. Mi húúnhun.
> Mi kó dafié. Mása fu alúnya. Ahunudé.
> Mi depó depó. Mása fu alúnya.
> Ké, mi mása! Mi deláo.
> Mása fu alúnya.

* The several fragments I have heard about Afadjé's city "enstoolment" come from Tebíni, Peléki, and Otjútju (all of whom see each other often) and from Faánsisónu, the senior captain who now holds Afadjé's staff. Until 1976, my notes show that these fragments were always phrased in terms of Gúnkamé, Afadjé's father (see *23–24*); my notes are consistent that the older man was depicted as the "giant" who made the separate peace, with the son dying on his way south after having taken over his late father's position. In 1978, however (almost as if there had been a discussion in my absence that had resolved the issue differently), each of them insisted that this story referred to the *son.* I cannot account for this apparent change except by accepting—as they insist—that they routinely use the name of the father in conversation to stand for that of the son (a rhetorical device that is common enough in reference to living Saramakas today).

The Separate Peace of Afadjé (197–201)

Saramakas preserve little memory of the intricate negotiations and political maneuvering that occurred during 1762 as a preliminary to the final treaty. Their vision of these events focuses on two moments: Wíi's bringing the Peace—preserved as a lively case of interclan rivalry—and the day that Saramakas collectively celebrated the official coming of the Peace in Sentéa. Nevertheless, embedded in oral fragments about other issues, preserved for other reasons, I find traces of some of the complex events of 1762. The briefest outline from contemporary documents helps set the stage and permits a perspective on Saramaka selectivity about the period. (Further details and documentation are provided in R. Price 1983 and in Price n.d.)

One month after Wíi returned to Djuka with the Saramaka delegation, the government negotiator, Louis Nepveu (who had been Creutz's spokesman in successfully setting up the ceasefire with "Adoe" in 1749), arrived there from Paramaribo to begin peace talks once again. The discussions between Nepveu and Chief Abíni ranged over a number of subjects of interest to the whites (the 1750 Picolet case, the Twofingers, the enumeration of Saramaka villages and headmen) as well as to the Saramakas (the precise provisions of the treaty, especially the number, quality, and kinds of "tribute" goods they would receive).* In April 1762, just before Nepveu returned to the city for the next stage of preparations, Abíni came to him to request a letter "to

* The Saramakas not only specified in detail the major kinds of goods they expected as tribute; they insisted that they did *not* want "various wishywashy [things] such as dolls' bells and other trifles [which the Djukas had received] but instead of these, salt and carpenter's tools" (SvS 154, 4 May 1762).

To beg the great *kúnu* [avenging spirit]. He said, "Great thanks. May the *kúnu* leave me alone, allow me to arrive [in Saramaka]. But if it kills me, it mustn't kill any of my kinsmen again." Then, it killed him. But it has never killed others, because Afadjé begged it so strongly. (Otjútju 13 August 1976)

200. Afadjé sang; he prayed:

> Vodu mekuta.
> Mekuta Afadjé.
> Huuhun, hunhun.
> Mi ko dafié.
> Ahunudé.
> Vodu Mekuta.
> Mekuta Afadjé.
> —(Peléki 31 August 1978)

201. Ever since my eyes could see, the elders said to me, "Tatá Afadjétosúme, of Gún-kamé, of the lineage of Dóti. He shouted a shout. And it stayed in Papá." It always used to protect Matjáus when they were away from home on journeys, but later, Matjáus began to die while away from home. (Otjútju spring 1976)   ✤

---

show to all the [other] headmen, as a sign . . . to make clear the intention of making Peace" (SvS 154, 4 May 1762 [15 April 1762]; for the full text of Nepveu's report, including this letter, see R. Price 1983:document 10). I believe that it is this letter, which singles out Abíni from all other headmen, that Matjáus commemorate in their oft-repeated formula, "Abíni received the letter at Sara Creek."* It was the receipt of this letter that contemporary Matjáus seem to have used as a key argument to bolster Abíni's accession, several months later, to the office of tribal chief of the Saramakas, the first to be officially recognized by the colonial government.

In mid-April, Abíni and his people returned to Saramaka, while Nepveu—accompanied by several Saramaka guests-of-the-government—went to Paramaribo to make arrangements for the treaty-signing itself. (Many of these preparations concerned ordering from the Netherlands the enormous quantity of goods to be given to the Saramakas as tribute—see Price and de Beet 1982, which includes a photo of the final list.) By September 1762, Nepveu had installed himself (without the tribute gifts, which had not yet arrived from overseas) at the agreed-upon treaty-signing site across from the mouth of the Sara Creek. Over a period of days, large numbers of Saramakas arrived, including Wíi and his "sister's son" Antamá, the Nasí leader Kwakú Étja, Abíni, a number of other headmen, and about two hundred men "almost all with snaphaunce muskets, of which several had four or five" (SvS 154, 27 September 1762 [17 September 1762]). After difficult negotiations, centering largely on the quantity of gunpowder and shot to be given to the Saramakas, the agreement was finally sealed on 19 September 1762.

> They took earth and water, and each chief placed a child or youth from his own family in front of him, calling on God Above and the Earth as witnesses. Then they swore, with considerable ceremony, that anyone who violated any of the articles would perish with his people, giving a little of the mixture to the youths to consume. (SvS 154, 27 September 1762 [20 September 1762])

On 24 September, Nepveu returned to Paramaribo from the Sara Creek, accompanied by sixteen Saramakas (SvS 154, 24 September 1762). He was greeted royally by the Council and given a gift of

* Matjáus today insert Abíni's receipt of the letter into several other stories, including the 1750 sinking of Picolet (see *158–61* above). He did in fact receive another "letter" or "paper"—a copy of the treaty itself—at Sara Creek a few months later. I suspect, however, it was the letter he persuaded Nepveu to give him that is the key document for Matjáus, as it would have been the means at that particular moment to establish his primacy, in Saramakas' eyes, over all other chiefs.

*f.*1,200 and an annual pension of *f.*600 (SvS 154, 29 September 1762); in addition, the Directors of the Societeit honored him with a "silver urn" to be used as a coffee cup (Hartsinck 1770:812). The Council quickly moved to ratify the Peace formally, and on 28 September the official ceremony was held at the Court of Policy. Present were the Saramakas who had accompanied Nepveu from the Sara Creek as well as Wíi. The Council gave Nepveu *f.*120 to buy for the chiefs whatever things they might want; and for the absent Chief Dabí, Abíni was given a flag as well as a drum (SvS 154, 28 September 1762). A day of public thanksgiving was proclaimed in all the churches for 5 December, to celebrate the signing of the Saramaka peace and "to ask Him to assure that the Peace be permanent and prosperous" (SvS 154, 29 September 1762; SvS 205, 5 December 1762; Wolbers 1861:159). Even Wíi got special recognition: on 7 October he was sent a "doucertje" for his help in making the peace (SvS 154, 7 October 1762), and a month later, the minutes of the Council record that he had requested and was granted "een extra doucertje" (SvS 154, 7 November 1762).*

After the September treaty signing at the Sara Creek, several groups of Saramakas appeared in Djuka—one led by Samsám and another, with thirty-seven men, known as "Matjari[s]" (Matjáus). Neither had been present at the treaty signing, and both now wanted special gifts from the whites (SvS 154, 24 September 1762, 2 October 1762, 8 November 1762). I have not seen further details about these delegations in the documents, though it is clear that some of these Saramakas did continue on from Djuka to the city with the intention of making a separate peace.

I now believe that it is to this set of obscure incidents that the Matjáu story of "The Separate Peace of Afadjé" (*197–201*) refers. Its importance for Matjáus concerns pan-tribal politics and succession: as discussed in 23C–24C, the matrilineal descendants of Dóti and Gúnkamé (Afadjé's parents) have twice held the office of tribal chief.

Matjáu traditions describe Afadjé's enstoolment in the city after the general treaty was signed and his death soon after, as he led his group south. I suspect that Afadjé—whose group was clearly separate from that of Abíni, in the documents as well as in Saramaka memories—treated separately in a preliminary way with the whites in Paramaribo during the summer of 1762 (as, probably, did Samsám's people). We know that early the following year, Afadjé and Samsám were in Saramaka to conclude a final peace—again separately from the other chiefs—with the white emissary to Saramaka who wrote: "On 13 January [1763] Samsam and the headman of Matjarie whose name is Avaje, bringing other Negroes with them, came to see me to conclude the Peace" (SvS 318, 15 January 1763—see also R. Price 1983:document 12). It must have been soon after that, returning from a visit to Paramaribo (possibly in connection with the distribution of tribute goods the next fall) that Afadjé's sudden and terrible death occurred. (I have seen no mention of his name in the documents after 1764.)

The death of a leader, so soon after his official recognition as captain by the whites, and far from home, must have been considered enormously evil and inauspicious. According to Saramakas, Afadjé's captain's staff remained unused for decades and his position unfilled. The Papá fragment that he sang as he lay dying, in great abdominal pain, is among the most dangerous that Matjáus know. I have only whispered and indistinct versions on tape, plus possibly-garbled fragments of a

---

* Wíi did not live to enjoy his privileged status with the government. Having publicly crossed Quakoe, his long-term host in Djuka, during the Peace preliminaries, he had decided to move back to Saramaka with his wife and children. In May of 1762, as a token of their gratitude for his role in making the Peace, the Court resolved to aid Wíi in this move. However, in the midst of his family preparations for the move, Wíi was shot by a Djuka, almost precipitating a Saramaka-Djuka war (see, for example, SvS 154, 13 May 1762, 8 November 1762; 317, 1 November 1762; 155, 20 April 1763 [passim]). I do not have detailed oral fragments about these matters, which are described at greater length in R. Price 1983 and Price n.d.

The Day They Celebrated the Peace at Sentéa

202. ([Tebíni to me:] I will do something special for you. Just like the day they celebrated the Peace at Sentéa. . . .)* When they had come to the very end of the meeting
[with the whites], well, we finally answered "Yes." As soon as we answered "Yes," everyone solemnly clapped their hands together *bólobólo* and then ceased [a sign of thanks-
giving or prayer]. And we sang out:

Ki-bén-de ki-bén-de o—— tjí-mba-ti kó - a. An-a-béén-sú o

ti-dé tjí-mba-ti kó - a. Ki-bén-de ki-bén-de o—— tjí-mba-ti kó - a.

An-a-béén— sú e tjí - mba - ti kó - a.

Tebíni explained the song's general meaning: "The heart is cool. There's no more fighting. Good things
have come. People's blood mustn't fall on the earth any more." A speculative, more literal translation of
these esoteric words would interpret "Kibénde" and "Anabéénsú" as the names of the gods being
addressed, and "tidé tjímbati kóa" as "today Tjímba's heart is cool"; separate traditions record that Tjímba
was an *apúku* (forest spirit) on whom the Matjáus depended heavily in their battles with the whites.

* For a recording of parts of this performance, see Price and Price 1977. In *202*, I have combined pieces of
several performances given me by Tebíni in 1976 and 1978.

---

second song—"Akwati logoso sawée madonu kaiwo fu naadji"—which were used to "beg" the
kúnu (avenging spirit) to desist. (I have been told—though I remain suspicious on other grounds
of its reliability—that this *kúnu* was none other than "the white plantation owner who Ayakô
killed. [that is, Imanuël Machado] It stayed in the lineage of Dóti. That's what killed Afadjé.")

The Day They Celebrated the Peace at Sentéa (202)

For Saramakas, all of the events recorded in this book culminate in what they remember as a
single climactic day, "when they celebrated the Peace at Sentéa." (Today, when a public meeting
is really large, Saramakas say, "It's as big as the one at Sentéa!") It was on this day that the "trumpet
of war" (to use Dabí's felicitous phrase, see above) was finally set aside, after nearly a century of
struggle. It was a day of victory and celebration. And in modern Saramaka consciousness, all of
history tends to be measured against it as either "before" or "after." Saramakas do not preserve
memories of the final formalities that led to Sentéa. As we have seen above, the actual treaty was
"signed" at the Sara Creek in September 1762 and ratified in Paramaribo soon afterwards. It was,
however, the arrival of the official government emissary at Sentéa in November that marked for
Saramakas the real end of the war, and that prompted the great celebration itself.

By the late 1970s, the "Matjáu elder" Tebíni was generally acknowledged to be the last living
person able to describe the great day in detail, using many of the songs actually sung at the event

My goodness! We clapped hands rhythmically *bólobólobólo*. Then they said, "The way things are, battles are all over, guns are a thing of the past, human blood will no longer stain the earth." This peace [freedom] just couldn't be enough for them! "Let the Supreme God send it to us as is really fitting. Let him continue to give us more." And they prayed to the Great God:

"Mulêlè" is said by Tebíni to be an esoteric word for stars. "Abíti abíti" means "a few." This haunting, immensely sweet song would then be saying, "A few stars for my ancestors/Let me [untranslatable by me] name of an *apúku*/But how will I ever reach the stars?" [Or, "But where will I ever find the stars?"]

---

more than two hundred years ago. It is only during rites for the earliest ancestors, at the Dángogó shrine of Awónêngè, that these songs are normally performed today. Tebíni was kind enough to sing them for me on several occasions (in the express hope of preserving them forever), and I have heard some of them as well from the greatest living *adunké* singer, Kandámma (who was born ca. 1897). Tebíni's accounts of the Peace sometimes sneak in an appropriate song or two from later periods; in the transcription/translation presented here, the only candidate for such anachronism is "Mbéi u án sáa môô," which I know was a favorite of the famous water spirit (the *wênti* Wanánzái) that was in the head of Kódji of Béndiwáta a half-century ago, and which may possibly have been composed by this god. (An excerpt from one of Tebíni's performances—as well as an *adunké* song sung by Kandámma—is included on our phonograph record [Price and Price 1977].)* Following the final and most complete of the special performances from which *202* is transcribed, Otjútju—who was one of the Saramaka men who had shared with me the privilege of hearing it—spontaneously thanked Tebíni's "soul" by presenting a shiny new machete and, in recognition of the fact that Tebíni was the only living Saramaka who still knew these songs, formally bestowed upon him a new name: "Matjáu Gold."

As should be clear from this section, Saramaka song represents a central medium for the preservation of historical experience. Among the many examples already cited in this book, we might recall Ayakô's "eagle" *óbia* song (*11*), Wámba's sung warning about Kwasímukámba (*174*), the *papá* about Folú firing Agbáila (*131*), or Wíi's triumphant Sángonomitólola (*185*). Today it is *sêkêti* songs that chronicle the loves and tragedies, the hopes and needs of Saramakas, and serve

---

* Johannes King, the nineteenth-century Matawái Christian evangelist, has left a moving account, in prose, of a very similar "thanksgiving" celebration, performed during his youth on the occasion of the triennial tribute distributions. Included is the firing of salutes, dance/song/drumming, playing "African trumpets," prayers to the gods and, separately, prayers and rites for the warrior ancestors who won the Peace. The original Sranan version is reproduced in King 1983; for an English translation, see Price 1979b:302–4.

"The Great God has caused us to emerge from the forest undergrowth to receive the Peace. Let's celebrate it and go still further. Let it go on and on." ([To me:] That's what this is all about. The time had come for peace. Sadness was no longer with us. We had found freedom.)

This song, addressed to the ancestors, literally means, "Let's not be sad any longer, come 'play' [dance/sing/drum] for [with] us./ Brother, [first line repeats]/ Well, when the time is right, you can come to us/[first line repeats].

---

as a major form of social commentary. Until the early twentieth century, it was often songs in the style of *adunké* that served this function, and it is the singing of these *adunké* songs at ancestor rites (in order to please those people with the songs they loved when they were alive) that keeps these once-topical events alive as well (see, for more detail, Price and Price 1980:174–78, and S. Price 1983). The final song in Tebíni's account of the Peace celebration is an excellent example of such an *adunké*, preserving for posterity an embarrassing domestic incident of more than two centuries ago.* In cross-cultural perspective, the commemoration of great events may take many forms; the preservation through song of a transient domestic squabble that happened to take place on the greatest day in Saramaka history somehow epitomizes for me a prototypically Saramaka way of at once humanizing (or individualizing) and celebrating their distant collective past.

Immediately after the Peace was ratified in Paramaribo, following the precedent established with the Djukas, the government appointed a white Postholder, Ensign J. C. Dörig, to take up residence among the Saramakas. He left Paramaribo in mid-October of 1762, accompanied by twenty-seven Saramakas who served as his escort, and had an often-frightening three-and-one-half-week canoe journey to the upper Gaánlío (punctuated by the bellicose but largely empty

---

* Kandámma has sung for me another *adunké*, apparently composed at Sentéa by the wronged woman, Diítawéndjèmánu, herself, to memorialize the very same incident: "Akámakásugóni [a person's name], the thing is ruined. That [expletive] husband of mine, Kwasí, didn't want me to come. *Hónzóó.*"

"Those people who didn't live to see the Peace, they must not be jealous. Their hearts must not be angry. There is no help for it. When the time is right, we shall get still more freedom. Let them not look at what they have missed. Let us and them be on one side together, those First-Time people! It is to them we are speaking."

There was a god called Tándo. We sang out:

Hón- dóó! Bái hón- dóó! Hón- dóó! Bái hón- dóó! Ti-dé u nyán kó-a e.

Nyán mi nyán soo-sóo bán-da- wa. É, bái hón- dóó!

"Hóndóó" is a now-obsolete exclamation of great joy, like the synonymous "Hóókóó" and "Hónzóó" (see below). The song is in Komantí language: "Joy! Shout out 'Joy'!/Today we eat [celebrate] kóa [coolness? peace?]/I am eating meat bándawa! Shout out 'Joy.'"

---

threats of Samsám). On 3 November, Dörig made his historic entry into Sentéa, the first peacetime visit of a white man to a Saramaka village. Even he was impressed by his reception:*

At 6 AM we set out [up river] passing several stony rapids, until at 8 o'clock I heard a horn blowing. Not knowing what it meant, I asked about it and was told that it was a signal that they were ready to receive me. At about 8:30 at a creek on the right hand side going upstream, at Darie [Dabí] or Abini's landingplace, I heard some musket salutes being fired and I saw Abini and some Negro men and women standing there to offer a warm welcome. Among others they included an old Negro woman painted completely white with a plantation-slave cutlass in her hand [the blade of] which she held in her [other] crooked arm, pacing back and forth making a racket, babbling in her language which I could not understand. The other nearby Negro women appeared very frightened and went to stand behind the men, using them as a barrier. After I had a talk with Abini, he had all my goods carried off, and at 9 o'clock we set off together accompanied by the sound of the horn and the firing of their muskets. At 10 o'clock, as we approached their village, the first [person] we saw was an old Negro right in our path, holding a calabash of water and a siebie siebie [scoparia dulcis] or wild plant in his hands, using it as a brush to sprinkle us with the water that was in the calabash, in accordance with their pretences [that it serves] against the evil spirits and further because of their religiosity. The second [person] who we met as we proceeded was an old Negro wearing a tall red hat who gave me his hand with the words, "Greetings, Master. If you curse me, I'll curse you back. That's the way this Peace works. . . . "

During our march, the other Negroes who accompanied me from the fort [Paramaribo], walked one behind the next, and we were all sprinkled by the old Negro with water from his calabash. This continued right up to [our arrival at] their shed which they call Gran Cassa. There, while we sat on low blocks of wood, the horn was blown and muskets fired with tremendous shouting and noise, clapping hands to the mouth and with [regular] handclapping. The spectacle was curious.

After being subjected to further "exotic" rituals, Dörig listened to a public speech of welcome from Abíni and began to answer politely in kind; but he was interrupted by

a great handclapping with other hand gestures toward both Heaven and Earth, and clapping them [hands] to the mouth. The horns were blaring and I was honored with the firing of several salutes.

---

* I present here only a few representative passages from Dörig's journal (SvS 155, 20 April 1763) to compare with Tebíni's account. The full document is presented in R. Price 1983.

THE EVENTS

European being brought upriver by Saramakas, 1779. Engraving from Johann Andreus Riemer, *Missions-Reise nach Suriname,* Zittau und Leipzig, 1801, plate 6. The original caption translates as "Master! Fear not."

We told the gods. The water god called Tándo. We were calling out to tell them that peace had come.

By the time they had finished praying, it was the dead of night. The women said that it was time to dance—until morning! The men said, "Let's dance. Let's celebrate. Peace [freedom] has come!" Then they sang out:

Fií kó, ——— kó dén-de fií ——— o. ——— Kó dén - de,

Peace has come, *kó dénde*, Freedom. *Kó dénde*, Peace.

Peace had come. . . . Then they said, "Well, women, it's time to show off [strut your stuff, *poólu*], to dance *aléle*." And they sang out:

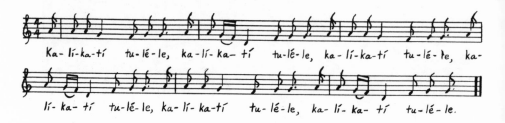

Ka - lí - ka - tí tu - lé - le, ka - lí - ka - tí tu - lé - le, ka - lí - ka - tí tu - lé - le, ka -

lí - ka - tí tu - lé - le, ka - lí - ka - tí tu - lé - le, ka - lí - ka - tí tu - lé - le.

When the ceremony had ended, I was conducted from there by the whole company to my lodgings, having asked Abini if I could rest, being weary from the tiring journey.

As Dörig settled in for the night, who would have been bustling around the village in preparation for the evening's celebration? Using documents from the later eighteenth century, I can infer the identity of a great many of the younger and middle-aged participants in these festivities, but these people are beyond the scope of the present book, since all remembered traces of their deeds date from after the Peace. But what about the men and women who have filled our stories to this point? How many of them would have been at Sentéa? From Dörig's journal we know that Abíni and Dabí were his primary hosts, and that Afadjé and Šamsám had made a special point of being absent. We can surmise that Abíni's elderly mother, Yáya, accompanied by his wife, Akoomí, and her Awaná relatives, were supervising the cooking. Abíni's son Alábi would have been helping with other practical arrangements (and possibly flirting with his future wife Sialôtò). The inseparable Nasí brothers, Étja and Kwádjaní, Wíi's "sister's son" Antamá, Kaási's son Alándo and his Lángu kinsman Bákisipámbo, Musínga and Bekú from Tuído in Matawái, the Dómbi Dóndo Kasá, Folú's grandson Alúbutu—all soon to be officially recognized as captains—would have been in solemn attendance. Adjágbò and his beautiful wife Paánza, Adugwé and his aged brother-in-law Kúngoóka (who was probably supervising ritual preparations), Ayakô's brother-in-law Ngweté and his Papútu in-laws, the Twofinger Indians—all would have been there. Many hundreds of others were there as well—some of their names known to us from later events, some still invoked in rituals at Saramaka ancestor shrines, but most now lost forever as individuals. But there was one final group whose presence weighed heavily on the celebrants that night: those men and women who did not live to see the Peace, but upon

THE EVENTS

Then the women danced *gilin gilin gilin* [intensifiers]. The men danced, moving their hips. . . . The house . . . the whole village was going "zzzz. . . . " [with excitement] Well, that night they played *aléle* . . . all night long, *gbele, gbele, gbele.* Everyone was dancing it! They played *aléle* at Sentéa. Then they went [another day] and played it at Baákawáta! That's what they did when the Peace came. ([To me, excitedly:] Friend, I am giving it all to you! If you have a tape recorder, turn it on because *that* day, there were no tape recorders!)

When they finished this celebration . . . one woman said to another, "Child [term of affection], with the size of our celebration at Baákawáta, with that fantastic *aléle,* how come *you* didn't show up?" [The other] said, "Oh! The man [my husband] locked me up and left me in the house [because he was jealous]. That's why I didn't come." Then the first woman sang out [composing a new *adunké* song, still sung today]:

Translation: Diítawéndjèmánu [the woman's play name], Why didn't you come to the *aléle? Hóókóó* [expression of joy]. [Expletive] Kwasí didn't want me to come. *Hóókóó.* ✣

---

whose sacrifices and heroism it was built. Among those names and deeds invoked that evening at the ancestor shrine of Sentéa would have been many now familiar to us—Lánu, Ayakô, and Sééi, Dóti and Gúnkamé, Kwémayón, Gúngúúkúsu, Kaála and Andolé, Kaási and Piyái, Talí and Amímba, Abámpapá and Adáumêni, Bíatiísi and Yebá, Vumá and Tjasíngbe, Momóimítji, Makambí, and so many others.

Dörig reported in his journal that while he found the lodgings that Abíni had provided for him comfortable, he was quite unable to sleep that night. First, "All the Negro men and women came and made an unbelievable uproar with muskets, and stayed for a long while near me, until Abíni finally chased them away" (SvS 318, 15 January 1763). Even after this helping hand from Abíni, however, Dörig still could not get to sleep because of what he described, in his gruff soldier's way, as "howling and shrieking figures shooting off guns the whole night" (ibid.). Seen through the foreign eyes of this European soldier, this description must refer to nothing less than the climactic ceremony-cum-celebration described so delicately by Tebíni: the night they played *aléle* at Sentéa.*

From village to village—from Sentéa to Baákawáta, from Dosú Creek to Tuído—women now danced the *aléle. Fií kó:* Peace had come at last. A new chapter of Saramaka history was about to begin. ✣

* The rest of the final peace negotiations, described in detail in Dörig's journal, include the "separate peaces" of Samsám and Afadjé (*197–201*), who represented the last of the groups that made up the Saramaka nation to come to terms with the whites.

REFERENCES

Archival references are abbreviated as follows in the text:

GA   Het oud-archief van de Gouvernements secretarie (Gouverneurs archief) der kolonie Suriname, Algemeen Rijksarchief, The Hague.

Hof   Archieven van het Hof van Politie en Crimineele Justitie, Algemeen Rijksarchief, The Hague.

SvS   Archieven van de Sociëteit van Suriname, Algemeen Rijksarchief, The Hague.

Anon.

1697   *Bericht en Antwoord Aen de Edele Achtbare Heeren Directeurs Van de Geoctroyeerde Sociëteit van Suriname door Jan van Scharphuysen, Oud-Gouverneur der selve Colonie, Overgegeven Op de Pointen en Artikelen, uit den naeme en van wegen haar Ed-Achtb. aen hem ter hand gestelt. Nevens de gemelde Pointen en Artikelen, hier achter gevoegt.* Amsterdam: Wed. e. van Aert Dirksz. Oossaen.

Anon.

1752   *Recueil van egte Stukken en Bewyzen door S. du Plessis . . . tegen Mr. Jan Jacob Mauricius,* 4 vols. Amsterdam.

Anon.

1830   "Naamlijst der plantaadjes en gronden (opgemaakt 1 September 1829)." In *Surinaamsche almanak voor het jaar 1830,* 51–110. Amsterdam: C. G. Sulpke.

Appadurai, Arjun

1981   "The Past as a Scarce Resource." *Man* 16:201–19.

Axtell, James, and William C. Sturtevant

1980   "The Unkindest Cut, or Who Invented Scalping?" *William and Mary Quarterly,* (3d ser.) 37:451–72.

Bakhuis, L. A.

1902   "Verslag der Coppename-expeditie." *Tijdschrift van het Koninklijk Nederlandsch Aardrijkskundig Genootschap,* 2e ser. 19:695–852.

Bastide, Roger

1965   "La théorie de réincarnation chez les Afro-Américains." In *Réincarnation et vie mystique en Afrique noire,* edited by Dominique Zahan, 9–27. Paris: Presses Universitaires de France.

de Beet, Chris, and H.U.E. Thoden van Velzen

1977   "Bush Negro Prophetic Movements: Religions of Despair?" *Bijdragen tot de Taal-, Land- en Volkenkunde* 133:100–135.

Benjamins, H. D., and Joh. F. Snelleman, eds.

1917   *Encyclopaedie van Nederlandsch West-Indië.* The Hague: Martinus Nijhoff.

Bijlsma, R.

1919   "Het archief der Nederlandsch Portugeesch-Israelitische Gemeente in Suriname tot omstreeks 1864." *Verslagen Omtrent 's Rijks Oude Archieven* 42 (1):297–329.

Bloch, Marc

1953   *The Historian's Craft*. New York: Vintage.

Brandt, Elizabeth

1980   "On Secrecy and the Control of Knowledge: Taos Pueblo." In *Secrecy: A Cross-Cultural Perspective,* edited by Stanton K. Tefft, 123–46. New York: Human Sciences Press.

Cohen, David William

1977   *Womunafu's Bunafu: A Study of Authority in a Nineteenth-Century African Community*. Princeton: Princeton University Press.

Dening, Greg

1980   *Islands and Beaches. Discourse on a Silent Land: Marquesas 1774–1880*. Honolulu: The University Press of Hawaii.

Dittelbach, Petrus

1692   *Verval en val der Labadisten*. Amsterdam: Daniel van den Dalen.

van Eeghen, Chr. P.

1946   "Dirk Valkenburg—boekhouder—schrijver—kunstschilder voor Jonas Witsen." *Oud-Holland* 61:58–69.

Fontaine, Jos

1972   *Zeelandia: de geschiedenis van een fort*. Zutphen: De Walburg Pers.

1980   "Joden Savanne." In *Uit Suriname's historie; fragmenten uit een bewogen verleden,* edited by Jos Fontaine, 32–39. Zutphen: De Walburg Pers [orig. 1973].

Green, Edward Crocker

1974   "The Matawai Maroons: An Acculturating Afro-American Society." Ph.D. Diss., Catholic University, Washington, D.C.

de Groot, Silvia W.

1980   "Boni's dood en Boni's hoofd: een proeve van orale geschiedenis." *De Gids* 143 (1):3–15.

1982   "Surinaamse Marrons in kaart gebracht 1730–1734." In *"Een andere in een ander": liber amicorum voor R.A.J. van Lier,* edited by B. F. Galjart, J. D. Speckman, and J. Voorhoeve, 19–45. Leiden: Instituut Culturele Antropologie en Sociologie der Niet-Westerse Volken.

Hartsinck, Jan Jacob

1770   *Beschrijving van Guyana of de Wilde Kust in Zuid-America*. Amsterdam: Gerrit Tielenburg.

Herlein, J. D.

1718   *Beschryvinge van de Volk-plantinge Zuriname*. Leeuwarden: Meindert Injema.

Herr, Michael

1977   *Dispatches*. New York: Knopf.

Herskovits, Melville, J., and Frances S. Herskovits

1934   *Rebel Destiny: Among the Bush Negroes of Dutch Guiana*. New York: McGraw-Hill.

Hoogbergen, Wim S. M.

1978   *De Surinaamse "weglopers" van de negentiende eeuw*. BSB 1. Utrecht: Centrum voor Caraïbische Studies.

Ijzerman, Robert

1931   *Outline of the Geology and Petrology of Surinam (Dutch Guiana)*. Utrecht: Kemink en Zoon.

Jozefzoon, O.J.R.

1959   *De Saramaccaanse wereld*. Paramaribo: Varekamp.

Junker, L.

1922/ "Eenige mededeelingen over de Saramakkaner-Boschnegers." *De West-Indische Gids* 4:449–80.
23

1923/ "Over de afstamming der Boschnegers." *De West-Indische Gids* 5:310–17.
24

Kahn, Morton C.

1931 *Djuka: The Bush Negroes of Dutch Guiana.* New York: Viking Press.

King, Johannes

1983 *Skrekiboekoe: de visioenen van Johannes King,* edited by Miriam Sterman. BSB 10. Utrecht: Centrum voor Caraïbische Studies.

Knappert, L.

1926/27 "De Labadisten in Suriname." *De West-Indische Gids* 8:193–218.

de Lavaux, Alexander

1737 *Generale Caart van de Provintie Suriname.*

Lichtveld, Ursy M., and Jan Voorhoeve, eds.

1980 *Suriname: spiegel der vaderlandse kooplieden. Een historisch leesboek.* (Tweede herziene druk, orig. 1958). The Hague: Martinus Nijhoff.

van der Linde, J. M.

1966 *Surinaamse suikerheren en hun kerk: plantagekolonie en handelskerk ten tijde van Johannes Basseliers, predikant en planter in Suriname, 1667–1689.* Wageningen: H. Veenman en Zonen.

Miller, Joseph C., ed.

1980 *The African Past Speaks.* Folkestone: Wm. Dawson & Sons.

Mintz, Sidney W.

1972 Introduction to the second English edition of *Voodoo in Haiti,* by Alfred Métraux. New York: Schocken Books.

Mintz, Sidney W., and Richard Price

1976 *An Anthropological Approach to the Afro-American Past: A Caribbean Perspective.* Philadelphia: ISHI.

Morssink, F.

n.d. "Boschnegeriana (misschien beter Silvae-nigritiana?)." MS. [1934?]

Nassy, David de Ishak Cohen, *et al.*

1788 *Essai historique sur la colonie de Surinam.* Paramaribo.

Oldendorp, Ch. G. A.

1777 *Geschichte der Mission der evangelischen Brüder auf den caraibischen Inseln S. Thomas, S. Croix und S. Jan.* Barby.

Pakosie, André R. M.

1972 *De dood van Boni.* Paramaribo.

Price, Richard

1970 "Saramaka Woodcarving: The Development of an Afroamerican Art." *Man* 5:363–78 (plus plates).

1973 "Avenging Spirits and the Structure of Saramaka Lineages." *Bijdragen tot de Taal-, Land- en Volkenkunde* 129:86–107.

1975 *Saramaka Social Structure: Analysis of a Maroon Society in Surinam.* Rio Piedras: Institute of Caribbean Studies of the University of Puerto Rico.

1976 *The Guiana Maroons: A Historical and Bibliographical Introduction.* Baltimore: Johns Hopkins University Press.

1979a "Kwasímukámba's Gambit." *Bijdragen tot de Taal-, Land- en Volkenkunde* 135:151–69.

1979b *Maroon Societies: Rebel Slave Communities in the Americas,* edited and introduced by Richard Price, 2d ed., rev. Baltimore: Johns Hopkins University Press.

1983   *To Slay the Hydra: Dutch Colonial Perspectives on the Saramaka Wars*. Ann Arbor: Karoma.

n.d.   *Alábi's World: The Making of an Afro-American People*. Book MS in preparation.

Price, Richard, and Chris de Beet

1982   *De Saramakaanse vrede van 1762: geselecteerde documenten*. BSB 8. Utrecht: Centrum voor Caraïbische Studies.

Price, Richard, and Sally Price

1972   "Saramaka Onomastics: An Afro-American Naming System." *Ethnology* 11:341–67.

1977   *Music from Saramaka: A Dynamic Afro-American Tradition*. (Phonograph record with ethnographic notes.) New York: Folkways FE 4225.

Price, Sally

1978   "Reciprocity and Social Distance: A Reconsideration." *Ethnology* 17:339–50.

1983   *Co-wives and Calabashes*. Ann Arbor: University of Michigan Press.

Price, Sally, and Richard Price

1980   *Afro-American Arts of the Suriname Rain Forest*. Berkeley and Los Angeles: University of California Press.

Price, Thomas J.

1970   "Ethnohistory and Self-Image in Three New World Negro Societies." In *Afro-American Anthropology*, edited by Norman E. Whitten, Jr. and John F. Szwed, 63–71. New York: Free Press.

Rodney, Walter

1981   *A History of the Guyanese Working People, 1881–1905*. Baltimore: Johns Hopkins University Press.

Rosaldo, Renato

1980   *Ilongot Headhunting 1883–1974: A Study in Society and History*. Stanford, Calif.: Stanford University Press.

Sack, J.

1911   "Mededeelingen over den ontdekker van het Quassiehout." *Pharmaceutisch Weekblad* 48: 1152–57, 1175–86.

Schiltkamp, J. A., and J. Th. de Smidt

1973   *Plakaten, ordonnantiën en andere wetten, uitgevaardigd in Suriname 1667–1816*. Amsterdam: S. Emmering.

Schumann, C. L.

1778   "Saramaccanisch Deutsches Wörter-Buch." In *Die Sprache der Saramakkaneger in Surinam*, Hugo Schuchardt. Verhandelingen der Koninklijke Akademie van Wetenschappen te Amsterdam 14(6), 1914, 46–116. Amsterdam: Johannes Müller.

van Sijpesteijn, C. A.

1854   *Beschrijving van Suriname*. 's Gravenhage: De Gebroeders van Cleef.

1858   *Mr. Jan Jacob Mauricius, Gouverneur-Generaal van Suriname van 1742–1751*. 's Gravenhage: De Gebroeders van Cleef.

Spalburg, J. G.

1913   *Bruine Mina, de koto-missi*. Paramaribo: J. N. Wekker.

Staehelin, F.

1913–   *Die Mission der Brüdergemeine in Suriname und Berbice im achtzehnten Jahrhundert*.
1919   Herrnhut: Vereins für Brüdergeschichte in Kommission der Unitätsbuchhandlung in Gnadau.

Stedman, John Gabriel

1988   *Narrative of a Five Years Expedition against the Revolted Negroes of Surinam. Transcribed for the First Time from the Original 1790 Manuscript,* edited by Richard Price and Sally Price. Baltimore: Johns Hopkins University Press.

1796   *Narrative, of a five-years' expedition, against the revolted Negroes of Surinam, in Guiana, on the Wild Coast of South America; from the year 1772, to 1777*. London: J. Johnson and J. Edwards.

Tardits, Claude
1964   "Allocution de M. Claude Tardits (Hommage à Alfred Métraux)." *L'Homme* 4 (2):15–19.

Vaillant, M.
1948   "Milieu culturel et classification des variétés de riz des guyanes française et hollandaise." *Revue Internationale de Botanique Appliqué et d'Agriculture,Tropicale* 28:520–29.

Valéry, Paul
1962   *History and Politics.* Bollingen Series, vol. 45, no. 10. New York: Pantheon Books.

Voorhoeve, Jan
1959   "An Orthography for Saramaccan." *Word* 15: 436–45.

Voorhoeve, Jan, and Ursy M. Lichtveld, eds.
1975   *Creole Drum: An Anthology of Creole Literature in Surinam.* New Haven: Yale University Press.

Wolbers, J.
1861   *Geschiedenis van Suriname.* Amsterdam: H. de Hoogh.

THANKS

Thanks-giving (*dá tangí*) is a class of Saramaka event set apart: a material thing of quite modest proportions is proffered in return for generously given goods or services. I would like to consider this book that thing, bearing in mind that the services that helped nurture it have been many and diverse. So, thanks first to the following organizations that, over the years, funded some portion of the research or writing: the American Council of Learned Societies, The Johns Hopkins University, the National Science Foundation (Grant BNS 76–02848), the Netherlands Institute for Advanced Study, the Netherlands America Commission for Educational Exchange, and the Nederlandse Organisatie voor Zuiver-Wetenschappelijk Onderzoek. Thanks to John Parker of the James Ford Bell Library for permission to quote passages from John Gabriel Stedman's original 1790 manuscript of his *Narrative,* which Sally Price and I are currently preparing for publication by the University of Minnesota Press. Thanks to Dean Pendleton, who did the final drafting of the complex maps that I prepared. And thanks too—far more than I can express here—to all those scholars who have helped me to explore and write about Saramaka history, especially Chris de Beet, Ken Bilby, Margot van Opstal, Miriam Sterman, Bonno Thoden van Velzen, Diane Vernon, and many other students and colleagues at Johns Hopkins and Utrecht. David Cohen raised some particularly challenging questions about the materials in this book. And Sally Price, who completed two other books about Saramaka while this one was in progress, never failed to be my most frequent, most generous, and toughest critic. To all these, but especially to the Saramaka people, living and dead—to whom this work is formally dedicated—I offer this book as a token of my deeply felt appreciation. *Gaán tangí tangí f 'únu.*

ABOUT THE AUTHOR

Richard Price was first drawn to anthropology during a Harvard freshman seminar about the Navajo, taught by the late Clyde Kluckhohn. Following Kluckhohn's advice to pursue undergraduate studies in history and literature, but at the same time to devote summers to anthropological fieldwork, he lived with highland Indians in Peru and Mexico, with fishermen in Martinique, and with cork and olive farmers in Andalusia. A year in France, studying with Claude Lévi-Strauss, led back to Harvard, where he received his Ph.D. in social anthropology in 1970. After teaching for several years at Yale, he moved to Johns Hopkins as professor of anthropology and chairman of that department. Since the mid-1960s, together with Sally Price, he has been exploring the past and present of the Suriname Maroons in the broader hemispheric context of Afro-American studies, and has spent three years doing fieldwork in Suriname and three additional years working in archives and museums on Suriname materials in the Netherlands. He currently lives in Martinique, where he is continuing his explorations of Afro-American historical consciousness.

RECENT TITLES IN THE SERIES

Keepers of their
own history

Review

1 level - comparative history
                 historiography

1 level - use of interdiscip.
(anthro) to inform history

1 level - history - as Price
respects Saramakas
as historians of
          First-Time

The function of history
as ideology

collective memory, in
particular references as
documentation

Language?

History as 'dangerous'
powerful.
In itself defining
authority & power
relations - compare to
          Wood

The Johns Hopkins University Press

FIRST-TIME

This book was composed in Garamond Linotron
by Brushwood Graphics,
from a design by Gerard A. Valerio.
It was printed on 60-lb. Glatfelter paper
by Thomson-Shore, Inc.